MW01110245

PIRANDELLO'S ONE-ACT PLAYS

Translated by William Murray

A SAMUEL FRENCH ACTING EDITION

SAMUEL FRENCH

FOUNDED 1830

New York Hollywood London Toronto

SAMUELFRENCH.COM

This volume of translations is dedicated to my mother, Natalia Danesi Murray, who first urged me to read Pirandello and who has devoted so much of her time to advancing the cause of this great playwright in the United States.

W.M.

FOREWORD

In about 1909, when Pirandello had already established himself as a writer with his novels and short stories, he wrote a brief autobiographical sketch of himself that was eventually published in the Roman periodical *Le lettere*, the issue of October 15, 1924. Here, in part, is what he said of himself:

"I was born in Sicily, and specifically on a country estate near Girgenti, on June 28, 1867. I came to Rome for the first time in 1886 and stayed there for two years. In October of 1888 I left for Germany and remained there two and a half years, that is until April of 1891. I took my degree there, at the University of Bonn, in letters and philosophy. In 1891 I came back to Rome and have not moved from here since. I have been teaching, alas, for fifteen years at the Istituto Superiore di Magistero Femminile [a girls' high school]. I say alas not only because teaching weighs on me enormously, but also because my greatest desire would be to retire to the country to work.

"I live in Rome as sheltered a life as possible; I go out only a few hours a day toward evening, to get a little exercise, and in the company, if possible, of a friend or two: Giustino Ferri or Ugo Fleres.

"I very seldom go to the theatre. By ten o'clock every night I am in bed. I get up early in the morning and habitually work until noon. After lunch, usually, I go back to my desk at two-thirty and stay there until five-thirty, but, after the morning hours, I do no more writing, unless there is some urgent necessity; I either read or study. In the evening, after dinner, I chat a bit with my little family,

I read the titles of the articles and the headlines in a few newspapers, and then to bed.

"As you can see, there is nothing in my life worth revealing: it is all interior, in my work and my thoughts, which . . . are not happy ones.

"I think life is a very sad piece of buffoonery, because we have in us, without being able to ascertain how or why or from whom, the need to fool ourselves continuously by the spontaneous creation of a reality (one for each and never the same for everyone) that from time to time reveals itself to be vain and illusory.

"Whoever understands the game can no longer fool himself, but if you cannot fool yourself, you can no longer derive any enjoyment or pleasure from life. So it goes.

"My art is full of bitter compassion for all those who fool themselves, but this compassion can't help but be succeeded by the ferocious derision of a destiny that condemns man to deception.

"This, succinctly, is the reason for the bitterness of my art, and also of my life."

The above is an accurate portrait of the artist as he was and would remain, factually and in spirit, to the end of his life. He was forty-two at the time and had not yet written a play, but the mood and philosophy of every one of his forty-three stage works is evident in these words. It should be necessary only to add, as background to his view of life and art at this time, that he had been forced to take up teaching by the ruin of his father's business, for, despite his early successes as a writer, it was not possible then (nor is it now) for anyone to make a living in Italy by purely literary activity. And since 1894, Pirandello had also been supporting a family of his own. His wife, Antonietta Portulano, was the daughter of a business colleague of his father's, and the marriage was dictated, to some extent at least, by expediency: Pirandello had not met his wife when the match was arranged and knew her only slightly at the time of the wedding. Three children, two boys and a girl, were born between 1895 and 1899, and his wife suffered a mental breakdown, so that in addition to the financial burdens he was suddenly forced to shoulder, Pirandello found himself living with a woman on the brink of madness. Her derangement focused itself on him and, from 1904 until she was committed to an asylum in 1919, Pirandello found himself living two lives: the one that seemed real to him and the one created for him by his wife's imagination. She was prone to frequent hysterical scenes in which she would accuse him of duplicity and unfaithfulness, and this condition became more severe with the years. According to his friend, the critic Domenico Vittorini, "Pirandello did all that a humane being could do to allay his wife's suspicions. He stayed home constantly, and gave up his friends, drawn into the whirl of his wife's insanity, patient and resigned, but letting his fantasy work in the immobility to which he condemned himself. He went so far as to give his wife every penny he made, keeping for himself sixty centimes a day for carfare to school. But it was of no avail."

Pirandello had begun by writing verse. His first volume of poems was published in 1889 and was soon followed by two others. Luigi Capuana, a well-known Sicilian novelist of the realistic school, encouraged him to write fiction and, in 1901, Pirandello's first novel, *L'esclusa* (*The Outcast*), was published serially in a Roman newspaper. It was soon followed by another one, *Il turno* (*The Turn*), and collections of the short stories he had begun to contribute to newspapers and magazines. In 1904 his most famous novel, *Il fu Mattia Pascal* (*The Late Mattia Pascal*), firmly established his literary reputation, and between then and about 1920 he produced several more novels, various collections of short stories, and a two-volume work of criticism, *Arte e scienza,* in which he elaborated his artistic creed.

He did not turn to the stage until 1910, and then only at the urging of Nino Martoglio, a Sicilian playwright and producer who had taken over a theatre in Rome and was casting about for something new and worthwhile to produce. In 1898 Pirandello had written a little play called *L'epilogo* (*The Epilogue*), which had been published but never produced. Retitled *La morsa* (*The Vise*), it was now turned over to Martoglio, along with another one-act play, *Lumie di Sicilia* (*Sicilian Limes*), which Pirandello had adapted from one of his own short stories. Martoglio produced them successfully at his theatre in December of 1910. It was the beginning of a new career, because for the rest of his life Pirandello was to devote the bulk of his time to writing plays, an activity that eventually freed him from his financial dependence on teaching and engaged him most deeply as an artist. He wrote thirty full-length and thirteen one-act plays, of which the best-known in this country are: *Six Characters in Search of an Author, The Man with the Flower in His Mouth, As You Desire Me, Right You Are If You Think You Are,* and *Henry IV.* When he wrote, he wrote intensively, as attested by his admission to his Italian biographer, Federico Nardelli, that he turned out nine plays in a single year, one of them in three days, another one in six. That he could have worked so quickly does not mean, of course, that he was a careless writer, but only that in his drama he seemed to have found the perfect cathartic expression for the turmoil of his inner life and philosophical musings.

What sort of drama was it? He himself defined it: "A serious theatre, mine. It demands the complete participation of the moral-human entity. It is certainly not a comfortable theatre. A difficult theatre, a dangerous theatre. Nietzsche said that the Greeks put up white statues against the black abyss, in order to hide it. I, instead, topple them in order to reveal it. . . . It is the tragedy of the modern spirit."

This spirit pervades all of the one-act plays, even such relatively lighthearted ones as *Chee-Chee* and *The Jar,* and a close reading of these thirteen little dramas will provide an excellent survey in miniature of Pirandello's work as a playwright. They span his career. He began in the theatre with two of them, and one of his last plays was *I'm Dreaming, But Am I?*, written in 1931 and not staged in Italy until December of 1937, the last of his works to be premiered in his native country. (There had been an earlier production of this play, however, in Lisbon.) They contain all of his most familiar themes, the ones that he elaborated in his longer plays, and they were written in the various styles with which he became identified: realistic melodrama, ironic comedy, philosophical discourse, the play of illusion and reality involving the participation of the audience, the use of fantasy and dream to reveal the truth behind a seemingly simple, even humdrum surface situation. About the question of style itself, Pirandello wrote: "Style can be defined as *the form of one's talent*. For each talent a different style; but by talent I mean that interior virtue of spirit by which a man discovers for himself what he has not learned from others. A talent without individuality is not a real talent. And style means individuality, one's own way of thinking, feeling, expressing. In short, a person has style who has things of his own to say and knows how to say them in his own way, with a completely personal attitude and manner that does not necessarily have to be beautiful."

Pirandello considered himself first and last an artist and he had strong ideas about what art was and what it was not. Among his papers was found the following revealing fragment:

"The realists limit art to the pure and simple imitation of nature. They make no pretense at saying anything; they wish to portray exactly what nature is. It follows that the masterpiece of masterpieces will be the image reflected by a mirror. But why repeat in a human and lesser voice what nature says in her powerful one? Can one perhaps succeed in taking from nature the sun, its warmth, the perpetual mobility of its successive aspects? To copy nature is impossible. Yes, one should study her and follow her, considering her as the greatest and most prolific teacher. Art is nature itself, but proceeding along its own lines in the human spirit. And it is from this resemblance that the artist's love of nature derives: he recognizes himself in her, and in contact with her he assumes consciousness of his own talent.

"In contrast to the realists, who have resolved to say nothing, there are those who want to say too much: philosophers, preachers, priests of the Idea. Before creating a picture, a poem, a melodrama, they write the commentary on it. And when the work is finished we are confronted by a sphinx, an enigma. Certain music called Wagnerian, certain dramas, certain novels or collections of verse of the so-called symbolistic school, certain pictures or rebuses without perspective, without color, aridly outlined, unfortunately provide us with painful examples of this. Art has nothing in common with this pedantic, obscure, and pretentious symbolism.

"Art does not derive from an abstract idea. But does this mean that thought has nothing to do with art? This is what the so-called aesthetes claim who say that the artist must in no way concern himself with the essence because the form is all. What does it matter what the artist expresses, if the expression is rich and powerful, the sounds, the lines, the colors joyfully beguile the senses and surprise the imagination by the fancy of their harmonious play? The aesthetes set themselves apart from the symbolists and the naturalists; they desire the cold representation of unalterable beauty, artifice for its own sake, for the pleasure of executing it. They distinguish the form from the idea and value only the former, without realizing that to separate these two terms – form and idea – is to suppress art, which consists in essence of the compenetration of these two terms. The idea has no value in art until it acquires feeling, until, in entire possession of the spirit, it becomes a desire strong enough to arouse the images capable of endowing it with a living expression. Art, in short, is life, not a reasoning process. Now, all the founders of a system condemn the artist to reason instead of to live.

The realists make an artisan of him, the idealists a philosopher, the aesthetes and the partisans of art for art's sake a kind of juggler who should divert his neighbor with words, sounds, lines, and colors in bizarre interplay, like so many little globes of colored glass. In each case we have the substitution of thought for nature. Instead of allowing the work to mature spontaneously in the spirit, they compose it externally by summing up various elements whose affinity they can study. Instead of abandoning themselves to the free movement of life, they assemble, they graft, they knowledgeably combine dead limbs in order to compose a living body. Art is the living idea, the idea that, in becoming the center of the interior life, creates the body of images in which it clothes itself. The idea is nothing without the form, but what is form without the idea, if the idea is what creates it? No formulas, then, for art. Whoever desires to create beauty by a formula deludes himself. Beauty can derive from anything except premeditated reasoning. Since, above all, the artist must be moved, out of his being moved the work of art will be born."

In 1925 Pirandello formed his own art theatre in Rome and later took it on tour to London, Paris, Basle, and various theatres in Germany. The enterprise was an artistic success and, as almost always happens in these cases, a financial disaster in which Pirandello himself lost a large sum of money. In his later years he traveled a good deal – to France, South America, the United States – and in 1934 he was awarded the Nobel prize. He continued to write plays until his death in Rome in 1936. His last wishes concerning his death and the disposal of his body were characteristically austere:

"I. Allow my death to pass in silence. To my friends, to my enemies, prayers that not only should they not write about it in the newspapers, but should not even mention it. No announcements or condolences.

"II. Dead, I do not wish to be clothed. Wrap me, naked, in a sheet. And no flowers on the bed and no tapers lit.

"III. The lowest class of funeral carriage, the one for the poor. Naked. And let no one accompany me, neither relatives nor friends. The carriage, the horse, the driver and that's all.

"IV. Burn me. And let my body, as soon as it has been consumed, be dispersed, because I want nothing, not even ashes, to be left of me. But if this cannot be done, let my funeral urn be taken to Sicily and walled up in some rough country stone of Girgenti, where I was born."

The playwright's ashes were placed in a Greek urn and kept in the municipal museum of Agrigento until, on the twenty-fifth anniversary of his death, his last wishes were honored and he was walled up in a rock underneath a pine he was particularly fond of, down the slope in front of the house in which he was born.

— William Murray

NOTES

The following bibliographical notes on each of the plays are based on the exhaustive bibliography compiled by Manlio Lo Vecchio-Musti for the complete edition of Pirandello's work published by the editor Arnoldo Mondadori of Milan. The facts occasionally conflict with those reported in various English-language books on Pirandello, notably the critical studies by Walter Starkie (*Luigi Pirandello*, 1926) and Domenico Vittorini (*The Drama of Luigi Pirandello*, 1935), but it seems evident that Lo Vecchio-Musti is the more reliable authority and has to be given the benefit of any doubts. I should mention in passing that, in addition to new translations of some of his more neglected work, there is a desperate need for a full-scale critical biography of Pirandello in English. Though he has been translated and written about extensively abroad, no such treatment has been accorded him in the English-speaking countries. In fact, it is safe to say that there is not a single full-length critical or biographical work in English devoted to this writer that is of much value today.

I have listed the plays chronologically in the order that they were first produced:

1) THE VISE. *La morsa*. First published in Rome, *Ariel*, March 20, 1898, under the title *L'epilogo;* Rome, *Noi e il Mondo*, March 1, 1914 in its present form. First produced in Rome, December 9, 1910.

2) SICILIAN LIMES. *Lumie di Sicilia*. First published as a short story in two issues of *Il Marzocco*, May 20 and 27, 1900. Published as a play in Rome, *Nuova Antologia*,

March 16, 1911. First produced in Rome, December 9, 1910.

3) THE DOCTOR'S DUTY. *Il dovere del medico*. First published as a short story in the collection *La Vita Nuda* (Treves, 1910), then as a play in Rome, *Nuova Antologia*, January 1912. First produced in Rome, June 20, 1913.

4) THE JAR. *La giara*. First published as a short story in the *Corriere della sera* of Milan, October 20, 1909. First produced in Rome in Sicilian dialect as *'A giarra*, text revised by the author, and starring the famous comedian Angelo Musco, July 9, 1917.

5) THE LICENSE. *La patente*. First published as a short story in the *Corriere della sera* of Milan, August 9, 1911, then as a play in Rome, *Rivista d'Italia*, January 31, 1918. First produced in Rome in Sicilian dialect as *'A patenti*, text revised by the author, February 19, 1919.

6) CHEE-CHEE. *Cecè*. This play was never published singly and was first produced at San Pellegrino, July 10, 1920.

7) AT THE EXIT. *All' uscita*. First published as a play in Rome, *Nuova Antologia*, November 1, 1916, and first produced in Rome on September 29, 1922.

8) THE IMBECILE. *L'imbecille*. First published as a short story in the *Corriere della sera* of Milan, September 11, 1912, and first produced in Rome, October 10, 1922.

9) THE MAN WITH THE FLOWER IN HIS MOUTH. *L'uomo dal fiore in bocca*. First published as a short story under the title "Caffè notturno" in *La Rassegna italiana*, August 15, 1918; then in the Mondadori edition as "La morte addosso." First produced in Rome on February 21, 1923.

10) THE OTHER SON. *L'altro figlio*. First published as a short story in *La lettura*, 1905. First produced in

Rome in the Tuscan vernacular, text revised by Ferdinando Paolieri, November 23, 1923.

11) THE FESTIVAL OF OUR LORD OF THE SHIP. *Sagra del Signore della nave.* First published as a short story, as "Il Signore della nave," in *Noi e il Mondo,* January 1916, and as a play in Milan, *Il Convegno,* September 30, 1924. First produced in Rome at the Teatro Odescalchi by the company of the Teatro d'Arte, Pirandello's own art theatre, and under the direction of the author, April 4, 1925.

12) BELLAVITA. *Bellavita.* First published in *Il secolo XX* of Milan, July 1928, and produced in Milan the year before, May 27, 1927.

13) I'M DREAMING, BUT AM I? *Sogno (ma forse no).* First published in *La lettura,* Milan, October 1929. First produced in Lisbon, Portugal, at the Teatro Nacional, September 22, 1931, in a Portuguese translation.

WILLIAM MURRAY, translator of another volume of Pirandello plays (*To Clothe the Naked and Two Other Plays*), was born in New York City in 1926. He was educated in Italy and France before returning to the United States to continue his studies at Phillips Exeter Academy and Harvard University. He is the author of five novels, including *The Sweet Ride* and *The Americano,* and an original play, *Witnesses,* first produced in 1968 by Center Theatre Group in Los Angeles. He has contributed short stories and many articles to *The New Yorker* and other magazines.

CONTENTS

THE VISE

(La morsa, 1910)

THE CAST

ANDREA FABBRI
GIULIA, his wife
ANTONIO SERRA, his lawyer
ANNA, a servant

A room in the Fabbri house, in a small provincial town.

A room in the FABBRI *house. At rear, the main entrance; at left, another exit; at right, two windows. Shortly after the curtain rises,* GIULIA, *who has been looking out the window, her back to the audience, starts in surprise and backs away from the sill. She puts the knitting she has been carrying down on a table and hurriedly but cautiously goes to close the door at left, then turns back to wait by the main entrance.* ANTONIO SERRA *soon enters the room.*

GIULIA
Throwing her arms around his neck, softly, happily.
Back already?

ANTONIO
Nervously fending her off.
No, please!

GIULIA
Aren't you alone? Where did you leave Andrea?

ANTONIO
Absently.
I came back ahead of him, last night.

GIULIA
Why?

ANTONIO
Annoyed by the question.
I made up an excuse. A real one, anyway. I had to be here this morning on business.

GIULIA
You didn't mention it to me. You could have let me know.
He looks at her but does not answer.
What's happened?

ANTONIO

In a low, tense voice, almost angrily.
What's happened? I'm afraid Andrea suspects us.

GIULIA

Surprised and frightened.
Andrea? How do you know? You didn't give us away?

ANTONIO

No. We both did, if anything.

GIULIA

When? Here?

ANTONIO

Yes. The night we left. On our way downstairs. Andrea was in front of me, remember? With his suitcase. You were standing in the doorway, holding a candle, weren't you? And as I went past – God, how stupid we can be sometimes!

GIULIA

He saw us?

ANTONIO

I thought he turned his head just then, on his way down.

GIULIA

Oh my God! And so you came to tell me – and?

ANTONIO

You didn't notice anything?

GIULIA

Me? No, nothing. But where's Andrea? Where is he?

ANTONIO

Tell me, had I started down the stairs when he called you?

GIULIA

And said good-by to me? Maybe he saw us when he turned on the landing.

ANTONIO

No, before, before.

GIULIA

But if he had seen us –

ANTONIO

Just a glimpse, if anything. A second at most.

GIULIA

And he let you come back last night, ahead of him? Is that possible? Are you sure he didn't leave right after you?

ANTONIO

Very sure, at least of that, very sure. And there's no other train from the city before eleven.

Looks at his watch.

He'll be here soon. Meanwhile, this uncertainty – like dangling over an abyss – do you understand?

GIULIA

Don't say it, don't say it, please! Keep calm. Tell me everything. What did he do? I want to know everything.

ANTONIO

What can I tell you? In this kind of situation the most casual remark seems significant – every look, every movement – the tone of his voice even –

GIULIA

Calm, we must keep calm!

ANTONIO

How? It's easy to say!

A brief pause. He tries to pull himself together.

Here, you remember? Before we left we were talking, he and I, about this damned business we had to take care of in town. He was getting all excited. . . .

GIULIA

Yes, well?

ANTONIO

As soon as we were out of the house, he stopped and walked along with his head down. I looked at him. He was disturbed about something, he was frowning. . . . He's seen us! I thought right away. I was trembling. But suddenly, very innocently, very naturally: "Sad, isn't it," he said, "to have to travel at night? To have to leave home at night . . ."

GIULIA

That's how he put it?

ANTONIO

Yes. He also said it was sad for those left behind as well.
Then came the phrase – I was in a cold sweat – "To have
to say good-by on a staircase, by candlelight . . ."

GIULIA

Ah! Like that? *How* did he say it?

ANTONIO

In the same tone of voice. Very naturally. I don't know.
. . . But he was doing it on purpose! He talked to me
about the children, how he'd left them in bed, asleep. But
not with the simple tenderness that reassures anyone. And
he mentioned you.

GIULIA

Me?

ANTONIO

Yes, and all the time he was looking at me.

GIULIA

What did he say?

ANTONIO

That you love your children so much.

GIULIA

That's all?

ANTONIO

On the train he brought up the business of the lawsuit
again. He asked me about Gorri, the lawyer, and whether
I knew him. Oh, among other things, he wanted to know
if he was married. He laughed. This, you see, had nothing
to do with the case. Or did I simply –

GIULIA

Quickly.
Quiet!

ANNA

Appearing at the main entrance.
Excuse me, madam. Shouldn't I go and get the children?

GIULIA

Yes – but wait a few minutes.

ANNA

Isn't Mr. Fabbri coming home today? I saw the carriages on their way to the station.

ANTONIO

Looking at his watch.
It's eleven o'clock. The train will be in any minute.

GIULIA

Really? Already?
To ANNA.
Wait a few minutes. I'll tell you when.

ANNA

Leaving.
Yes, madam. Meanwhile I'll finish setting the table.
Exits.

ANTONIO

He'll be here soon.

GIULIA

And you can't tell me anything, you weren't able to find out anything for certain?

ANTONIO

Yes! That he's a very good actor, if he really does suspect.

GIULIA

Him? With that violent temper of his?

ANTONIO

And yet, and yet . . . Could my own nervousness have blinded me to that extent? Is that possible? At times, you see, I thought I could detect a double meaning in his words. The next moment I'd take heart and tell myself, "It's your own fear!" I studied him, watched him every chance I got: how he'd look at me, talk to me. . . . You know he usually doesn't talk much. Well, you should have heard him these past three days! Often, however, he'd lapse into a long, uneasy silence, but he'd always come out of it by getting back to talking business again. . . .

Then I'd ask myself, "Is that what he was worried about, or was it something else? Perhaps he's just talking now to cover up. . . ." Once I even thought he didn't want to shake my hand. I know he was aware that I had my hand stuck out. He pretended not to notice. He was really a little strange, the day after we left. No sooner had I turned away than he called me back. He's changed his mind, I immediately thought. And, in fact, he said, "Oh, excuse me, I forgot to shake hands, but it doesn't matter, does it?" Other times he'd talk to me about you, the house, but for no obvious reason I could make out. Just talking. Nevertheless, I had the impression he avoided my eye. Often he'd repeat the same phrase three or four times, for no reason at all . . . as if he was thinking of something else. . . . And when he talked about things that had nothing to do with you, he'd suddenly find a way to come back to you or the children, and he'd ask me questions. . . . On purpose? Who knows! Trying to catch me by surprise? He'd laugh, but there'd be an ugly look in his eyes. . . .

GIULIA

And you?

ANTONIO

Oh, I was always on my guard.

GIULIA

He must have noticed how nervous you were.

ANTONIO

If he already had his suspicions –

GIULIA

You must have confirmed them. Well, anything else?

ANTONIO

Yes. The first night, at the hotel – he insisted on taking one room with two beds – we'd been in bed for some time and he noticed I wasn't asleep. That is, he couldn't have noticed – we were in the dark – he guessed it! And bear in mind – well, you can imagine – I hadn't moved an inch, there in the dark – in the same room with him and suspecting that he knew – imagine! – I lay there, my eyes wide open, waiting – I don't know – to defend myself, I suppose. . . . Suddenly, in that silence, I heard him speak these exact words: "You are not asleep."

GIULIA

What did you say?

ANTONIO

Nothing. I didn't answer. I pretended to be asleep. A minute later he said it again: "You are not asleep." So then I answered him: "Did you say something?" I asked. And he said, "Yes, I wanted to know if you were asleep." But he hadn't been asking me a question; he had spoken the phrase in the certainty that I wasn't sleeping, that I couldn't sleep, do you see? At least, that's how it seemed to me.

GIULIA

Nothing else?

ANTONIO

Nothing. I haven't slept for two nights.

GIULIA

Afterward, was he the same as always with you?

ANTONIO

Yes, just the same.

GIULIA

All this pretending, him? Andrea? If he had really seen us –

ANTONIO

And yet I know he turned back, on his way down the stairs.

GIULIA

But he couldn't have noticed anything? Could he?

ANTONIO

He may not be sure. . . .

GIULIA

Even so, you don't know him. Control himself like that? Him? So that he gives nothing away? What do you really know? Nothing. Suppose he had seen us, saw you stop and bow toward me. If he'd had the slightest suspicion that you had kissed me, he'd have come back up. Oh yes! Imagine, imagine what would have happened! No, listen, no! Think about it! It just isn't possible! You were afraid, that's all. He couldn't have suspected. He has no reason to suspect us. You've always treated me familiarly in front of him.

ANTONIO

Yes, but a suspicion can flower from one minute to the next. Then you know what? A thousand other things you've barely noticed, paid no attention to, suddenly take on significance. The slightest hint becomes definite proof, every doubt a certainty. That's what I'm afraid of.

GIULIA

We have to be careful.

ANTONIO

That's what I told you from the very beginning!

GIULIA

Are you blaming me now?

ANTONIO

I'm not blaming anyone, but haven't I told you a thousand times? You see, you –

GIULIA

Yes? I what?

ANTONIO

I don't know how we could have done it, giving ourselves away like this – for nothing – for a foolish whim – like the one three nights ago. . . . You were the one who –

GIULIA

It's always me, yes.

ANTONIO

If you hadn't –

GIULIA

You're afraid.

ANTONIO

You think we have nothing to worry about, you and I? You especially!

A pause. He paces up and down the room, then stops.
Yes, I'm afraid! You think it's only for myself? I'm afraid,
you say? If that's what you think . . .

A pause. He resumes his pacing.
We were too sure of ourselves, that's all! And now I can
look back and see how careless we were, how crazy, and
I ask myself how we could have gotten away with it as
long as we did! How could we? Making love right here,
under his very eyes – taking advantage of everything, of
the least little opportunity – whenever he left us alone for a
moment, but even when he didn't – by our gestures, the
way we'd look at each other – madness!

GIULIA

After a long pause.
You do blame me. And why shouldn't you? I betrayed a
man who trusted in me more than in himself. Yes, you're
right, the blame is mine, mostly mine.

ANTONIO

*Stopping to stare at her, then resuming his pacing,
curtly.*
That isn't what I meant at all.

GIULIA

But it is, it is, I know it. And you might even add that it
was I who chose to run away from home with him, that
it was I who pushed him into eloping with me, and that
it was I who then betrayed him with you! You're right to
blame me now, absolutely right!

Coming up to him and speaking feverishly.
But listen, I ran away with him because I loved him, not
because I wanted to live such a dull, respectable life here,
not because I wanted all the comforts, all the luxuries of
a new home. I already had all that. I never would have
gone off with him if I hadn't loved him. But – but, you
see, he felt he had to atone for what he'd done. He was a
serious, respectable man and – and he had behaved rashly.
He'd pay for it, make it up to everybody and quickly. How?
By dedicating himself to his job, by making a rich, com-

fortable home for me, with plenty of free time at my disposal. So he's worked like a dog for me, thought only of his work, always, wanting nothing from me but praise for his industry, his honesty, and even — even my gratitude! Yes, because I could have done worse for myself. . . . He was an honest man, he'd make me rich, he would, as rich as before, richer than before. . . . All this for me, for me, and every night I'd wait impatiently, happily, for him to come home. He'd come back tired, exhausted, happy with his day's work and already worrying about tomorrow's. . . . Well, in the end I got tired, too, tired of having practically to force the man to love me, to return the love I had for him. . . . There are times when a husband's respect, his trust, his friendship can seem like insults to a woman. . . . And you, who took advantage of this situation, now you blame me for having loved you, for having betrayed my husband, now that we're in danger! You're afraid, I can see you're afraid! But what have you got to lose? Nothing! While I —

She buries her face in her hands.

ANTONIO

After a brief pause.

You urge me to keep calm. . . . If I'm afraid, it's — it's for you — for your children.

GIULIA

Proudly, almost shouting.

Don't you even mention them!

Bursting into tears.

My poor innocent babies!

ANTONIO

Go on and cry. I'm leaving.

GIULIA

Yes, get out! There's nothing to keep you, is there?

ANTONIO

Quickly, seriously.

You're being unfair. I loved you, just as you loved me. You know that. I warned you to be careful. Was I wrong?

More for your sake than for mine. Yes, because if anything happened, I'd have nothing to lose. Your very own words.

A short pause, then emphasizing each word.

I've never reproached you, never blamed you for anything. I have no right to. . . .

He passes a hand over his eyes, then changes his tone of voice and attitude.

Come on now, get hold of yourself. Maybe he doesn't know anything. That's what you think, isn't it? And maybe you're right. Even I can't believe that he could have controlled himself to such a point. He couldn't have noticed anything. So – come on. Nothing's over. You and I can still –

GIULIA

No, no, impossible! How could you even want to now? We – we'd better, we'd better end it.

ANTONIO

Whatever you say.

GIULIA

Yes, I can see how much you love me.

ANTONIO

Are you trying to drive me out of my mind?

GIULIA

No. We'd better end it and right now, no matter what happens. It's all over for us. And we'd better tell him everything.

ANTONIO

Are you crazy?

GIULIA

Yes, we'd better, really! What kind of a life can I have now? I no longer have the right to love anyone! Not even my children! If I bend down to kiss them, I seem to see the shadow of my blame fall across their innocent faces! No! No! Would he kill me? I'd do it myself, if he didn't.

ANTONIO

You're talking nonsense!

GIULIA

You think so? I always said I would. It's too – too . . .
There's nothing left for me now.
Making an effort to control herself.
Go, please go. He mustn't find you here.

ANTONIO

Must I? And leave you? I came on purpose to – Wouldn't
it be better if I –

GIULIA

No, he mustn't find you here. Come back after he gets
home. It's necessary. Come back soon and be calm, casual,
not like this. Talk to me in front of him, turn to me often.
I'll second you.

ANTONIO

Yes, yes.

GIULIA

Quickly. And in case –

ANTONIO

In case what?

GIULIA

Nothing. Anyway . . .

ANTONIO

What?

GIULIA

Nothing, nothing. Good-by, that's all.

ANTONIO

Giulia –

GIULIA

Go now.

ANTONIO

I'll be back soon.
He exits. GIULIA *remains in the middle of the room, her
eyes lost in gloomy thought. Then she raises her head,
sighs with utter weariness, and presses her hands to her*

*face. But she fails to rid herself of her obsession. She
strolls wearily about the room, stops in front of a mirror
and is briefly distracted by her reflection in the glass.
She moves away, then finally sits down and buries her
head in her arms. She remains like this for some time,
then raises her head and sits there, thinking.*

GIULIA

To herself.

Couldn't he have come back up the stairs? Made some excuse . . . He'd have found me there – by the window –
looking out. . . .

A pause.

If only Antonio weren't so afraid – so afraid.

*She shakes her head in contempt and disgust. Another
pause. She rises, paces again about the room, goes back
to the table, seems undecided, finally rings the bell
loudly twice.*

ANNA

Entering.

You rang?

GIULIA

Thoughtfully.

Yes. I want you to make sure that everything's ready,
Anna.

ANNA

It is, madam.

GIULIA

After a pause.

The table?

ANNA

It's set.

GIULIA

Mr. Fabbri's room?

ANNA

All ready.

GIULIA

Go and get the children, then.

ANNA

At once, madam.
  Starts to go.

GIULIA

Anna!

ANNA

Anything else?

GIULIA

  Undecided, then after a moment's thought.
Let them stay a little longer. You can get them after Mr.
Fabbri arrives.

ANNA

That might be best. He should be here any minute. In fact,
if you want me to go down and wait for him, I could help
with his bag —

GIULIA

No, wait! Wait a minute!

ANNA

The children are so happy their daddy's coming home. He
promised to bring them presents. A little horse this high for
Carluccio. Of course Ninetto says he wants it. They were
already fighting over it this morning on their way to their
grandmother's. "Daddy loves me better than you!" Carluccio would say. And Ninetto would answer, "Yes, and
Mommy loves me better!"

GIULIA

The darling!

ANNA

And just beginning to talk, too!

GIULIA

Go and get them!

ANNA

  Listening.
Wait — the carriages. . . .

Going to the window.
The carriages are coming back. Shall I go downstairs?

GIULIA

Yes, yes, go on. . . .
ANNA *exits. Very uneasy,* GIULIA *now resumes her pacing about the room. She stops and listens, then goes back to the table and almost mechanically picks up her knitting.*
I'll know right away.
Again she stops to listen, then begins to work feverishly. Suddenly, almost without being aware of it, she stops to listen once more.

ANNA

Off stage.
He's here, madam!
Enters carrying a suitcase that she puts down on a chair near the entrance.
Mr. Fabbri!
GIULIA *rises and moves casually toward the door, still holding her knitting.* ANDREA *enters.*

GIULIA

Holding out her hand to him.
I've been waiting for you.
To ANNA.
Go and get the children.

ANNA

Hesitating.
Mr. Fabbri said —

ANDREA

They're at my mother's? Well, let them stay a while. First I want to unpack. So they'll find their presents when they get here.

GIULIA

As you like.
ANNA *exits.*

ANDREA

I'm so tired. A bad headache.

GIULIA

Was the window open in your compartment?

ANDREA

No, they were all closed. But the noise – I didn't sleep a wink.

GIULIA

Crowded?

ANDREA

Yes, packed.

GIULIA

And my little pillow?

ANDREA

Isn't it here? Oh Lord, I must have left it on the train! Well, too bad. Can't be helped now, never mind. . . . How are you? And the children?

GIULIA

Going back to her work.
We're all fine.

ANDREA

And – you've been expecting me, you say? Serra must have told you.

GIULIA

Yes, he came by a little while ago. You didn't even write me once.

ANDREA

I know, but for three days I've – Serra came back last night.

GIULIA

So he told me. He's going to drop in and see you.

ANDREA

He is? Good. I'm glad you sent the children over to Mother's. She loves to have them. You didn't go and see her?

GIULIA

No, you know I only go there with you.

ANDREA

Yes, but by this time you could have –

GIULIA

Changing the subject.
How did your business go?

ANDREA

Didn't Serra tell you?

GIULIA

Yes, he did mention it, but he was here such a short time. . . .

ANDREA

Oh, it looks like the whole thing is well under way. At least – but our dear Antonio left me holding the bag. . . . Oh, by the way, Gorri, the lawyer, talked to me about him, you know, praised him to the sky. Oh yes. He's talented, very talented, that boy! He handled the whole thing very skillfully. No one could have done it any better.

Breaks off and begins again in another tone of voice.
And if everything goes as well as I hope it does, as well as it ought to, then – well, guess what I'm thinking? Once it's done, I'd wind everything up here, yes, without a second thought, and – zoom! – off we go! Oh, no more headaches for me, no more work! We'll pack up and move out! To the city! What do you say? We'll go and live in town. What do you say?

GIULIA

In town?

ANDREA

Well, look at her! You don't like the idea?

GIULIA

It isn't that.

ANDREA

Ah, the city! The city! I want to live it up a little! It's high time! Enjoy myself!

GIULIA

What made you decide all this?

ANDREA

I haven't exactly decided yet. If I can – well, I'm certainly not going to stay here. I'm sick of it! After what
they've done to me! And anyway, it's for your sake, too.

GIULIA

Oh, as far as I'm concerned, anywhere . . .

ANDREA

Oh, go on now! You'd have so many things you can't
ever have in the country. It would be good for you, too. If
only to breathe a little city air, all that activity. Then here
there's my mother, and you and she never –

GIULIA

I hope that isn't the reason you want to go away.

ANDREA

No, I didn't mean that.

GIULIA

You know very well that it's your mother who doesn't like
me –

ANDREA

I know, I know, and that would be one good reason to
move. But there are others.
    A brief pause.
You know, in town I bumped into your brothers once or
twice and every time –

GIULIA

What did they do?

ANDREA

To me? Nothing. What could they do? I'd like to see them
try – well, never mind. But, as usual, they pretended not
to see me. Oh yes!
    Gaily.
It's no good, they just can't get over it! What pride! But
anger, too, now. Yes, because I'm not the penniless no-
good I used to be, you see? So they've been deprived of
the satisfaction of seeing you in misery, pining away for
the home you abandoned to run off with me. That's what

they can't stand! And now, you see, I'm going to set myself up in town for their benefit! That'll please them! They'll
enjoy it! I think Serra would gladly come along, don't you?
What's to keep him here?

GIULIA

His practice.

ANDREA

Yes, some practice! You have to go to the city for that.
What's here? Nothing, no one, a herd of sheep, once we
leave! Oh, by the way, I'll have to think of some way to
pay him for all his trouble. Of course, I've done him some
favors, plenty of them, but they don't count.

GIULIA

Maybe he thinks they do.

ANDREA

Don't you believe it! Business is business and personal favors have nothing to do with that. In business you buy
your friendships! After all, he deserves something. If you
could have heard some of the reasons he came up with to
back up my claims! Sound ones to boot! Sometimes they
even deny me the merit here of having done some good for
the town! But if gratitude – well, never mind! I don't say
I've enriched the place, though I could make that claim,
but at least I helped clean things up, got rid of the malaria. . . . Why won't they grant me that much?

GIULIA

They don't understand.

ANDREA

No, of course not. When it's a question of gratitude, no
one ever understands. They turned over a swamp to me –
you remember what it was like – when we came here, you
remember – running away from the city. . . . All it grew
were some weeds not even the sheep would graze on. I
risked all my capital on it, that is, your capital, to drain it,
fertilize it, put it to work. I made it the richest property in
the county, fine! My lease ends and not only do they try
to take it away from me, but they even deny me the honor

of having put the town on its feet again. "You got rich out of it," they said. Thank you! Who took the chance, gambled everything he had? I suppose they expected us to impoverish ourselves permanently for their benefit! Well, never mind! Anyway, it was your money.

GIULIA

Now what does that have to do with it?

ANDREA

No, it was yours. And if I became a rich man, I owe it all to you.

GIULIA

I didn't do the work. You did.

ANDREA

I worked, yes, I worked all right. And I wasn't afraid either. On the train I could look out the window at this land. Everyone on board was full of admiration for what I'd done. And they used to say I was crazy. A swamp! Yes, to them. To me it looked like California! I'd been obsessed with the idea ever since I was a boy. To think that people here used to die like flies from malaria. Old Mantegna happened to be in our compartment. Do you know him? Two of his girls died of it. He told us about it, crying all the time. His wife also died of it.

GIULIA

Still knitting.

She wasn't living with him then.

ANDREA

I should hope not! How could they go on living together after what —

He laughs.

But he mourned her more than his own children. And, of course, we all had a good laugh over that. He's not all there any more, poor man. They make fun of him here now. Did you know they beat him up?

GIULIA

Really?

ANDREA

Yes. Not recently. His wife's lover did it. He told us about
it on the train. Just like that, very calmly. You can imagine how we laughed! "Try to put yourselves in my
shoes," he told us. Then he turned to Sportini – he was
there, too, sitting next to me, the man from the customs,
you know him. "Ah, Mr. Sportini," he said, "you're the
only one here who can appreciate what I went through."
All hell broke loose! Luckily, there was a young man with
us, you know the kind, one of these supersophisticated
young dandies – Aren't you listening?

GIULIA

Yes, but I wanted to ask you –

ANDREA

To go in to dinner? Is it ready? In a couple of minutes. But
listen to this first: the young man starts to talk. "You
wanted to catch them together?" he said. "Good Lord,
what a prehistoric idea! Where's the fun in that? This gentleman gets himself beaten up. The usual unexpected trip,
the usual wrong train, the silly stunts of old-fashioned husbands who pretend to have lost a train when what they've
really lost is their heads. There's no psy-cho-lo-gy to it!
Let me explain: You suspect your wife and you want proof.
Well, why do you have to catch them at it? Isn't that
ridiculous? To bother two people who are having such a
good time together. . . ." Very witty, don't you think?
"If I had a wife," the young man continued, "God help
me, and I suspected her" – I thought he was pulling Mantegna's leg here – "I'd pretend I hadn't noticed anything.
I wouldn't look around for proof or make her prematurely
uneasy in any way. I'd only see to it – and here's the trick!
– that she gives herself away to me, that she herself becomes the living, the blinding proof of her own guilt, right
up to the crucial moment." Interesting idea, don't you
think?

He pulls his chair up close to her.

Listen to what else he said: "When that moment comes,

I'd turn to my wife, I'd ask her to sit down, and then, very casually, as if it were nothing at all, I'd tell her in the nicest way a little story about one of these affairs – some interesting, sophisticated little tale, you know the kind – and it would have to do with her own guilt. Gradually, very gradually, I'd screw the vise tighter and tighter until, at a certain point, I'd thrust a mirror under her nose and ask her very politely, 'Why are you so pale, my dear?' "

He begins to laugh a little strangely.

Delightful, isn't it? "You see, my dear, I know everything –"

GIULIA
Disturbed, she rises, but forces a smile, pretends indifference.

What nonsense!

ANDREA
Don't tell me I bored you? You weren't interested?

GIULIA
What's so interesting about – about Mantegna's wife?
She starts to go.

ANDREA
Well now, about Serra –
Very pale, GIULIA *stops and turns slightly to look back at him over her shoulder.* ANDREA *controls himself, changes tone again.*

Yes, I'll tell him, "Listen, old man, I really don't know what to do about you. Let's not stand on ceremony. We're friends, aren't we? So tell me, tell me what I owe you and I'll give it to you." How does that strike you?

GIULIA
Do what you think best.

ANDREA
Only, you see, I'm afraid that if I say it like that –

GIULIA
He'll refuse?

ANDREA
Rising, with a sigh.
Ah, the human conscience, my dear, often has such odd

scruples. Having made love to my wife, he'll refuse my money.

GIULIA

What did you say?

ANDREA

Frowning, but still in control of himself, almost gaily.
Isn't it the truth?

GIULIA

Are you mad?

ANDREA

It isn't true? Well, well, she denies it.

GIULIA

Are you mad?

ANDREA

Mad? You mean it isn't true?

GIULIA

You think you can frighten me? How can you say such a thing? What right do you have to insult me like this?

ANDREA

Suddenly grabbing her.
Insult you? You're trembling!

GIULIA

It's not true! What proof —

ANDREA

Proof! Right! Do you think I'm a fool? An idiot? And you the innocent, the victim! I saw you, understand, I saw you. With my own two eyes —

GIULIA

It's not true! You're crazy!

ANDREA

I am? You think I'm *that* stupid? I tell you I saw you with my own eyes and you dare to deny it? Whore! You're shaking like a leaf — like him — like him — on the trip! Three days I tortured him! And he ended by running away — couldn't stand it any more. He came here and told you,

didn't he? Didn't he? I let him come! Why didn't you go
off with him? Deny it, deny it now, if you can!

GIULIA

Andrea — Andrea!

ANDREA

You can't, can you?

GIULIA

Please!

ANDREA

Please?

GIULIA

Kill me, do what you like —

ANDREA

Seizing her again, furiously.
You'd deserve it, you bitch! You'd deserve it! Yes, yes — I
don't know what's holding me back — No! You see —
Letting go of her.
I'm not going to soil my hands with you! For the children's
sake! No! You didn't think about them, did you? Bitch,
bitch!
He seizes her and flings her toward the front door.
Get out! Get out of my house!

GIULIA

Desperately.
Where do you want me to go?

ANDREA

Why ask me? Go to your lover! You betrayed your own
family to come with me, to run away with me — with me!
So now if they slam the door in your face, they'll be right
to do it! Go to your lover! I'll give you everything, everything. Take him your money, too! You think I want your
money? It would dirty my hands now! I'll begin all over
again, for my children! Get out!

GIULIA

Andrea, kill me instead! Don't talk to me like this! I beg
you to forgive me, for their sake! I promise I'll never even
look you in the face again, only for their sake —

ANDREA

No!

GIULIA

Let me stay, for them –

ANDREA

No!

GIULIA

I'll do anything –

ANDREA

No!

GIULIA

I beg you!

ANDREA

No, no, no! You'll never see them again!

GIULIA

Do what you want to me –

ANDREA

No!

GIULIA

But they're mine, too!

ANDREA

You think of that now, do you? Now you think of it!

GIULIA

I was out of my mind –

ANDREA

So was I!

GIULIA

I was crazy! There's no excuse for what I've done, I know! I blame only myself. But I was out of my mind. Please believe me! I loved you, yes! I felt neglected by you – I'm not blaming anyone, only myself. I know, I know – but I ran away with you – doesn't that prove I loved you?

ANDREA

So you could betray me? Tell me now I was the first man in your life. You'd have done the same with anyone.

GIULIA

No! But I'm not trying to find excuses —

ANDREA

Then get out!

GIULIA

Wait! I don't know what else I can say to you! I'm in the wrong with you, with my children — yes — yes, it's true — but if there's no way I can make it up to you, let me at least find some way for their sake. You can't deny me that! You can't take me away from them!

ANDREA

Ah, now it's my fault! Don't try to get around me that way! You'll never see them again!

GIULIA

No! No, Andrea! I'm asking you for the last time, I'm begging you! Look — like this. . . .

She kneels before him.

ANDREA

Violently.

No! I said no! Stop it! Get up! I don't want to listen to you or ever see you again! The children are mine alone and they'll stay with me. As for you, get out!

GIULIA

All right then — kill me. . . .

ANDREA

Shrugs indifferently.

Do it yourself.

He goes to the window and gazes out. GIULIA, *crushed by these events, slowly bows her head and begins to sob.* ANDREA *turns slightly to look at her, then turns back to the window and remains motionless.* GIULIA *slowly gains control of herself, then rises and, very pale, choking back an occasional sob, approaches her husband.*

GIULIA

Then listen —

ANDREA *turns again to look at her and again she bursts into tears. He turns his back on her.*

ANDREA
You're only acting.

GIULIA
No. Listen – if I'm never to see them again – not even one last time – now – I beg you – please!

ANDREA
No. I said no.

GIULIA
One last time – just to give them a kiss – to hold them in my arms – and – and that's all!

ANDREA
No.

GIULIA
How cruel you are! All right – all right – then promise me at least – when they come home – and later on – promise me you'll never tell them – you'll never speak badly of me – promise me that! Don't let them know! And when –

ANDREA
In an odd tone of voice, turning to GIULIA *and inviting her to look out the window.*
Come here, come here now. . . .

GIULIA
Hesitating, terrified.
Why?
Then almost hysterically.
Ah! The children!

ANDREA
Seizing her by the arm and forcing her to look out.
No, no. Look! Look! Down there! See him?

GIULIA
Clutching him.
Andrea! Andrea! For God's sake!

ANDREA

Pushing her toward the door at right.
Go in there! What are you afraid of?

GIULIA

Andrea, please!

ANDREA

In there! In there! Afraid for him?

GIULIA

No! No! He's a coward —

ANDREA

Wait for him in there! You're two of a kind!

GIULIA

Her back against the door.
No! No! — Good-by, Andrea! — Good-by!
*She kisses him quickly and rushes into the next room,
shutting the door behind her.* ANDREA *remains stunned,
bewildered, facing the closed door, his hands to his face.*
ANTONIO *enters. Seeing* ANDREA, *he hesitates in the doorway. The sound of a shot from the next room.* ANTONIO
shouts.

ANDREA

Whirling suddenly on him.
Murderer!

Curtain

SICILIAN LIMES

(Lumie di Sicilia, 1910)

THE CAST

MICUCCIO BONAVINO, a band musician
SINA MARNIS, a singer
MARTA MARNIS, her mother
FERDINANDO, a servant
DORINA, a maid
GUESTS AND OTHER SERVANTS

In a city of northern Italy.

A waiting room sparsely furnished with a table and a few chairs. A corner of it, at left, is hidden by a screen. Side exits left and right. At rear, the main exit leads through a glass door, now open, into a darkened room through which can be seen another glass door leading into a splendidly illuminated salon where a table has been sumptuously set. It is late evening and the room is dark.

Shortly after the curtain rises, FERDINANDO *enters at right holding a lamp. He is in shirtsleeves but has only to put on his serving jacket to be ready to wait on table. He is followed by* MICUCCIO BONAVINO, *evidently a peasant from the look of him: he wears a rough coat with a cape pulled up around his ears, has heavy knee-length boots, carries a filthy sack in one hand and an old suitcase in the other. Tucked under his arm is the case of some musical instrument, but he is so worn out from cold and fatigue that he is barely able to keep his hold on it. As soon as the room is lighted, the snoring ceases and* DORINA'S *voice is heard from behind the screen.*

DORINA

Who is it?

FERDINANDO

Putting the lamp on the table.

Hey, Dorina, wake up! Can't you see Mr. Bonvicino's here?

MICUCCIO

Shaking his head to rid himself of a last drop of water on the end of his nose.

It's Bonavino, really.

FERDINANDO

Bonavino, Bonavino.

DORINA

Yawning, still behind the screen.
And who's he?

FERDINANDO

A relative of Miss Marnis.
To MICUCCIO.
What are you, anyway? A cousin maybe?

MICUCCIO

Embarrassed, hesitantly.
Well, no, not really. We're not related. I'm – I'm Micuccio
Bonavino. She knows.

DORINA

*Her curiosity aroused, still half-asleep, appearing from
behind the screen.*
A relative of Miss Marnis?

FERDINANDO

Annoyed.
Of course he isn't! How could he be?
To MICUCCIO.
You're from her home town, is that it? So why did you ask
me if "Aunt" Marta were home?
To DORINA.
You see? I thought he was a relative, a nephew or some-
thing.
To MICUCCIO.
I can't let you in, see.

MICUCCIO

Can't let me in? After I've come all this way?

FERDINANDO

What for?

MICUCCIO

To see her!

FERDINANDO

But you can't see her at this hour. Anyway, she isn't here.

MICUCCIO

Can I help it if the train arrives so late? What did you want
me to do? Tell it to go faster?

Smilingly, as if to persuade them to be understanding.
A train's a train. It arrives when it's supposed to. I've been
traveling two whole days.

DORINA

Looking him over.
Oh, I can tell that!

MICUCCIO

You can, huh? It shows? How do I look?

DORINA

Terrible, dear. Don't be offended.

FERDINANDO

I can't let you in. Come back tomorrow morning and you'll
find her. Right now she's at the theatre.

MICUCCIO

Come back tomorrow? Where am I supposed to go at this
time of night, a stranger? If she isn't here, I'll wait for her.
Oh, that's a good one! I can't wait for her in here?

FERDINANDO

I tell you that without her consent —

MICUCCIO

The hell with her consent! You don't know who I am!

FERDINANDO

Exactly, because I don't know who you are. I'm not going
to catch it on your account!

MICUCCIO

Smilingly wagging a finger at him.
Don't you worry about it.

DORINA

To FERDINANDO.
Oh sure, she'll be dying to see him, tonight of all nights!
To MICUCCIO.
See that, darling?
Indicating the room at rear.
There's going to be a party!

MICUCCIO

Oh yes? What kind of party?

DORINA

A gala . . .
Yawning.
A gala evening in her honor.

FERDINANDO

And God knows when we'll get through here, at dawn maybe!

MICUCCIO

Fine, so much the better! I'm sure that as soon as Teresina sees me —

FERDINANDO

To DORINA.
Hear that? He calls her Teresina, no less. He asked me if this was where "Teresina the singer" lives.

MICUCCIO

What's wrong with that? Isn't she a singer? Isn't that her name? *You* aren't going to try to teach me about *her,* are you?

DORINA

So you really do know her well?

MICUCCIO

Well? We grew up together, the two of us!

FERDINANDO

To DORINA.
What'll we do?

DORINA

Oh, let him wait.

MICUCCIO

Indignantly.
You're damn right I'll wait! What is this? You don't think I came to —

FERDINANDO

All right, sit down over there. I wash my hands of it. I have to finish setting the table.
He starts out.

MICUCCIO

This is really something! As if I were — I suppose it's because you see me like this, with the smoke and dust of the train all over me. If I told Teresina about this, when she gets home from the theatre . . .

He experiences a moment of doubt and looks around.
This place — I mean, who owns it?

DORINA

Looking at him, teasingly.
It's ours, for as long as we live in it.

MICUCCIO

Well, then!
He looks toward the salon again.
Is the house very big?

DORINA

So so.

MICUCCIO

That's the living room?

DORINA

Usually. Tonight they're dining in there.

MICUCCIO

Oh. Quite a spread! All those candles . . .

DORINA

Beautiful, eh?

MICUCCIO

Rubbing his hands happily.
So it's true!

DORINA

What?

MICUCCIO

Oh — I can tell — they're pretty well off. . . .

DORINA

Do you know who Sina Marnis *is*?

MICUCCIO

Sina? Oh yes! That's her name now. Aunt Marta wrote me about it. Teresina — sure — Teresina: Sina . . .

DORINA

Wait a minute – now that I think about it – you're –
Calling FERDINANDO *from the other room.*
Hey, Ferdinando, come here! Know who he is? He's the
one her mother writes to all the time!

MICUCCIO

She can just about write at all, poor woman.

DORINA

Yes, yes, Bonavino. But – Domenico! Is your name Domenico?

MICUCCIO

Domenico, Micuccio, it's all the same. We say Micuccio
where I come from.

DORINA

And you've been sick, haven't you? Just recently.

MICUCCIO

Very sick, yes. I almost died. I *was* dead! They had the
candles lit for me.

DORINA

And didn't Mrs. Marnis send you a money order? Yes, I
remember. We went to the post office together.

MICUCCIO

A money order, yes. And that's another reason I came. I
have the money with me, in here.

DORINA

You're giving it back to her?

MICUCCIO

Vehemently.
Money, never! I don't even want to listen to talk about
money! But tell me, will it be long before they come home?

DORINA

Looking at the clock.
Oh, still some – Tonight, well, you can imagine!

FERDINANDO

Passing through with a load of dishes, shouting.
Brava! Brava! Encore! Encore! Encore!

MICUCCIO

Smiling.

A great voice, eh?

FERDINANDO

Oh, sure. The voice, too . . .

MICUCCIO

Again rubbing his hands.

I can be proud of that! M; work!

DORINA

The voice?

MICUCCIO

I discovered it!

DORINA

You did?

To FERDINANDO.

Hear that, Ferdinando? He discovered it – her voice.

MICUCCIO

I'm a musician, you know.

FERDINANDO

Ah, a musician? Good for you! And what do you play?
The trombone?

MICUCCIO

Very seriously.

No, not the trombone. The piccolo. I'm in the band, the
town band. In our town –

DORINA

Which is called – wait, I'll remember. . . .

MICUCCIO

Palma Montechiaro, there's only one.

DORINA

Ah, yes, Palma. Of course.

FERDINANDO

So you were the one who discovered her voice?

DORINA

Come on, come on, tell us how you did it! Listen to this,
Ferdinando.

MICUCCIO

Shrugging.

How I did it? She used to sing and . . .

DORINA

And because you were a musician, you knew right away, eh?

MICUCCIO

No, not right away. In fact . . .

FERDINANDO

It took you a while?

MICUCCIO

She used to sing all the time. Just to forget.

DORINA

Really?

FERDINANDO

Forget what?

MICUCCIO

A lot of things.

FERDINANDO

Like what?

MICUCCIO

She was unhappy. She had a lot of bad luck, poor thing. Those were the days! Her father had died. I – well, I used to help her, both her and her mother, Aunt Marta. But my mother was against it and – well . . .

DORINA

So you were in love with her?

MICUCCIO

Me? With Teresina? Don't make me laugh! My mother wanted me to drop her because, poor thing, she had nothing, after her father died. While I, for better or for worse, I had my little post in the band. . . .

FERDINANDO

But – so there was nothing? You weren't engaged?

MICUCCIO

My family wouldn't hear of it then! And so Teresina used to sing out of spite.

DORINA

Is that so? And so you . . .

MICUCCIO

Pure luck! I must have been inspired! No one had ever paid any attention to her voice before, not even me. Suddenly, one morning –

FERDINANDO

Talk about luck!

MICUCCIO

I'll never forget it! It was a morning in April. She was singing at the window, over the rooftops. She was living in an attic then!

FERDINANDO

Hear that?

DORINA

Keep quiet!

MICUCCIO

What's wrong with that? From little acorns –

DORINA

Sure, sure. Well? She was singing and –?

MICUCCIO

I must have heard her sing that little song a hundred thousand times –

DORINA

What song?

MICUCCIO

Just a little local song! I'd never paid any attention before. But that morning – an angel, that's what she sounded like, an angel! Without saying a word to anyone, not even to her or her mother, that evening I brought the leader of our band – he's a good friend of mine – up to her room. Oh, he's a very good friend of mine, old Saro Malaviti, such a nice man. . . . Well, he listens to her – he's very good,

a very good musician – everyone knows him in Palma –
and he says: "This is a God-given voice!" You can imagine
the joy! I rented a piano and what a time we had getting
it up there – well, never mind! I bought music and right
away the maestro begins giving her lessons, but just like
that – happy with whatever I could give him from time
to time – What was I? What I am today: a poor man. The
piano cost money, the music cost money – and Teresina
had to eat. . . .

FERDINANDO

Oh, I'll bet!

DORINA

She needed her strength to sing.

MICUCCIO

Meat every day! I'm proud of that!

FERDINANDO

You ought to be!

DORINA

And so?

MICUCCIO

She began to learn. And you could tell even then – she was
up in heaven, you might say – and you could hear her all
over town, that great voice. People would gather – like this,
down below in the street, to listen. She was on fire, really
on fire in those days. And when she'd finish singing, she'd
grab me by the arms – like this –

Grabbing FERDINANDO.

– and shake me – like a madwoman. Because she already
knew, she knew what she'd become. The maestro used
to tell her, too. And she didn't know how to show her
gratitude. Aunt Marta, instead, poor woman –

DORINA

She was against it?

MICUCCIO

Not exactly. She didn't believe in it, that's all. She'd had
such a hard time, poor soul, such a hard life that she didn't
even want Teresina to get the idea that things might get

better, she'd become so resigned to the way they were
living. She was afraid, that's all. And then she knew what
it was costing me – and that my family – But I broke with
everyone, my father, my mother, when a certain maestro
passed through our town. He was giving some concerts –
or maybe just one – I don't even remember his name any
more, but he was fairly well known – it doesn't matter!
Anyway, when he heard Teresina and said it would be a
shame, a real shame if she couldn't finish her studies in a
city, at a real conservatory – well, I caught fire, too! I
broke with everyone, sold the piece of land an old uncle
of mine, a priest, had left me when he died, and I sent
Teresina to Naples, to the conservatory there.

FERDINANDO

You? You did that?

MICUCCIO

Sure, who else?

DORINA

To FERDINANDO.
At his own expense, get it?

MICUCCIO

I kept her there for four years. I haven't seen her since.

DORINA

Never?

MICUCCIO

Never. Because – because then she began to sing in theatres, understand? Here and there. Once she began to fly,
it was from Naples to Rome, from Rome to Milan, then to
Spain – then Russia – then back here again. . . .

FERDINANDO

A sensation!

MICUCCIO

Oh, I know! I have all her clippings, a suitcase full of
them. And then I also have her letters in here –
*Takes a packet of letters from the inside pocket of his
jacket.*
– hers and her mother's. Here they are. And here's what she

wrote when she sent me that money, when I was dying: "Dear Micuccio, I have no time to write you. Mother will write you for me. Take care of yourself, get well soon, and love me. Teresina."

FERDINANDO

And – and did she send you enough?

DORINA

A thousand lire, wasn't it?

MICUCCIO

That's right, a thousand.

FERDINANDO

And that property you sold, forgive me, but what was it worth?

MICUCCIO

What could it be worth? Not much. It was just a little piece of land.

FERDINANDO

Knowingly to DORINA.

I see.

MICUCCIO

But I have the money right here, every cent of it. I don't want anything. The little I did, I did for her. We agreed to wait two or three years until she could make a little headway. Aunt Marta always reminded me of that in her letters. I have to admit I didn't really expect to get this money. But if Teresina sent it to me, it's a sign that she's doing all right, that she's made a name for herself.

FERDINANDO

And what a name!

MICUCCIO

So I guess it's time –

DORINA

To get married?

MICUCCIO

Here I am.

FERDINANDO

You came here to marry Sina Marnis?

DORINA

Shut up! If she promised to! You don't understand anything! Of course they're going to get married!

MICUCCIO

I don't say that. All I say is, here I am. I left everything and everyone back home: my family, the band, everything. I fought with my relatives over this thousand lire, which arrived without my knowing about it, when I was more dead than alive. I had to tear the check away from my mother. She wanted to keep it. Oh no, sir, no money, nothing! No one owes Micuccio Bonavino a cent! Wherever I go, to the ends of the earth, I'm never going to starve, not me. I have my art. I have my piccolo with me and –

DORINA

You do? You brought it with you?

MICUCCIO

Of course! We're inseparable, him and me!

FERDINANDO

She sings and he plays, get it?

MICUCCIO

I couldn't get a job in some orchestra, maybe?

FERDINANDO

Of course! Why not?

DORINA

And – and you play well, I'll bet!

MICUCCIO

Not bad. I've been at it about ten years.

FERDINANDO

Why don't you let us hear something?
He goes to get the instrument case.

DORINA

Yes, yes, good idea! Play something for us!

MICUCCIO

No! What could I play? It's too late.

DORINA

Some little thing, come on! Be nice!

FERDINANDO

Any little tune . . .

MICUCCIO

No! I can't!

FERDINANDO

Don't make us beg.
Opens the case and takes out the instrument.
Here we are!

DORINA

Come on now! We want to hear you.

MICUCCIO

But it's impossible. I mean, like this – with no accompaniment –

DORINA

It doesn't matter! Come on! Try!

FERDINANDO

Otherwise, look out, *I'll* play!

MICUCCIO

I don't mind, if you insist. . . . I'll play the little song Teresina sang, in the attic that day. All right?

FERDINANDO AND DORINA

Yes! Yes! Good! That one!
MICUCCIO *sits down and begins very seriously to play.*
FERDINANDO *and* DORINA *try hard to keep a straight
face. Another* WAITER, *the* COOK, *and a* KITCHEN BOY
join them and are signaled to keep quiet and listen.
MICUCCIO's *playing is suddenly interrupted by the loud
ringing of a bell.*

FERDINANDO

Oh, there they are!

DORINA

To the other WAITER.
Hurry up, you go and open the door!
To the COOK *and* KITCHEN BOY.

And you, get a move on! She said she wanted to eat as soon as she got here.

The other SERVANTS *exit quickly.*

FERDINANDO

My jacket, where did I put it?

DORINA

In there!

She points to the screen and runs out. MICUCCIO *gets up, dismayed, holding the piccolo.* FERDINANDO *goes to get his jacket, puts it on hurriedly, then, seeing that* MICUCCIO *is about to follow* DORINA *out, rudely stops him.*

FERDINANDO

You stay here! I have to let her know first.

He exits. MICUCCIO *remains behind, ill-at-ease, confused, oppressed by a gloomy presentiment.*

MARTA'S VOICE

Off stage.

Not here, Dorina! In there, in there!

FERDINANDO, DORINA, *and the other* WAITER *re-enter from the room at right and cross the stage, headed toward the room at rear and holding magnificent masses of flowers.* MICUCCIO *sticks his head out to peer into the banquet room and now he can see a number of gentlemen in evening dress talking to each other.* DORINA *re-enters in a great hurry, heading for the exit at right.*

MICUCCIO

Touching her arm.

Who are they?

DORINA

The guests!

Exits. MICUCCIO *again peers inside. His gaze becomes misty, partly out of amazement, partly out of emotion; he isn't even aware himself that his eyes are full of tears. He closes them and withdraws into himself, almost as if to resist the anxiety and pain caused in him by the sound of a brassy laugh: Sina Marnis laughs like that,*

from the other room. DORINA *returns with two more baskets of flowers.*

DORINA

Without stopping, headed for the banquet room.
What? Are you crying?

MICUCCIO

Me? No. All those people . . .
AUNT MARTA *enters from the right. She is wearing a hat
and is all but overwhelmed, poor woman, by a costly,
resplendent velvet cape. As soon as she catches sight of*
MICUCCIO, *she immediately smothers the cry that rises
instinctively from her throat.*

MARTA

What? Micuccio! You here?

MICUCCIO

Uncovering his face and staring at her, almost frightened.
Aunt Marta . . . Oh God! . . . You? Like that?

MARTA

Like — like what?

MICUCCIO

That hat. You?

MARTA

Oh, yes . . .
She nods distractedly. Then, suddenly alarmed.
But what are you doing here? Without letting us know!
What's happened?

MICUCCIO

I — I came to —

MARTA

Tonight, of all nights! Oh Lord, Lord . . . Wait — what'll
we do? What'll we do? You see all those people? It's for
Teresina —

MICUCCIO

I know.

MARTA

In her honor, understand? Wait – now wait here a moment. . . .

MICUCCIO

If you – if you think I ought to go –

MARTA

No, wait a moment, I said.

She starts for the banquet room.

MICUCCIO

I wouldn't know – I mean, here –

AUNT MARTA *turns back, signals with her gloved hand that he is to wait, and exits into the other room, where there is suddenly a complete silence.* SINA MARNIS'S *voice is now heard clearly and distinctly.*

SINA

One moment, gentlemen!

Again MICUCCIO *hides his face in his hands, but* SINA *does not appear. Instead, after a little while,* AUNT MARTA *returns, minus hat, gloves, and cape, less embarrassed than before.*

MARTA

Here I am, here I am.

MICUCCIO

And – and Teresina?

MARTA

I told her. I told her. Now, as soon as – as soon as she has a moment – she'll come. Meanwhile, we'll stay here together, won't we? All right? Happy now?

MICUCCIO

Oh, as for me, I –

MARTA

I'll stay here with you.

MICUCCIO

You don't have to if – if you don't want to – if you're needed in there, I –

MARTA

No, no. They're going to have dinner, understand? Her admirers – the impresario – Her career, you understand? We'll stay in here, just the two of us. Dorina will set the table for us and – and we'll eat together, you and I, right here, eh? What do you say? Just the two of us. We'll talk about the old days. . . .

DORINA *returns with a tablecloth, plates, and silverware.* Come, come, Dorina. Here, quick now. For me and this dear boy of mine. My dear old Micuccio! I can't believe it's really you!

DORINA

Here. Meanwhile, you can sit down.

MARTA

Sitting.

Yes, yes. Here, all by ourselves, just the two of us. In there, you understand – all those people . . . Poor child, she can't get out of it – her career – what can you do? Did you see the papers? They're just raving about her, Micuccio! Raving! And I, you know, I'm all at sea, it's too much. . . . I can't believe I'm sitting here alone with you tonight like this.

She rubs her hands and smiles, gazing at him tenderly.

MICUCCIO

Gloomily, in a hurt tone.

And – and she'll come, she said? I mean – I mean, just to – to see her, at least.

MARTA

But of course she'll come! As soon as she can catch her breath, didn't I tell you she would? But for her, too – imagine what a joy it would be for her to stay here with us – with you, after all this time. . . . How many years is it? So many, so many . . . Ah, Micuccio, it seems only yesterday and it seems ages ago, too. . . . So many, many things I've seen – things that – that don't seem real. I never would have believed it if someone had told me, when we were still back in Palma and you used to come and see us – in that attic with swallows nesting in the rafters, remember? Remember how they'd fly all over the house? Into our faces sometimes. And those beautiful pots of basil I used to keep on the window sill. And Annuzza, old Annuzza? Our neighbor? Whatever became of her?

MICUCCIO

Oh . . .

With two fingers he makes the sign of the benediction to indicate that she is dead.

MARTA

Dead? I might have known. She was an old crone even then, older than me. Poor old Annuzza. With her "little pinch of garlic." Remember? That was always her excuse – to borrow a little pinch of garlic, just as we were about to sit down and eat and – poor old thing! And who knows how many others are gone now, eh? Back in Palma . . . Well, no matter. Dead or not, at least they're resting in their own ground, beside their own people. While I – who knows where I'll rest these poor old bones of mine? Well, never mind, let's not think about it!

DORINA *arrives with the first course and offers the serving plate to* MICUCCIO.

Oh good, Dorina . . .

MICUCCIO *looks at* DORINA, *then at* AUNT MARTA, *confused, embarrassed. He raises his hands to serve himself, sees how dirty they are from the trip and, more confused than ever, lowers them out of sight again.*

Here, here, Dorina! I'll do it, I'll do it.

She serves him.

Like that? Enough?

MICUCCIO

Yes, yes. Thanks.

MARTA

Serving herself.

There we are.

MICUCCIO

Smacking his lips, making an effort to be jolly.
Ah hah! Looks good!

MARTA

For the party in her honor, you see. Come on, let's eat! But
first —
She makes the sign of the Cross.
I can do it here with you.
He also makes the sign.
Good boy! You, too . . . Good old Micuccio, you're just
the same, you haven't changed! Believe me, when — when
I have to eat in there — without making the blessed sign —
I feel — I feel like the food is a lump of lead inside. . . .
Eat, eat!

MICUCCIO

I'm starved! I haven't eaten for two days, you know!

MARTA

What? Didn't you eat on the train?

MICUCCIO

I brought something to eat — in my suitcase — but —

MARTA

But what?

MICUCCIO

You won't believe me. I — I was ashamed, Aunt Marta. It
didn't seem like much and — and I thought everyone would
stare at me. . . .

MARTA

How silly! And so you went without eating? Come on, eat
now, my poor old Micuccio. Of course you must be starved!
Two days . . . And drink, drink . . .
She pours him some wine.

MICUCCIO

Thanks. That's fine.
*From time to time, as the servants go back and forth
from the kitchen to the banquet room, opening and closing the inner door, a sudden wave of sound — phrases,*

bursts of laughter – invades the room. MICUCCIO *looks up, disturbed by it, and finds himself staring into the afflicted and loving eyes of* AUNT MARTA, *as if seeking some explanation from them.*

They're laughing. . . .

MARTA

Yes. Drink, drink. . . . Oh, that good wine of ours, Micuccio! How I miss it, if you only knew! The wine Michelà used to have, right under us . . . What about Michelà? What's happened to him?

MICUCCIO

Michelà? He's fine, fine. . . .

MARTA

And his daughter, Luzza?

MICUCCIO

She got married. She has two kids already.

MARTA

Really? She used to come up and see us, remember? Always so gay! Oh, little Luzza – imagine that – married. . . . Who did she marry?

MICUCCIO

Totò Licasi, the fellow who used to work at the customs house, remember?

MARTA

Oh yes? Good . . . And so Mariangela's a grandmother, eh? A grandmother already! Lucky woman! Two children, you said?

MICUCCIO

Yes, two . . .

Another wave of sound from the party.

MARTA

More wine?

MICUCCIO

Yes. Now – what –

MARTA

Don't pay any attention. You know, it's a party. They

laugh, that's all. That's life, isn't it? What can you expect?
Her career. The impresario's there. . . .

    DORINA *returns with another course.*

Here, Dorina. Give me your plate, Micuccio. You'll like
this, too.

    Serving him.

Say when.

MICUCCIO

You do it, you do it!

MARTA

There, how's that?

    Serves herself. DORINA *exits.*

MICUCCIO

How well you've learned! I can't get over it!

MARTA

I had to.

MICUCCIO

When I saw you with that velvet thing on – and that hat –

MARTA

I had to! Don't make me think about it!

MICUCCIO

I know, I know. You have to put on a show! But if they
could see you, if they could see you dressed like this in
Palma, Aunt Marta!

MARTA

    Hiding her face in her hands.

Oh my God, don't make me think of it! Believe me – if I
think about it – I feel so ashamed! I look at myself, I say:
"That's me? Looking like that?" And it all seems like a
game. . . . But what can I do? I can't help it!

MICUCCIO

So then – so I mean – she's – she's a big success? Yes, I
can see she is! A big success! Do they – do they pay her
well, eh?

MARTA

Oh, yes. Very well.

MICUCCIO

How much each night?

MARTA

It depends. According to – to the seasons – the – the theatre, understand? But you know, Micuccio, it's expensive,
it's very expensive, this life. There never seems to be
enough money! It costs so much, so much, if you only
knew! It goes – it goes as fast as it comes – clothes, jewels –
all kinds of expenses –

She is interrupted by a burst of sound from the party.

VOICES

Where? Where? We want to know! Where?

SINA'S VOICE

One moment! I said one moment!

MARTA

Here she is! It's her – she's coming!

*SINA enters hurriedly, a vision in rustling silk, splendidly
bedecked in jewels, her gown cut very low to reveal her
bosom, her naked shoulders and arms. It's as if the little
room were bathed suddenly, violently in light. MICUCCIO,
who had been about to reach for his glass, freezes, his
face aflame, his eyes bulging, his mouth sagging open.
Overwhelmed by her appearance, he stares at her as if
she were a figure from a dream.*

MICUCCIO

Stuttering.
Te-Teresina . . .

SINA

Micuccio? Where are you? Oh, there you are! How are
you? How are you? Are you well now? Good, good! You
were sick, eh? Listen, I'll see you again in a little while.
Anyway, Mother's here. All right? See you soon. . . .

*She rushes out again. MICUCCIO remains frozen in amaze-
ment, while from the party SINA's return is greeted with
renewed shouting.*

MARTA

After a long pause, timorously, breaking the spell.
You're not eating?

MICUCCIO *looks at her uncomprehendingly.*

Eat. . . .

Points at his plate.

MICUCCIO

*Tugging at his dirty, wrinkled collar with two fingers
and sighing.*

Eat?

*He indicates with a gesture that he can't eat another
mouthful. Another pause as he remains bitterly absorbed in what he has just seen, then he speaks in a low
voice.*

What she's done to herself . . . I – I couldn't believe it was
her. . . . All – all – like this . . .

He refers, without scorn but with disbelief, to SINA'S
nudity.

A dream . . . Her voice – her eyes . . . She isn't – she isn't
the same – that's not Teresina. . . .

Noticing that AUNT MARTA *has also stopped eating and
has sadly bowed her head.*

The same? Not even – not even to think about! All over –
and for who knows how long it's been over! And I, like a
fool – like an idiot . . . They tried to warn me back home
and I – I broke my back to get here. Thirty-six hours on a
train to – to make – That's why that waiter and that girl,
that Dorina – what a laugh! Me, with my . . .

*He smiles sadly, nodding, indicating by a gesture that
he knows how foolish he has been.*

But how could I have known? I came because – because
she, Teresina – because she promised me. . . . But
maybe – oh yes! – how could she have guessed that one
day she'd become like this? While I – back there – while I
was stuck with – with my piccolo – in the town square – she
– such a long way . . . No! It's out of the question!

He turns swiftly to stare at AUNT MARTA.

Maybe I did once help her out, Aunt Marta, but I don't want anyone to think I came here to live off her. . . .

Rising, becoming increasingly excited.

In fact, wait a minute!

He pulls out his wallet.

I also came to give you back the money you sent me. What was it supposed to be? My salary? Paying me back? For what? I see Teresina's become a – a queen! I see she's – never mind! It's out of the question! But this money, no! I didn't deserve that from her. . . . For what? It's over and that's all there is to it, but money, no! Money to *me*, never! I'm only sorry it's not all –

MARTA

Trembling, her eyes full of tears.

What do you mean, what are you saying, my child?

MICUCCIO

Cutting her off with a gesture.

I didn't spend it. My relatives did, while I was sick, without telling me. But that'll make up for the few lire I spent on her, remember? It was nothing. Let's forget about it. Here's most of it. And I'm going now.

MARTA

What? So soon? At least wait until I tell her. Didn't you hear her say she wanted to see you? I'll go call her –

MICUCCIO

Restraining her.

No, it won't do any good. Listen!

From the party comes the sound of a piano and a bawdy operetta chorus being noisily sung, with much laughter, by all the guests.

Let her stay in there. She's fine, she belongs in there. . . . As for me, I've – I've seen her and that's enough. . . . Hear how they laugh? I don't want – I don't want them to laugh like that at me. I'm going. . . .

MARTA

Interpreting his decision as contempt and jealousy.
But I – I can't watch over her any more, Micuccio. She
does what she wants now. . . .

MICUCCIO

*Suddenly reading in her eyes a truth he had not yet
suspected, shouting, his face clouding over.*
What do you mean?

MARTA

*Confused, she hides her face in her hands but fails to
halt the flow of tears. Her voice is smothered in sobs.*
Yes, yes, go, Micuccio, go. She's not for you any more,
you're right. If you'd only listened to me –

MICUCCIO

*Interrupting, leaning over her and tearing a hand away
from her face.*
So – so then she's not worthy of me any more, is that it?
The chorus in the other room continues.

MARTA

*Crying, in torment, she nods yes, yes, then raises her
hands so prayerfully to* MICUCCIO *that his rage is dis-
pelled at once.*
Please, please, for my sake, Micuccio!

MICUCCIO

All right. I'll go anyway. In fact – in fact – all the more rea-
son now . . .
At this point, SINA *returns. Immediately,* MICUCCIO *turns
to face her. He seizes her by the arms and drags her
forward.*
Ah, that's why – that's why all this – all this. . . .
He alludes with contempt to her nakedness.
Breasts – arms – shoulders . . .

MARTA

Supplicatingly, terrified.
Please, Micuccio!

MICUCCIO

No. Don't worry. I'm not going to do anything. I'm going.

What a fool I was, Aunt Marta! I didn't realize it. Don't
cry, don't cry. Anyway, what harm did it do? In fact, I was
lucky! Lucky . . .

*So saying, he picks up his suitcase and the sack, and he
starts to leave, but suddenly he remembers that the sack
contains the beautiful limes he has brought Teresina
all the way from home.*

Oh, I forgot. Look, Aunt Marta! Look here. . . .

*He opens the sack and empties the contents on the
table.*

SINA

Starting for them.

Oh! The limes! The limes of Palma!

MICUCCIO

Immediately stopping her.

Don't you touch them! Don't you even look at them!

He picks one up and holds it under MARTA'S *nose.*

Smell it, smell the air of our town. . . . And now, what if
I threw them, one by one, at the heads of all those fine
gentlemen in there?

MARTA

No, please!

MICUCCIO

Don't worry. They're for you, Aunt Marta. Only for you,
remember! I brought them for her –

Indicates SINA.

And to think I even paid the tax on them . . .

*He notices the money he left on the table. He grabs it
and stuffs it into the bosom of* SINA's *dress as she bursts
into tears.*

This is what you want now! Here! Here! Take it! And
stop it, don't cry! Good-by, Aunt Marta! Good luck!

*He stuffs the empty sack into his pocket, picks up his
suitcase, his instrument case, and exits.*

Curtain

THE DOCTOR'S DUTY

(Il dovere del medico, 1913)

THE CAST

TOMMASO CORSI
ANNA, his wife
MRS. REIS, Anna's mother
DR. TITO LECCI
FRANCO CIMETTA, a lawyer
ROSA, the maid
A POLICEMAN
A MALE NURSE (nonspeaking)

In a city of Southern Italy.

A room in the Corsi house, with cupboards, a wash-basin, a sofa, a large antique armchair, a clothes rack, chairs, other objects. At left, a window flanked by curtains. Two exits, one at rear, leading into the bedroom, the other at right.

At curtain, the room is occupied by MRS. REIS *and the* POLICEMAN. *The latter is seated beside the door at right. He is evidently on guard duty, but he seems bored and tired. The woman is standing by the sofa and fidgeting moodily, impatiently. She is dressed in black, with a widow's bonnet on her woolly hair. Her eyes, peering out from under thick, frowning eyebrows, glitter with hatred and suspicion in a pallid, bitter face pinched and worn by anguish and grief. She is evidently waiting for someone or something, and two or three times she glances at the* POLICEMAN *as if she wants to ask him something, but restrains herself.*

MRS. REIS
Finally making up her mind, in a hard voice.
Will you be on guard here much longer?

POLICEMAN
No, madam. We may be through today.

MRS. REIS
Today? At last! You'll take him away?

POLICEMAN
I'm not sure. I think that's what they said.
ROSA, the maid, enters from the rear, quickly closing the door behind her.

ROSA
To MRS. REIS.
She's coming now.
She indicates the door behind her and exits at right.

Quite a long pause. Finally, the door at rear opens again and ANNA *enters, also immediately closing the door behind her. She is about thirty, undone by her desperation and the suffering she has been through. Her hair is uncombed and her eyes seem to burn from the effect of tears and sleepless vigils. She runs to her mother and throws herself into her arms, trying to smother her sobbing.*

ANNA

Mother! Mother! Oh, Mother!
She gradually gets control of herself, draws back, and turns to the POLICEMAN.
Would you mind leaving us alone for a minute? Couldn't you wait behind the door?

POLICEMAN

Really, my orders are to keep a sharper eye out here, not ease the watch.

ANNA

But he can't even move in bed without help!

POLICEMAN

Doubtfully.
I know, but . . .
Making up his mind.
Just for a moment then.

ANNA

Thank you. Take the chair with you.
The POLICEMAN *nods and exits at right, taking the chair with him.*

ANNA

Turning back to her mother and embracing her again.
Oh, Mother! I'm so grateful you came back! No, I don't blame you for having left me alone.

MRS. REIS

You wouldn't listen to me. You wanted to stay here, to take part in this lovely business. Look at the state you're in!

ANNA

How could I leave him, Mother? What are you saying?
Thank you for taking the children away. How are they?
Didì? Federico?

MRS. REIS

They're all right.

ANNA

Even Didì?

MRS. REIS

Both of them. But you'll be joining us soon, I hear. I was
told they're going to take him away today.

ANNA

Stunned, frantic.
Today? Who told you that?

MRS. REIS

The guard.

ANNA

Today? But that's impossible! He told you that?
She runs to the door at right and calls the POLICEMAN.
Officer, come in here, please.
And immediately the POLICEMAN *returns, embarrassed.*
Is it true? Today? You're going to take him away today?

POLICEMAN

I'm not sure, madam. I think that's what I heard.

ANNA

But he's still in bed! The wound hasn't even closed. The
doctor will never allow it. He's still under the doctor's care.
Only last night he said he'd try and get him out of bed for
a few minutes today.

MRS. REIS

He's all right. He can get up.

ANNA

No, he can't! He can hardly stand! He can't even sit up
unless someone helps him.
Going to the door at right and calling.
Rosa! Rosa!

To the others.
It would be a crime!
Quickly, to ROSA, *who has appeared in the doorway.*
Send Enrico at once to the doctor's house and tell him to
come here. Quickly, without wasting time!

ROSA

I understand. Yes, madam.
She exits.

ANNA

Just when he's barely beginning to be himself again! After
doing everything we could to save him!

POLICEMAN

You asked me to come in, madam. I could go back out, if
you want.

ANNA

Yes, please. Don't worry, he can't move.
The POLICEMAN *exits again.*

ANNA

Spreading her arms wide and looking up, desperately.
And now this! After all we've been through, another tor-
ture!

MRS. REIS

He didn't want to die! The murderer!

ANNA

Oh, Mother, you hate him. You won't forgive him.

MRS. REIS

Giving vent to her feelings.
Yes, I hate him. I hate him for everything he's made you
go through, for the shame he's caused you, your children,
our whole family! And it's still not over! The least he
could have done was die!

ANNA

Yes, it would have been better, even for him, if he'd died
on the spot. But believe me, Mother, he *did* want to die.

MRS. REIS

All I see is that he knew how to kill Neri, all right, but that
he himself is still alive.

ANNA

He aimed the gun into his own heart.

MRS. REIS

He should have aimed at his head, his head!

ANNA

And three, four times he tore the bandages off the wound.
The doctors, of course, wanted to save him. What didn't
they do here, night and day, to keep him alive! But believe
me, believe me, he tried his very best *not* to live.

MRS. REIS

I don't wonder! He knows what's in store for him!

ANNA

No, Mother. To punish himself. You won't look beyond the
mere facts.

MRS. REIS

Does that make him any the less a murderer, because he
did want to die? Didn't he kill Neri? Wasn't he betraying
you with Neri's wife?

ANNA

Yes, yes.

MRS. REIS

And you tell me I don't look beyond the facts!

ANNA

But there are so many things you can't know and that I do
know.

MRS. REIS

Now you sound like him! My God, it's almost like hearing
him speak! Facts that aren't really facts, empty sacks that
won't stand up . . . That's how he's always fooled you,
blinded you. . . .

ANNA

No, Mother.

MRS. REIS

Yes, yes, blinded, blinded!

ANNA

It was a hunger for life, that's all. He didn't think.

MRS. REIS

He had no scruples.

ANNA

Yes, put it any way you like. So many times I've tried to judge one of his acts, but he never gave me time to judge, just as he never attached any importance to anything he did. It was useless to call him to account. A shrug of the shoulders, a smile and off he'd go. No matter what, he had to keep going. No hesitating to weigh right from wrong.

MRS. REIS

Oh, you admit that!

ANNA

But, you see, there was nothing ever really bad in this constant rage for life of his. He was always himself, always happy, everybody's friend. At thirty-eight he was still a boy, able to play like a child with Didì and Federico, even to lose his temper. And after ten years with me he was still – still – No, no. Maybe he did stray once in a while, deceive me from time to time. But lie to me, no. Never. He could never lie with those lips, those eyes, that smile that every day used to light up the whole house. Angelica Neri? Do you really expect me to believe that between her and me Tommaso would – Look, it was nothing more than the whim of the moment for him, nothing, merely proof of a weakness perhaps all men share. Nor would you expect him to have any scruples over his friendship with the husband, who knew perfectly well what kind of woman his wife was and how she dishonored him openly with everyone. Even here, I tell you, in our own house, right under my own eyes, she used to try and seduce Tommaso with her sick monkey tricks. Here, right here! I noticed it and so did he. We used to laugh about it, Tommaso and I! Yes, yes, we laughed, we laughed!

She bursts into hysterical laughter.

MRS. REIS

Anna! Anna! You're going mad!

ANNA

You're driving me mad! Facts! Facts! The facts are that Neri knew, and not only about Tommaso but about everyone else, and he never gave the slightest hint of caring. At the last minute he decided to create a tragedy, when what he should have done was to kill her like a mad dog! It wouldn't have cost him a thing! The facts . . . Then I suppose they'll claim Tommaso was carrying a gun to kill Neri? He always carried one because of the work he had to do, the business of the leases and so on in the country.

LECCI *and* CIMETTA *enter at this point. The former is tall, stiff, wears thick eyeglasses; the latter is older, with a nearly white pointed beard and long hair that is still black and combed straight back.*

ANNA

Ah, here's the doctor! And you too, Cimetta?

LECCI

Why this sudden call? Anything new?

ANNA

Indicating her mother to CIMETTA.

My mother.

Turning to LECCI.

Doctor, they're trying to drive me mad. They want to take him away today!

LECCI

Of course not. Who told you that?

ANNA

The policeman out there. Ask him. That's what he said.

LECCI

Oh, we'll put a stop to that, don't you worry. I'll go to the Commissioner myself, right now. Will you come too, Cimetta?

ANNA

Yes, yes, you go too, please!

CIMETTA

Any time you say. Right this minute. It's just down the street.

LECCI

Don't even think about it. Without my consent they can't move him. That would be the last straw, at this point.

To CIMETTA.

We accomplished a miracle here, my friend, a real miracle.

ANNA

You see, Mother, it's true. They did it in spite of him, against his wishes.

LECCI

Without attaching any importance to the matter.
Yes, that's true. There was some resistance. Perhaps in his delirium. The real trouble, my friend, came from an accumulation of complications, one more serious than the next and all of them quite unforeseen. I was forced to improvise remedies that were quite often opposed to each other, and all so risky that, believe me, they'd have discouraged and stopped anyone else in my place. If I'd allowed myself for a moment to hesitate or doubt even slightly, good-by! I can tell you that I've never in my whole career had a satisfaction to equal this one.

CIMETTA

To ANNA.

You must excuse me, Mrs. Corsi, for not having come to see you earlier. But I was absolutely stunned by this unexpected disaster. It's shocked the whole town. Until today you've needed a doctor. Now that, unfortunately, you're also going to need a lawyer, I came without waiting for you to call me, because I know the confidence Tommaso has always placed in what little ability I have.

LECCI

I asked our dear friend to come here today with me, because I think it's time we started to prepare the patient for some of the hard facts he's going to have to face.

ANNA

It's going to be horrible, Doctor. I don't think he has the slightest idea, up to now. He's like a child. He's easily moved, cries, laughs at nothing. And just this morning he was telling me that, as soon as he's well, he wants to take a month's vacation in the country.

MRS. REIS

Oh, of course! Why shouldn't he have a vacation?

CIMETTA

Poor Tommaso.

LECCI

Let's give him a couple of days. Meanwhile we'll let him see Cimetta. I can't believe he won't eventually realize what's ahead for him.

ANNA

To CIMETTA.
How serious is it?

CIMETTA

Closing his eyes, spreading his arms.
My dear Mrs. Corsi . . .
    ANNA *hides her face in her hands.*

LECCI

Come, come, this is no time to worry about that. For now he's all right. Anything new since last night?

ANNA

No, nothing.

LECCI

Good. Go in there and ask the nurse to help you get him dressed and out of bed. Take your time, eh? And see if, once he's on his feet, you can get him to take a few steps. Meanwhile, Cimetta and I will go see the Commissioner. We'll be back in a few minutes. Come, come, courage, Anna. You've been very brave till now.

ANNA

Her face still covered.
I can't! I can't any more!

CIMETTA

You've got to!

LECCI

Please, Anna.

ANNA

Getting control of herself.
I'm all right.
Tries to smile.
How's this? All right? Until later, then.
Shakes CIMETTA's *hand. Then, to* LECCI.
Good-by. And you, Mother?

MRS. REIS

Vehemently.
I'm going, I'm going!

ANNA

I know. . . .

MRS. REIS

Good-by, Anna.

ANNA

The children — kiss them for me.
ANNA *exits at rear.*

CIMETTA

Poor woman, I hardly recognize her.

MRS. REIS

Whirling on him.
Get him out of here right away! Right away! To jail! That
murderer! Please, please, for Anna's sake!

LECCI

It's a question of a day or two, Mrs. Reis. If not today,
tomorrow.
To CIMETTA.
It was an extraordinary concession to leave him here under
our care until now. Guarded, yes, but with all the freedom

and consideration possible. Especially when you remember
who the victim was!

CIMETTA

It's incredible! It's a dream, a nightmare! For that woman!
A man like Neri, ugly, apathetic, a worm, who used to
drag himself around, utterly indifferent to everything! For
years he knew his wife betrayed him openly with everybody and he never cared! When he talked, it was all he
could do to whine a few words in that mewing voice of his!
And all of a sudden – yes, sir! – his blood boils and over
whom? Why, poor Tommaso.

To MRS. REIS.

Tell me, how is it, why is it that Tommaso was a friend of
his?

MRS. REIS

They met through that judge, the one who was trans-
ferred, Judge – what was his name? Làrcan, I think.

CIMETTA

Ah, yes, Làrcan. Judge Làrcan.

MRS. REIS

He lived here, a few houses away. When he was trans-
ferred, he wrote a letter of introduction to my son-in-law
for Neri, who was taking his place. That's how they met.

CIMETTA

And wasn't Neri also godfather to one of Tommaso's children?

MRS. REIS

Yes, the last one, the one that died.

CIMETTA

To LECCI.

You see? The man was a jinx. And you can be sure that,
with his temperament, death must have been a joy for
him. And now a whole family into the abyss because of it.

ANNA *returns hurriedly.*

ANNA

Tell me, Doctor, is it safe to let him leave his room for a
few minutes? He wants to.

LECCI

If he can, but he mustn't make the slightest effort. See to it.
Hold a chair behind him, in case his legs go out from under
him. And be careful.

To MRS. REIS.

Are you coming, too, Mrs. Reis?

MRS. REIS

Yes. I'll go ahead. Good-by, Anna.
She exits.

LECCI

We'll go, too. After you, Cimetta.

CIMETTA

Good-by, Mrs. Corsi.

ANNA

Good-by.
To LECCI.

Please, Doctor, tell the guard to stay out there.

LECCI

Don't worry. Although, maybe –

ANNA

No! He mustn't see him!

LECCI

Then you try and tell him. No one can do it better than
you.

CIMETTA

He's right.

LECCI

When you get a chance.

ANNA

But how? How?

LECCI

Never mind. We'll be back right away. Good-by.
They exit. ANNA *arranges the chair for the patient and
exits out the rear, leaving the door open and the curtain
drawn aside. Soon after,* TOMMASO CORSI *enters, sup-*

ported by ANNA *and a* MALE NURSE. CORSI *is tall and handsome. His face is very pale and has a waxy sheen, with deep hollows under the eyes. But his gaze is laughing, almost childish in its innocence. He has difficulty breathing, but belies it by a sweet smile. His jacket is thrown over his shoulders. Through the open collar of his shirt can be seen the bandages on his chest.* ANNA *and the* NURSE *lead him to the chair into which he sinks with a sigh of relief.*

TOMMASO

Ah, how nice it is in here. And all our things seem so new to me. The sink over there, yes. And my closet. And this is my chair, where I read the papers.

Looking around at the furniture.

Here all the time, silently waiting.

Indicating a wardrobe.

But that one, when you open it, will squeak.

To his wife.

Open it, open it. I want to hear it.

Reacting, as if in pain.

Ah!

ANNA

What is it?

TOMMASO

Nothing. Made a wrong move. It's over. Wait. I'll lean back. I'll lean back in the chair.

ANNA

You'd better have a pillow behind your shoulders.

TOMMASO

No. Well, maybe you're right.

The NURSE *runs to get a pillow from the next room.*

ANNA

Calling after him.

And get a blanket, too!

TOMMASO

The green one on the bed.

ANNA

At the rear door.
The one on the bed, yes.
The NURSE *returns with a pillow and the green blanket.*
ANNA *arranges the pillow on the chair while the* NURSE
spreads the blanket over the patient's legs.

TOMMASO

Stroking the blanket.
This one, this one. If you only knew how I love it. The
dreams I've had with it. I first saw my hand again on this
green surface. Then I held it up. It seemed even whiter. It
trembled. Ah, I felt as if I were in a void. But a peaceful,
gentle void, as if in a dream. And this downy green here
seemed like a countryside. The blades of grass of an endless field. And I lived in the middle of it, happily, lost in
delights I can't even describe to you. Everything new. My
life was beginning all over again. Perhaps it was the same
for everyone else. But no – there – I could hear a carriage
pass by. No – I said to myself – out there, in the streets, life
all this time has gone on. This upset me. And so I'd resume
staring at this blanket: here, yes, life was really beginning
all over again, among all these blades of grass. And so for
me, too, a new beginning. Ah, if I could only breathe a
little fresh air!
He turns to look at his wife.
You're crying?

ANNA

Turning her head away so as not to be seen.
No, it's nothing.

TOMMASO

To the NURSE, *almost smiling.*
She's crying.
A pause.
Please, leave us alone for a moment.
The NURSE *exits out the back.*

TOMMASO

Anna.

And as ANNA *turns quickly and bends over him, her eyes full of tears.*

Why?

A pause. Then, hesitantly.

You still – you still haven't forgiven me?

He takes her hand and places it over his eyes. ANNA *presses her trembling lips together as fresh tears flow from her eyes and she cannot find her voice to answer him. He removes her hand from his eyes.*

Have you?

ANNA

In anguish, timidly.

Yes, I have. . . . I have. . . .

TOMMASO

Well then?

Taking her face in his hands and drawing it close to his, very tenderly.

You understand, you know it's true when I tell you that never, never in my heart, in my thoughts, never have you been out of them, my saint, my love.

ANNA

Gently drawing away from him and stroking his hair.

Yes, yes, but hush now. You'll tire yourself out.

TOMMASO

It was an outrage.

ANNA

Don't, please. Don't think about it.

TOMMASO

No, it's better if I tell you.

ANNA

I don't want to hear anything about it. No, don't tell me anything. I know. I know everything.

TOMMASO

Just to clear away every cloud between us.

ANNA

But there aren't any.

TOMMASO

It was an outrage that he should catch me in that shameful, stupid moment.

ANNA

Don't, please don't, Tommaso.

TOMMASO

You'll understand, if you really have forgiven me.

ANNA

Yes, yes, but please don't go on.

TOMMASO

A stupid mistake, which the fool wanted to compound by
trying to kill me, twice.

ANNA

He did? Really?

TOMMASO

Twice. He rushed at me, holding the gun, and fired. He
was trying to kill me. I had to, I had to defend myself. He
gave me no choice. I couldn't – you understand – I couldn't
let myself be killed over her. I couldn't, for your sake. And
I told him so. But he was out of his mind, he was all over
me. And I couldn't get to my feet, to get out of bed, for –
for shame. He fired and the first shot broke the glass in a
picture over the bed. I turned and shouted at him, "What
are you doing?" I was almost laughing, it seemed so impossible that he couldn't see what an outrage, what madness it
was to try and kill me like that, in that very moment, to kill
me when I didn't even want to be there. I was there only
by accident; she had sent for me, with some excuse.

ANNA

You see, you're getting all excited. Please, Tommaso, that's
enough. It's bad for you.

TOMMASO

My whole life was at stake and had nothing to do with
what was going on there: you, the children, my business.
He shot again, point-blank. Oh, you will, will you? Then
take this, you bastard! But I don't remember shooting him.

He sat down with a thud on the floor. Then he rolled over on his face. That was when I noticed I was holding the gun, still hot and smoking, in my hand. I felt something rising in my chest. . . . I don't know, something awful, horrible. I looked at the corpse on the floor, at the window through which she had jumped. I heard the noise in the street below and – and with that same weapon I . . .

Exhausted, he falls back against the pillow.

ANNA

You see, you see what you're doing, Tommaso? Oh, God!

TOMMASO

It's nothing. I'm a little tired.

ANNA

Do you want to go back to bed?

TOMMASO

No, I'm fine here. It's over now. I'm strong enough. Now I have to get well right away. I just wanted to tell you how – how it was and – and that I had to. . . .

ANNA

Please, please don't start in again. All this you –

She is interrupted by the entrance of LECCI *and* CIMETTA. Ah, the doctor's here again. All this you'll tell – you'll tell the judges, and you'll see, they –

At these words, TOMMASO *suddenly leans up on one elbow and stares at* LECCI *and* CIMETTA *as they come forward.*

TOMMASO

But I – oh, yes – the trial . . .

He turns very pale and falls back, exhausted.

LECCI

Going to him.

Come, come, mere formalities!

TOMMASO

Under his breath, staring at the ceiling.

And what more can they do to me than I've already done with my own hands?

CIMETTA

Instinctively, with a sigh.

Ah, my friend, it's not enough.

TOMMASO

Noticing him and trying to find a reply.

Not enough? So then . . .

Immediately sinking back again.

Oh, I see, yes. . . . Would you believe it? I thought it was all over.

Desperately throwing his arms about ANNA'S *neck.*

Anna, Anna, I'm lost! I'm lost!

LECCI

Now, now, of course you aren't! What makes you think so? Who told you that?

TOMMASO

Lost. The trial. Now they'll arrest me. And how could I have forgotten? Of course! And it'll be all the worse for me, won't it, Cimetta, because I didn't kill just anybody, but an assistant district attorney, isn't that so, Cimetta?

CIMETTA

If we could only prove that he knew all about his wife's previous affairs!

ANNA

But there are lots of people who could testify to that.

CIMETTA

Ah, but not Neri himself! And you can't, unfortunately, summon the dead to testify on their word of honor. The worms, Mrs. Corsi, feed on the honor of the dead. What weight can hearsay evidence have against factual proof? He may have known all about his wife, but the facts indicate the contrary: that he would not accept his wife's behavior and rebelled against it. You say, "But could I have let myself be killed by him?" No. But if you did not wish to be deprived of this right to live, then you should not have been caught making love to his wife. By acting as you did — bear in mind now that I'm speaking for the prosecution — you yourself abrogated your right. You exposed yourself to a risk and therefore you had no right to react. Understand? Two counts against you.

TOMMASO

Trying to interrupt.
But I —

CIMETTA

Let me finish. On the first count, the charge of adultery, you should have let yourself be punished by him, by the wronged husband, but instead you killed him.

TOMMASO

I had to! Instinctively! To keep him from killing me!

CIMETTA

But immediately afterward you tried to kill yourself by your own hand!

TOMMASO

And isn't that enough?

CIMETTA

How can it be? In fact, it's another point against you!

TOMMASO

It is? Even that?

CIMETTA

By trying to kill yourself you implicitly acknowledged your guilt.

TOMMASO

Yes. And I punished myself.

CIMETTA

No, Tommaso. You tried to escape your punishment.

TOMMASO

By taking my own life? What more could I have done?

CIMETTA

True enough, but you would have had to die! Since you didn't die . . .

TOMMASO

Oh, so that's my real offense?
Pushing ANNA *aside so as to confront* LECCI.
But I would have died if he hadn't decided to save me.

LECCI

Amazed at being thus drawn into the discussion.
What? Me?

TOMMASO

Yes, you! You! I didn't want your attentions! You insisted
in forcing them upon me, in bringing me back to life!
Why did you bring me back to life, if now –

LECCI

Easy, keep calm. It's bad for you to get so excited.

TOMMASO

Thank you, Doctor. I see you really are concerned over my
health! Listen, Cimetta, I want to get to the bottom of this.
Calmly, so we won't upset the good doctor. I killed myself.
He came along and saved me. By what right, I want to
know?

LECCI

Evidently disturbed, though trying to smile.
Excuse me, but after all, I mean, this is a fine way to thank
me.

TOMMASO

Thank you? For what? Didn't you hear what Cimetta just
said?

LECCI

What was I supposed to do? Let you die?

TOMMASO

Yes, you should have let me die, if you didn't have the
right to dispose of the life I gave up and which you re-
stored to me.

LECCI

What do you mean, dispose? We couldn't simply ignore
the law!

TOMMASO

I had gone beyond the law, punishing myself more harshly
than even the law provides for! We've abolished the death
penalty in this country. And if it hadn't been for you, I
would be dead.

LECCI

But I had my professional duty, Corsi. It was my duty to do everything I could to save you.

TOMMASO

To hand me over to the law and have me condemned to prison? And by what right – this is what I want to know – by what right do you perform your duty as a doctor on a man who wanted to die, if in exchange society has not granted you the right to let this man live the life you give back to him?

CIMETTA

But excuse me, what about the crime you committed?

TOMMASO

I washed myself clean of it in my own blood! Isn't that enough? I killed a man and I killed myself. He wouldn't let me die. I fought against his attentions. Three times I tore the bandages away. Now here I am, alive again, thanks to him. A new man! How do you expect me to remain bound by a moment in another life that no longer exists? I'm free of the remorse of that moment; I paid for it in an hour that could have become an eternity! Now I have nothing to pay for any more! I have to live again for my family, to work for my children! How can you expect me to go to jail for a crime I never dreamed of committing, that I never would have committed if I hadn't been dragged into it? While those who reap the benefits of your skills, of your duty to keep me alive only to be imprisoned, will now coldly commit the crime of condemning me to spend the rest of my life in enforced, brutish idleness, and condemn my children, my innocent children, to poverty and shame! By what right?

He raises himself up, driven by a rage that the sense of his own helplessness transforms into fury, screams and tears at his face. Then he flings himself back against the arm of the chair. He tries to sob but cannot. The very futility of his tremendous effort leaves him momentarily stunned, as if suspended in a strange void. The others stare at him in mute horror. His face shows the long red marks of his fingers. Frightened, ANNA *runs to him. First she raises his head, then, helped by* CIMETTA, *she tries to lift him to his feet, but immediately she recoils with a cry of disgust and terror. His shirt is red with blood from the wound.*

ANNA

Doctor! Doctor!

CIMETTA

The wound's opened again!

LECCI

Becoming pale, staring, confused.
The wound?
Instinctively he starts for the chair, but is immediately stopped by a hoarse, threatening cry from CORSI. *Then, almost in a faint, he lets his arms fall to his side.*
No, no. He's right. Didn't you hear? I can't. I mustn't.

Curtain

THE JAR

(La giara, 1917)

THE CAST

DON LOLÒ ZIRAFA
UNCLE DIMA LICASI, a tinker
SCIMÈ, a lawyer
FRIEND PÈ, a farmhand
TARARÀ ⎫
FILLICÒ ⎭ olive shakers

TANA ⎫
TRISUZZA ⎬ olive pickers
CARMINELLA ⎭

A MULE DRIVER
NOCIARELLO, an eleven-year-old peasant boy

A Sicilian countryside.

A grassy yard in front of the farmhouse of DON LOLÒ
ZIRAFA, *on the crest of a slope. At left, the front of the
rustic, one-story house. The door, a slightly faded red,
is in the middle and a small balcony hangs directly over
it. There are windows above and below, those at ground
level with gratings. At right, an ancient olive tree whose
gnarled and twisted trunk is encircled by a stone seat.
Beyond the tree, the yard is entered by a dirt road.
At rear, the tops of other olive trees slope away down the
hill. It is October.*

At curtain, FRIEND PÈ *is standing on the stone seat and
gazing down the road up which the* WOMEN *come,
carrying baskets of olives on their heads or in their
arms, and singing a working song of the fields.*

PÈ

Shouting.

Hey, watch what you're doing! You there, snotnose! Take it
easy, goddamn it to hell – you're spilling them all over the
road!

The WOMEN *and* NOCIARELLO *stop singing and enter up
the road.*

TRISUZZA

So what's eating you, Friend Pè?

TANA

Saints preserve us, where did you learn to swear like that?

CARMINELLA

It won't be long before the trees begin to swear in this
place.

PÈ

You expect me to sit here quietly and watch you spill the
olives all over the road?

TRISUZZA

What do you mean? I haven't spilled one, not one.

PÈ

If Don Lolò, God help us, had been watching you from the balcony . . .

TANA

So let him watch! Night and day, if he wants to! You do your job right, there's nothing to worry about.

PÈ

Sure, singing with your nose up in the air like that.

CARMINELLA

What is this? We can't even sing now?

TANA

No, but it's all right to swear. They're having a contest, him and his boss, to see whose mouth is dirtier.

TRISUZZA

Why the good Lord hasn't struck down the place and every tree in it I just don't know!

PÈ

All right, that'll do! Damned cacklers! Go and unload, and stop your bellyaching!

CARMINELLA

You want us to go on picking?

PÈ

What do you think this is, a half-holiday? You still have time for two more trips. Come on, quick now, get going!

He shoos the WOMEN *and* NOCIARELLO *around the corner of the house. On their way out, one of them, out of spite, starts to sing again.* PÈ *looks up at the balcony.*

PÈ

Calling.
Don Lolò!

DON LOLÒ

From within.
What is it?

PÈ

The mules with the manure are here!

DON LOLÒ *comes storming out of the house. He's a big, angry-looking man of about forty, with the eyes of a suspicious wolf. He has two small gold bands in his ears and wears an old, battered white hat with a broad brim. He is coatless and his coarse checkered shirt is open to reveal a hairy chest; the sleeves are rolled up to the elbow.*

DON LOLÒ

The mules? At this hour? Where are they? Where'd you send them?

PÈ

They're over there, take it easy. The driver wants to know where to unload them.

DON LOLÒ

Oh, is that so? Unload them before I get a chance to see what he's brought me? Well, I can't right now. I'm talking to my lawyer.

PÈ

Ah, about the jar?

DON LOLÒ

Listen, so who promoted you?

PÈ

I only said —

DON LOLÒ

You just say nothing! Obey and shut up! And where'd you get the idea I was talking to my lawyer about the jar?

PÈ

Because I'm worried — I mean, I'm scared sick — at the idea of leaving the new jar back there in the mill house.

Pointing off left.

Get it out of there, for God's sake!

DON LOLÒ

No! I've told you a hundred times! I want it there and no one's to touch it!

PÈ

It's right by the door, and with all these women and boys coming and going –

DON LOLÒ

By the blood of all the – what are you trying to do, drive me crazy?

PÈ

Just as long as nothing happens to that jar.

DON LOLÒ

I don't want to be bothered until I've finished talking to my lawyer. Where do you want me to put this jar? We can't put it in the storeroom until we take the old barrel out of there, and I haven't time now.

The MULE DRIVER *enters at right.*

DRIVER

All right now, where do you want me to dump this manure? It'll be dark any moment.

DON LOLÒ

Another one! Sweet Jesus, I hope you break your fool neck, you and all your damn mules! At this hour you show up?

DRIVER

I couldn't come before.

DON LOLÒ

No? Well, I'm not buying any pig in a poke. I want you to pile it up around the fields where and when I tell you to. And now it's too late.

DRIVER

You know what, Don Lolò? I'm going to dump it right where they're standing, behind the wall over there, and then I'm going to clear out of here.

DON LOLÒ

Try it! I'd like to see you try it!

DRIVER

Just watch me!

He starts out in a rage.

PÈ

Holding him back.
Hey now, what a temper!

DON LOLÒ

Let him go, let him go!

DRIVER

He's not the only one around here who can get mad! It's
impossible to deal with him! This happens every time!

DON LOLÒ

You want to mess around with me, huh? All right, look!
See this?

He produces a little red book from his pocket.
Know what that is? Looks like a prayer book, doesn't it?
It's the Civil Code, that's what it is! My lawyer gave it to
me, the one who's here with me now. And I've learned how
to read it. I know what it says in this little book and no
one messes around with me any more, not even God the
Father! It's all provided for in here, case by case. And be-
sides, I pay my lawyer a nice fat yearly fee!

PÈ

Here he comes now.
SCIMÈ, *the lawyer, emerges from the house. He wears
an old straw hat and holds an open newspaper.*

SCIMÈ

What's up, Don Lolò?

DON LOLÒ

This clown here shows up with his mules and his load of
manure for my fields when it's getting dark, and instead of
apologizing –

DRIVER

Interrupting, to the lawyer.
I told him I couldn't come earlier –

DON LOLÒ

– he threatens –

DRIVER

What? I did not!

DON LOLÒ

You did, too! He threatens to dump his load behind my wall –

DRIVER

– because you –

DON LOLÒ

I what? I want you to dump it where I need it, where you're supposed to, in regular piles all the same size.

DRIVER

Go on! Why doesn't he come and tell me, then? There's still two hours of daylight left. It's because he wants to count it and measure it himself, turd by turd. I know him!

DON LOLÒ

Never mind the lawyer! He's here to advise me, not you! Pay no attention to him, Scimè. Take your regular walk down the road over there, sit down under your mulberry tree, and read your paper in peace. We'll finish our discussion about the jar later.

To the DRIVER.

Let's go, let's go now. How many mules have you got?

Starts off with the DRIVER *at right.*

DRIVER

Following him.

Didn't you say twelve? So I've got twelve.

They both disappear behind the house.

SCIMÈ

Raising his hands and waving them about in despair.

Out, out, out! First thing in the morning, out of here and home! He's making my head spin like a top!

PÈ

Not a moment's peace for anyone. And that's a fine present you gave him, let me tell you, with that little red book! First, when something happened, he used to shout, "Saddle up the mule!"

SCIMÈ

Yes, so he could gallop into town to see me and fill my head full of hot air like a balloon. That's the reason I gave him that little book, my friend. He digs it out of his pocket, looks it up himself, and leaves me in peace. Still, it must have been the devil himself who inspired me to come and spend a week here! But what could I do? When he found out my doctor told me to spend a few days in the country, he nailed me up on a cross and kept pestering me to accept his hospitality. I told him I'd come only if he promised not to talk to me about anything. For five days now he's been gassing steadily about some jar – I don't know what kind of jar –

PÈ

Yes, sir, the big jar for the olive oil. It arrived only a few days ago from Santo Stefano di Camastra, where they make them. It's a beauty, big around like this and as high as my shoulder – a Mother Superior of a jar! What's up? He wants to sue the maker?

SCIMÈ

That's right. Because, for the price he paid, he says it should have been bigger.

PÈ

Astounded.
Bigger?

SCIMÈ

That's all he's been talking about for five days.
He starts off down the road at right.
Ah, but tomorrow, good-by, so long, out!
He exits. From somewhere in the distance, beyond the olive grove, the singsong cry of DIMA LICASI *can now be heard.*

DIMA

Off stage.
Cups to mend, plates to mend . . .
TARARÀ *and* FILLICÒ *enter from the road at right, carrying ladders and poles.*

PÈ

Seeing them.
Hey, what are you doing? You've stopped already?

FILLICÒ

The boss told us to. He came by with the mules.

PÈ

And he told you to go home?

TARARÀ

Oh, no, not him! He said we should wait around to do some
kind of job in the storeroom.

PÈ

To take out the old barrel?

FILLICÒ

That's right. And make room for the new jar.

PÈ

Good! I'm glad he listened to me at least once. Come on,
come with me.

They start off at left, but the WOMEN *reappear from behind the house, carrying their empty baskets.*

TANA

Seeing the two olive shakers.

What? Finished shaking them down already?

PÈ

Finished for today, that's all.

TRISUZZA

And what about us? What are we supposed to do?

PÈ

Wait till the boss comes back. He'll tell you.

CARMINELLA

And till then we stand around here and count our fingers?

PÈ

What do you want me to tell you? Go and start sorting out.

TANA

Oh, no, not unless he says so. I'm not taking any chances.

PÈ

Then one of you go and ask him.

The MEN *exit.*

CARMINELLA

You go, Nociarello.

TANA

Tell him this: the men have stopped shaking the trees and the women want to know what they're supposed to do.

TRISUZZA

Ask him if he wants us to start sorting. Ask him that.

NOCIARELLO

All right.

CARMINELLA

Hurry up, run!

NOCIARELLO *runs out down the road.* FILLICÒ, TARARÀ, *and* FRIEND PÈ *reappear, one after the other, in a state of alarm, waving their arms about.*

FILLICÒ

Holy Mother of God, what'll we do now?

TARARÀ

He'll kill us, he'll kill us!

PÈ

God help us, God help us!

WOMEN

Crowding around and all talking at once.
What happened? What is it? What's wrong?

PÈ

The jar! The new jar!

TARARÀ

Broken!

WOMEN

All together.
The jar? Really? Oh, Holy Mother!

FILLICÒ

Split in half! Like you would with a knife: zing!

TANA

How's that possible?

TRISUZZA

No one touched it!

CARMINELLA

No one! But wait till you hear what Don Lolò has to say!

TRISUZZA

He'll go right off his rocker!

FILLICÒ

I'm not going to stick around to find out!

TARARÀ

What do you mean? You're running away? Stupid! Then
he'll never believe we didn't do it! Everyone stay right here!
    Turning to PÈ.
And you go and call him. No, no, better call him from here.
Give a shout.

PÈ

Climbing on the stone seat around the olive tree.
All right, like this, from here.
    *Cups his hands around his mouth and calls out several
    times.*
Don Lolò! Hey, Don Lolò-o-o! He can't hear us. He's shouting like a madman behind those mules. Don Lolò-o-o! It's
no good. I'd better run and get him.

TARARÀ

But for God's sake don't give him the idea –

PÈ

Don't worry. How could I blame you?
    He exits on the run down the road.

TARARÀ

Now remember, we're all agreed and we all stick together: the jar broke by itself!

TANA

It's happened before –

TRISUZZA

Right! New jars are liable to do that!

FILLICÒ

Because very often – you know how it is – when they bake
them in the oven, a spark gets caught and forms a little
bubble, then suddenly – wham! – it blows up on you.

CARMINELLA

That's right. Just like a gunshot.

The voices of DON LOLÒ *and* FRIEND PÈ *are heard approaching at right.*

God help us now!

She makes the sign of the Cross.

DON LOLÒ

Off stage.

By Christ, I want to know who did it!

PÈ

Off stage.

No one, I swear it!

TRISUZZA

Here he comes!

TANA

God help us!

DON LOLÒ, *pale with fury, enters, followed by* FRIEND PÈ *and* NOCIARELLO.

DON LOLÒ

Rushing first at TARARÀ, *then at* FILLICÒ, *grabbing each of them by the shirt front and shaking them.*

Was it you? Who did it? You or you, one of the two of you must have done it and by God you'll pay for it!

TARARÀ AND FILLICÒ

Simultaneously freeing themselves.

Me? You're crazy! Let go of me! Take your hands off me or I swear to God I'll –

During the above exchange, all the others crowd around, shouting in chorus.

OTHERS

It broke by itself! It's nobody's fault! We found it broken! I told you over and over!

DON LOLÒ

Still in a fury, addressing first one, then the other of them.

So I'm crazy, eh? Oh, sure, you're all innocent! It broke by itself! I'll make you pay for it, all of you! Now go and get it and bring it here!

The MEN *rush out to fetch the jar.*

In the light we'll see if there are any marks on it. And if someone kicked it or pushed it over, I'll eat him alive! You'll pay for it, every damn one of you!

WOMEN

In chorus.

What? Us? You're out of your mind! Make us pay for it, too? When we haven't even so much as seen it?

DON LOLÒ

You were going in and out of there, all of you!

TRISUZZA

Oh, sure, we broke the jar for you by brushing it like this, with our skirts!

She takes her skirt in one hand and contemptuously flicks it against his leg. Meanwhile, FRIEND PÈ, TARARÀ, *and* FILLICÒ *return, carrying the broken jar.*

TANA

Oh, too bad! Look at that!

DON LOLÒ

Wailing.

My new jar! After what I paid! And where will I store the oil? Oh, my beautiful new jar! The envy, the meanness of it! All that money thrown away! And this such a good year for the olives! Oh, God, what a disaster! What'll I do now?

TARARÀ

No, look —

FILLICÒ

It can be fixed —

PÈ

It's just one piece —

TARARÀ

Just one —

FILLICÒ

A clean break –

TARARÀ

There must have been a crack in it.

DON LOLÒ

What do you mean, there must have been a crack in it? It rang like a bell!

PÈ

He's right. I checked it myself.

FILLICÒ

It'll be as good as new, take my word for it, if you send for a good tinker. You won't even see the mark.

TARARÀ

Call Uncle Dima, Uncle Dima Licasi! He's around here somewhere. I heard him.

TANA

He's the best. He has a marvelous cement. Not even a hammer can dent it, once it takes hold. Hurry, Nociarello, he's around here somewhere! Try Mosca's place.

NOCIARELLO *exits on the run.*

DON LOLÒ

Shouting.

Shut up, all of you! I can't hear myself think! I don't believe in miracles! For me, the jar is gone!

PÈ

Ah, I told you, didn't I?

DON LOLÒ

In a fury again.

What did you tell me, you horse's ass? What did you tell me, if it's true the jar broke by itself, without anyone touching it? Even if we'd stored it in church, it would have broken just the same, if it broke all by itself!

TARARÀ

He's right. Don't waste your breath.

DON LOLÒ

Damn me, what an imbecile!

FILLICÒ

Just a few lire and it'll be all fixed, you'll see. And you know what they say: a broken jug lasts longer than a sound one.

DON LOLÒ

Goddamn it to hell, I've still got the mules on my hands back there!

To FRIEND PÈ.

What are you standing around for with your mouth open? Go and keep an eye on them at least!

FRIEND PÈ *exits down the road.*

My head, my head's spinning! To hell with this Uncle Dima! It's the lawyer I have to see! If it broke by itself, it means there was something wrong with it. But it rang, it rang like a bell when it got here! And I was sure it was all right. I even signed for it. All that money thrown away. I can kiss it good-by.

UNCLE DIMA LICASI, *a hunchback, enters at left, followed by* NOCIARELLO.

FILLICÒ

Ah, here's Uncle Dima!

TARARÀ

Softly to DON LOLÒ.

Listen, he doesn't say much.

TANA

Almost mysteriously.

A man of very few words.

DON LOLÒ

Is that so?

To UNCLE DIMA.

Don't you even say good evening? Where are your manners?

DIMA

You want my manners or my help? Don't waste my time. Tell me what to do and I'll do it.

DON LOLÒ

If words are so precious to you, why don't you save others the trouble, too? Can't you see what you have to do?
Indicates the jar.

FILLICÒ

Mend this big jar, Uncle Dima, with that cement of yours.

DON LOLÒ

They say it works miracles. Make it yourself?
UNCLE DIMA *looks at him sullenly and doesn't answer.*
Hey, answer when I talk to you! And let's have a look at it!

TARARÀ

Softly to DON LOLÒ.
If you approach him like that, you won't get anything out of him.

TANA

He won't let anyone see it.

DON LOLÒ

What the hell is it? Holy or something?
To DIMA.
Just tell me if you think you can fix it.

DIMA

Putting his toolbox down and taking out a small bundle wrapped in an old blue handkerchief.
Just like that? Have to look at it first. Need time.
He sits down on the ground and slowly, very cautiously opens the bundle. Everyone looks at him curiously and attentively.

TANA

Softly to DON LOLÒ.
It must be the cement.

DON LOLÒ

Indicating his stomach.
It gets me right here.
UNCLE DIMA *finally produces from the bundle an old pair of broken eyeglasses held together by bits of string.*

ALL

Laughing.

Oh, his eyeglasses! God knows what we thought it was!
We thought it was the cement! Looks like he sat on them!
UNCLE DIMA *polishes the lenses very deliberately with a
corner of the handkerchief, then sets the glasses on the
end of his nose and examines the jar.*

DIMA

It can be fixed.

DON LOLÒ

Boom! The court has handed down its sentence! But I'm
telling you now, I don't trust this marvelous cement of
yours. I want rivets.

UNCLE DIMA *turns to look at him; then, without a word,
he drops his handkerchief and his glasses angrily into
the toolbox, picks it up, and starts out.*

Hey! What are you doing?

DIMA

I'm going.

DON LOLÒ

In a pig's – you're what?

FILLICÒ

Detaining him.

Come on, Uncle Dima, take it easy!

TARARÀ

Do what he says, Uncle Dima!

DON LOLÒ

Who does he think he is, Garibaldi? Miserable damned
jackass, I'll tell the world! I have to put oil in it and it'll
soak through! Split a mile long and he wants to fix it with
cement alone! It needs rivets! Cement *and* rivets! I'm the
boss here!

DIMA

All the same! All the same! Ignoramuses! A jug, a bowl, a
cup, a plate – rivets! Like an old woman's teeth gnashing
at the world, saying: "Look, I'm busted and they fixed me
up!" I offer you something good and no one wants it. And

I'm never allowed to do a job the way it ought to be done!

Going up to DON LOLÒ.

You listen to me. If this jar doesn't ring like a bell with the cement alone –

DON LOLÒ

I said no! And that's all there is to it!

To TARARÀ.

And you said he didn't talk!

To UNCLE DIMA.

It's no good preaching! Save your breath! If everyone wants rivets, it's because rivets are called for. Their judgment against yours!

DIMA

What judgment? Sheer ignorance!

TANA

It may be ignorance, but it looks to me like you do need rivets, Uncle Dima.

TRISUZZA

Sure, they hold better.

DIMA

But they make holes. Can't you understand? Every stitch is two holes; twenty stitches, forty holes. With the cement alone –

DON LOLÒ

Christ, what a head! Worse than a mule! They make holes, but I want them! I'm the boss here!

Turning to the WOMEN.

Come on, come on, let's go. You start sorting.

To the MEN.

And the rest of you, come with me. Let's get the barrel out of there. Let's go!

Shoos them off toward the house.

DIMA

Hey, wait a minute!

DON LOLÒ

We'll settle up when you're done. I haven't any time to waste on you.

DIMA

You're leaving me all alone here? I need somebody to help me hold the broken piece in place. It's a big jar.

DON LOLÒ

Oh, well then –

To TARARÀ.

– you stay here.

To FILLICÒ.

And you come with me.

He exits with FILLICÒ. *The* WOMEN *and* NOCIARELLO *have already gone.* UNCLE DIMA *immediately sets to work with bad grace. He takes out his tools and begins to punch holes in the jar and along the edge of the broken fragment.*

TARARÀ

Chattily.

Thank God he took it as easy as he did! I can't believe it. I thought the world was going to come to an end tonight! Don't take it so hard, Uncle Dima. He wants rivets? Give him rivets. Twenty, thirty of them –

DIMA *looks up at him.*

More? Thirty-five?

DIMA *continues to stare at him.*

How many, then?

DIMA

You see this bit? Every time I use it – ping, ping, ping! – it punches a little hole, right here in my heart!

TARARÀ

Tell me, is it true the formula for your cement came to you in a dream?

DIMA

Working.

In a dream, yes.

TARARÀ

And who appeared to you in the dream?

DIMA

My father.

TARARÀ

Ah, your father! He came to you in the dream and told you how to make it?

DIMA

Blockhead!

TARARÀ

Me? Why?

DIMA

You know who my father is?

TARARÀ

No, who?

DIMA

The devil, and he's going to get you!

TARARÀ

Oh, so you're the son of the devil?

DIMA

And what I've got in there is the pitch you're all going to boil in.

TARARÀ

So it's black, is it?

DIMA

White. It was my father who taught me to make it white. You'll find out how strong it is when you're boiling in it. But down there it's black. Stick it on your fingers and you'll never get them apart again. And if I glue your lip to your nose, you'll look like a Ubangi for the rest of your life.

TARARÀ

Then how come you can touch it and nothing happens?

DIMA

Idiot! Does a dog bite its own master?
    Drops his tools and gets up.
Come here now.
    Makes him hold the broken piece.
Hold this.
    From his box he takes out a smaller one of tin, opens it,

scoops out some of the cement on his fingers and displays it.

See? Looks like any other cement, eh? Watch.

He spreads the cement first along the broken edge of the jar, then along the detached fragment itself.

Three or four good smears like this – just enough . . . Hold it in place. Now I'll get inside.

TARARÀ

Inside the jar?

DIMA

Of course, jackass. If I have to use rivets, I have to stitch them from the inside. Wait.

Rummages in his box.

Wire and pliers.

Takes what he needs and climbs inside the jar.

Now you – wait till I get set in here – set the piece carefully in place, so it fits just right – easy – good – like that.

TARARÀ *carries out* DIMA's *orders and so encloses him in the jar. Shortly after,* DIMA's *head emerges from the mouth of the jar.*

Now pull, pull! No rivets yet. Pull as hard as you can. See? You can't pull it away, can you? Ten pairs of oxen couldn't pull it away now. Go, go tell your boss!

TARARÀ

Excuse me, Uncle Dima, but are you sure you can get out of there now?

DIMA

Why not? I always have out of all the other jars.

TARARÀ

But this one – I don't know – the neck looks a little narrow for you. Try it.

FRIEND PÈ *returns up the road.*

PÈ

What's the matter? Can't he get out?

TARARÀ

To DIMA, *inside the jar.*

Easy now. Wait. That side.

PÈ

Your arm, get one arm out first.

TARARÀ

His arm? What do you mean?

DIMA

Now what the hell! I'm stuck in here?

PÈ

So big around in the middle and so narrow up top.

TARARÀ

What a laugh, if he can't get out now that he's fixed it!
Laughs.

DIMA

What's so funny? Goddamn it, give me a hand!
Bouncing furiously up and down in the jar.

PÈ

Wait! Don't do that! Let's see if by tilting it –

DIMA

No, that's worse! Stop it! It's too tight in the shoulders.

TARARÀ

Of course. You've got a little hump on one of them.

DIMA

Me? You said yourself the jar was too small!

PÈ

Well, now what?

TARARÀ

If this isn't something to write home about!
Laughs and runs toward the house, calling.
Fillicò! Tana! Trisuzza! Carminella! Come here, come here!
Uncle Dima's stuck in the jar!

FILLICÒ, TANA, TRISUZZA, CARMINELLA, *and* NOCIARELLO
enter at right.

ALL

In chorus, laughing, skipping, clapping their hands.
Stuck in the jar? Great! How'd it happen? Can't he get out?

DIMA

Simultaneously, snarling like an animal.
Get me out! Give me my hammer! It's in the box!

PÈ

Your hammer? You're crazy! I have to tell the boss first!

FILLICÒ

Here he comes, here he comes!
DON LOLÒ *enters on the run.*

WOMEN

Running to meet him.
He's walled himself up in the jar! By himself! He can't get
out!

DON LOLÒ

In the jar?

DIMA

Simultaneously.
Help! Help!

DON LOLÒ

How can I help you, you old imbecile, if you forgot to
measure your hump before getting in?
All laugh.

TANA

Look what happens to him, poor old Uncle Dima!

FILLICÒ

Funniest damn thing I ever saw!

DON LOLÒ

Wait. Easy now. Try to get one arm out.

PÈ

It's no good. We tried everything.

DIMA

Who has with difficulty managed to get one arm out.
Ouch! Easy! You're dislocating it!

DON LOLÒ

Patience! Try to —

DIMA

No! Let go of me!

DON LOLÒ

What do you want us to do then?

DIMA

Take my hammer and break the jar!

DON LOLÒ

What? Now that it's fixed?

DIMA

You don't think you're going to keep me in here, do you?

DON LOLÒ

First we have to see what can be done.

DIMA

What's there to see? I want to get out! I want to get out, damn it!

WOMEN

In chorus.

He's right! You can't keep him in there! If there's no other way!

DON LOLÒ

My head! My head! Shut up, all of you! This is something new! Nothing like this has ever happened before!

To NOCIARELLO.

Come here, boy. No, you, Fillicò.

Points down the road.

The lawyer's down there, under his tree. Tell him to come here right away. . . .

As FILLICÒ *leaves, turning to* UNCLE DIMA, *who is bouncing about in the jar.*

Stand still, you!

To the others.

Hold him still! That's no jar! It's the devil himself!

To DIMA *again, who continues to writhe about.*

Hold still, I said!

DIMA

Either you break it or I'll smash it up against a tree! I want to get out! I want to get out of here!

DON LOLÒ

Wait till the lawyer comes. He'll solve the case. Meanwhile I'm going to protect my jar and begin by doing my duty.

Takes a big, old leather wallet out of his pocket and produces a ten-lire note.

You're all witnesses! Ten lire for the work done on the jar!

DIMA

Keep your money! I don't want it! I want to get out!

DON LOLÒ

You'll get out when the lawyer says you can. Meanwhile I'm paying you.

He drops the money into the jar. SCIMÈ, *laughing, enters, followed by* FILLICÒ.

DON LOLÒ

Seeing him.

What's so funny? It's no skin off your nose! The jar is mine!

SCIMÈ

Unable to stop laughing any more than the rest of them.

What do you think – think you're do – doing? Keep – keep him – him in there? Keep him in there so you – ah ha ha! – so you won't lose the jar?

DON LOLÒ

So you think it's up to me to pay, huh?

SCIMÈ

You know what this is? Kidnapping, that's what!

DON LOLÒ

Kidnapping? Who kidnapped him? He did it himself! Is that my fault?

To UNCLE DIMA.

Who's keeping you in there? Get out!

DIMA

You get me out, if you think you can!

DON LOLÒ

Why should I? I didn't put you in! You did it all by yourself! Now come out of there!

SCIMÈ

Ladies and gentlemen, please! May I say something?

TARARÀ

Speak up! Let the lawyer speak! Quiet!

SCIMÈ

There are two aspects to this case. I want you to listen carefully and come to an agreement.

Turning first to DON LOLÒ.

On the one hand, you, Don Lolò, must immediately set Uncle Dima free.

DON LOLÒ

Quickly.

How? By breaking the jar?

SCIMÈ

Wait. Then there's the other aspect. Let me finish. But you must realize you can't hold him. That's kidnapping.

Turning now to UNCLE DIMA.

On the other hand, you, Uncle Dima, have to answer for the damage you've caused by getting into the jar without first making sure you could get out of it.

DIMA

I didn't make sure, Mr. Scimè, because during all the years I've been at this job I've fixed hundreds of jars, and every one of them from the inside, to put the rivets in the way you're supposed to. Not once have I ever been unable to get out. So it's up to him to go and see the man who made this jar with such a narrow damn neck! It's not *my* fault.

DON LOLÒ

And what about your hump? I suppose the man who made the jar stuck it there so you wouldn't be able to get out! If we try and sue, Scimè, and he shows up in court with that hump of his, the judge will laugh himself sick! I'll have to pay all the expenses and that's that!

DIMA

No, that's not true! Because hump or no hump, I never had any trouble getting in and out of all those other jars! Just like walking in and out of my own house it was!

SCIMÈ

I'm sorry, Uncle Dima, but that's not good enough. It was up to you to make sure you could get out before going in.

DON LOLÒ

So he has to pay for the jar, right?

DIMA

What?

SCIMÈ

Easy, easy. Pay the price of the jar as new?

DON LOLÒ

Certainly. Why not?

SCIMÈ

Because it was already broken, for God's sake!

DIMA

And I fixed it for him!

DON LOLÒ

You fixed it? So then it's as good as new. Not broken. Now if I break it so you can get out, I won't be able to have it fixed again and I'll have lost the jar for good. Right, Scimè?

SCIMÈ

That's why I said Uncle Dima would have to pay his share! Now let me handle this!

DON LOLÒ

Go on, go on.

SCIMÈ

My dear Uncle Dima, one of two things: either your cement is good for something or it isn't.

DON LOLÒ

In ecstasy, to the others.

Listen, now you're going to hear something! The trap is closing! When he starts off like this . . .

SCIMÈ

If your cement is no good, then you're just an ordinary crook. If it is good, then the jar, just as it is, has to be worth something. What is it worth? You tell me. Give us an estimate.

DIMA

With me in it?
All laugh.

SCIMÈ

No jokes now! Just as it is.

DIMA

I'll tell you. If Don Lolò had let me fix the jar with cement only, as I wanted to do, then I wouldn't be in here in the first place, because I would have been able to fix it from the outside. So then the jar would have been as good as new and worth just as much as before, no more, no less. Patched up as it is now and full of holes like a sieve, what can it be worth? Maybe a third of what he paid for it.

DON LOLÒ

A third?

SCIMÈ

Quickly to DON LOLÒ, *signaling him to be silent.*
A third! Quiet! A third – meaning?

DON LOLÒ

I paid four big bills for it, so that makes one and a third.

·DIMA

Maybe less, certainly not more.

SCIMÈ

I'll take your word for it. Pay it to Don Lolò.

DIMA

Who? Me? Pay him?

SCIMÈ

So he'll break the jar and let you out. You'll pay him exactly what you yourself estimated it was worth.

DON LOLÒ

In cash.

DIMA

Me pay him? You're crazy! I'll let the worms eat me first. Hey, Tararà, get my pipe, from the box over there.

TARARÀ

Doing so.
This one?

DIMA

Thanks. Give me a light.
   TARARÀ *strikes a match and lights* DIMA's *pipe.*
Thanks. And I kiss your hands, all of you.
   Puffing on his pipe, he disappears into the jar, amid general laughter.

DON LOLÒ

Dumbfounded.
Now what do we do? Suppose he won't come out?

SCIMÈ

Scratching his head and smiling.
Well, that's true. As long as he wanted to come out, we
could deal. But if he doesn't . . .

DON LOLÒ

Going up to the jar and addressing UNCLE DIMA.
Hey, what are you going to do? Live in there?

DIMA

Sticking his head out.
I like it in here. It's nice and cool. Paradise, in fact.
   *He disappears again. Puffs of pipe smoke drift up out
   of the jar.*

DON LOLÒ

Furiously, as all laugh.
Stop laughing, by God! And you're all witnesses that he
won't come out now, so he won't have to pay me what he
owes me, while for my part I'm ready to break the jar!
   To the lawyer.
Couldn't I sue him for squatting on my property?

SCIMÈ

Laughing.
Sure, why not? Get yourself an eviction notice.

DON LOLÒ

But he's keeping me from using the jar.

DIMA

Sticking his head out again.

You're wrong. I'm not here because I want to be. Let me out and I'll go, dancing and singing. But as for making me pay, forget it. I'll stay here forever.

DON LOLÒ

Grabbing the jar and shaking it furiously.

Oh, you will, will you! You will, eh!

DIMA

What a cement! No rivets in there, you know.

DON LOLÒ

Crook! Swindler! Villain! Who's responsible for this, you or me? And you expect me to pay for it?

SCIMÈ

Pulling him away.

Don't do that. You only make it worse. Let him spend the night in there and tomorrow morning, you'll see, he'll beg to be let out.

To DIMA.

All right, you – pay up or else!

To DON LOLÒ.

Let's go now. Forget about him.

He and DON LOLÒ *start toward the house.*

DIMA

Hey, Don Lolò!

SCIMÈ

To DON LOLÒ *as they walk away.*

Pay no attention. Come on.

DIMA

Before they exit into the house.

Good night, Mr. Scimè. I've got my ten lire right here!

As soon as they've gone, turning to the others.

Now we'll have a party, all of us! My housewarming party! Tararà, run to Mosca's and buy wine, bread, fried fish, and salted peppers! We're going to celebrate!

ALL

Clapping their hands as TARARÀ *runs off.*
Hurray for Uncle Dima! Hurray for Uncle Dima! A party!

FILLICÒ

And a full moon to boot! Look! There it is!
   Points off left.
Like daylight!

DIMA

I want to see! I want to see! Carry me over there, but take
it easy.
   They all help roll the jar slowly toward the road.
That's it – easy – like that. Ah, what a beauty! I see it, I
see it! Like the sun? Who'll sing us a song?

TANA

You, Trisuzza!

TRISUZZA

Not me! Carminella!

DIMA

We'll all sing! Fillicò, play your harmonica, and the rest of
you, a song. All together now, a nice song, while you dance
around the jar!
   FILLICÒ *produces his harmonica and begins to play. The
   others, singing and shouting, hold hands and dance
   wildly around the jar, egged on by* UNCLE DIMA. *After
   a few moments, the door of the house is flung open and*
   DON LOLÒ *rushes out, screaming.*

DON LOLÒ

Goddamn it to hell, where do you think you are, in a tav-
ern? Here, you old devil, go and break your fool neck!
   *He delivers a tremendous kick on the jar, which topples
   over and rolls away down the slope. Screams, shouts.
   Then the noise of the jar smashing into a tree.*

TANA

With a scream.
Ah, he's killed him!

FILLICÒ

No! There he is! He's out! He's getting up! He's all right!
The WOMEN *all clap their hands gaily.*

ALL

Hurray for Uncle Dima! Hurray for Uncle Dima!
They lift him to their shoulders and carry him off across the stage in triumph.

DIMA

Waving his arms.
I win! I win!

Curtain

THE LICENSE

(La patente, 1919)

THE CAST

The chambers of JUDGE D'ANDREA, in a small provincial town of southern Italy.

The chambers of JUDGE D'ANDREA, *an examining magistrate in a small provincial town of southern Italy. The rear wall consists almost entirely of shelves full of green letter-files, which, one imagines, are crammed with documents. Right rear, a desk covered with papers; next to it, against the wall, more crowded shelves. The* JUDGE'S *leather armchair is in front of the desk and there are other old chairs scattered about. The main entrance is at right. At left, a broad, high casement window framed by large shutters. In front of the window, a tall stand supporting a big bird cage. Also at left, a small secret doorway. The over-all impression is one of shabby disorder.*

At curtain, JUDGE D'ANDREA, *in hat and overcoat, enters through the main door, carrying a cage not much larger than his fist. He goes up to the stand, opens the door of the large cage, and transfers a goldfinch into it from the small cage.*

D'ANDREA

Go on, get in there! In with you, you lazy thing! Oh, at last . . . Now, you keep quiet, as usual, and let me dispense justice to these poor, ferocious little human beings.

He removes his hat and coat and hangs them up on a rack, then he sits down at his desk, picks up a sheaf of documents pertaining to a case he is supposed to try, waves it impatiently about, and snorts.

The fool!

He pauses, lost in thought for a moment, then he rings a bell and the porter, MARRANCA, *enters through the main door.*

MARRANCA

You rang for me, Your Honor?

D'ANDREA

Look, Marranca: I want you to run down the street – it's not far – to Chiàrchiaro's house –

MARRANCA

Leaping backward and making the sign against the Evil Eye, a downward thrusting of a closed fist with index and little fingers extended in the shape of horns.

For the love of God, don't even mention that name, Your Honor!

D'ANDREA

Very annoyed, pounding on his desk.

That's enough, by God! I forbid you to behave like an animal in my presence! And at the expense of a poor innocent man! Don't let this happen again!

MARRANCA

I'm sorry, Your Honor. I – I did it for your own good, too, you know.

D'ANDREA

Oh, so you insist –

MARRANCA

Not another word, Your Honor. What – what do you want me to do at this – this gentleman's house?

D'ANDREA

You'll tell him the public prosecutor wants to talk to him and you'll bring him here at once.

MARRANCA

At once, Your Honor. Yes, of course. Anything else?

D'ANDREA

That's all. You may go.

MARRANCA *exits, holding the door open as he leaves to admit three other magistrates, all dressed in their judicial robes and hats. They exchange greetings with* D'ANDREA, *then cluster about the goldfinch's cage.*

FIRST JUDGE

Well, and what does Mr. Goldfinch have to say for himself, eh?

SECOND JUDGE

You know, D'Andrea, you're becoming something of a joke, carrying this bird around with you everywhere.

THIRD JUDGE

You're known all over town as Judge Goldfinch.

FIRST JUDGE

Where is it? Where's that little cage you keep him in?

SECOND JUDGE

Picking it up from the desk.

Here it is! Gentlemen, look: a child's toy! And you a grown man!

D'ANDREA

I'm a child, am I? Just because of this little cage? And what about the rest of you, then, all dressed up like that?

THIRD JUDGE

Now, now, a little respect for the toga!

D'ANDREA

Go on, don't make me laugh! Nobody can hear us in here. As a boy, I used to make a game of this with my friends. One of us would play the defendant, somebody else would be the judge, the rest of us would be lawyers or members of the jury. . . . You must have played that game or something very much like it. . . . Well, I can tell you we took it much more seriously then than we do now.

FIRST JUDGE

Oh, you're right about that!

SECOND JUDGE

It always ended in a fight, I remember!

THIRD JUDGE

Displaying an old scar on his forehead.

Look at this: I still have a scar from a rock one of the defense lawyers threw at me while I was prosecuting his client!

D'ANDREA

The best part of the game was the robes we used to wear. They made us feel big and important, and under them we

were still children. Now it's just the opposite: we're grown
up and the robes belong to the game we played when we
were little. You have to have a lot of nerve to be able to
take it seriously.

He picks up the documents pertaining to CHIÀRCHIARO'S
case.

For example, my friends, I'm supposed to try this case.
Nothing could be more iniquitous than this trial. Iniquitous
because here a poor wretch is trying desperately to rebel
against the cruelest injustice, with no possibility of winning. A victim with no way of fighting back. By going to
court he's doing his best to fight back: he's demanding justice from the first two people who happened to come along.
And justice – justice, my friends – is the one thing he'll
never, never have. The court is bound to rule mercilessly
against him, thus confirming, and ferociously, too, the very
wrong by which this poor man has been victimized.

FIRST JUDGE

What case is it?

D'ANDREA

The suit brought by Rosario Chiàrchiaro.

At the mention of that name the three JUDGES *behave
exactly like* MARRANCA: *they leap backward, making
signs against the Evil Eye.*

ALL THREE

Shouting.

Holy Mother of God! – Touch iron, touch iron! – Don't
mention that name!

D'ANDREA

There, you see? And you're the very people who are expected to make certain that this poor fellow receives justice.

FIRST JUDGE

Justice has nothing to do with it! The man's gone crazy!

D'ANDREA

He's a poor unfortunate wretch, that's all.

SECOND JUDGE

Unfortunate, yes, but you'll have to admit he's also more

than a little mad! He's actually dared to bring a libel suit against the mayor's son, no less, as well as against that other fellow, what's his name. . . .

D'ANDREA

Fazio. Alderman Fazio.

THIRD JUDGE

A libel suit?

FIRST JUDGE

Yes, and you know why? He says he caught them making signs against the Evil Eye as he walked by.

SECOND JUDGE

How can it be libel when for two years now the whole town knows he has the Evil Eye and brings everybody bad luck?

D'ANDREA

And countless witnesses can appear in court to swear that many and many a time he's shown that he was well aware of his reputation by protesting violently against it.

FIRST JUDGE

Ah, you see? You admit it yourself.

SECOND JUDGE

Honestly, how can you condemn the mayor's boy and Fazio as slanderers for having done what everybody else has been doing openly for months now?

D'ANDREA

And you three along with the rest.

ALL THREE

Of course! — He's really terrible, you know! — God help us!

D'ANDREA

And then you wonder, my friends, why I carry this little goldfinch around with me. I've had him, you know, ever since last year, when my mother died. He used to be hers, and to me he's a living remembrance of her. I wouldn't know what to do without him. I talk to him, imitating his song, like this, and he answers me. I don't know what I'm saying to him, but if he answers, it means he probably gets something out of the sounds I make. Exactly like us, my friends. We think nature speaks to us, in the beauty of her flowers or in the stars above us, while in reality nature probably isn't even aware of our existence.

FIRST JUDGE

Keep on, keep on with that line of reasoning, my friend, and you'll see how happy it will make you!

Someone knocks at the main door. After a moment, it opens and MARRANCA *thrusts his head in.*

MARRANCA

Excuse me.

D'ANDREA

Come in, Marranca.

MARRANCA

He wasn't there, Your Honor. I told one of his daughters to send him over as soon as he comes home. Meanwhile, the youngest one, Rosinella, she came along with me. If Your Honor wants to see her –

D'ANDREA

No, no. I want to talk to him.

MARRANCA

She says she has something very important to ask you, Your Honor. She's very upset.

FIRST JUDGE

We'll be going along now. See you later, D'Andrea.

An exchange of good-bys and the three JUDGES *leave.*

D'ANDREA

To MARRANCA.
Show her in.

MARRANCA

Right away, Your Honor.

MARRANCA exits. ROSINELLA *now appears in the doorway. She is about sixteen, poorly but neatly dressed, her face half hidden by a black woolen shawl.*

ROSINELLA

May I come in?

D'ANDREA

Come in, come in.

ROSINELLA

Your servant, Excellency . . . Oh, please, sir! Oh, my sweet
Jesus! Your Excellency sent for my father? What's happened? Why? We're scared to death, Your Honor!

D'ANDREA

Calm yourself. What are you afraid of?

ROSINELLA

It's just that we've never had anything to do with the law
before, Excellency.

D'ANDREA

The law terrifies you?

ROSINELLA

Yes, sir. I tell you, we're scared to death! Only wicked
people, Excellency, have anything to do with the law.
We're not wicked, sir, just unlucky. And now if the law
turns against us, too . . .

D'ANDREA

What gave you that idea? There's nothing to worry about.
Nothing at all. The law is not turning against you.

ROSINELLA

Then why did Your Excellency send for my father?

D'ANDREA

Because your father wishes to set himself up against the
law.

ROSINELLA

My father? What do you mean?

D'ANDREA

Don't be frightened. Can't you see I'm smiling? . . . Do
you mean to say you don't know that your father is bringing a libel suit against the mayor's son and Alderman
Fazio?

ROSINELLA

My father? Oh, no, sir! We don't know anything about it!
My father is suing somebody?

D'ANDREA

Here are all the documents.

ROSINELLA

My God, my God! Don't pay any attention to him, Your
Honor! For more than a month now he's been like a crazy
man! He hasn't worked for over a year, did you know
that? Because they sent him away, they threw him
out in the street! He's been kicked around by everybody,
shunned like the plague by the whole town! He's suing
somebody? The mayor's son, you said? He's gone crazy!
Crazy! This horrible way they're all treating him, the
things they say about him, it's no wonder he's out of his
mind! Please, Your Honor, make him drop this suit! Make
him drop it!

D'ANDREA

Of course, my child. That's exactly what I want him to do.
And that's why I sent for him. I hope I can convince him.
Still, you know, it's so much easier to do evil than good in
this world.

ROSINELLA

Really, Your Excellency? For you, too?

D'ANDREA

Yes, for me, too. Because evil, my dear child, can be done
to anyone and by everyone, but good can only be done to
those who need it.

ROSINELLA

And you don't think my father needs it?

D'ANDREA

I do, I do. But it's this very need that makes it so difficult.
The people who need help, my child, are very often those
who have been so embittered by life that it becomes almost impossible to give it to them. Do you understand?

ROSINELLA

No, sir, I don't understand. But please do everything you
can, Excellency. There isn't any good or any peace for us
in this town any more.

D'ANDREA

Couldn't you go somewhere else?

ROSINELLA

Where? Your Honor doesn't know what it's like. Anywhere we'd run to people would find out about us and talk about us. We can't get rid of this thing, even if we tried to cut it out with a knife. If you could see my father, what he's become! He's grown a beard, a great big horrible beard that makes him look like an owl . . . and – and he's made himself a kind of suit, Excellency, that when he puts it on, he'll scare people, even dogs will run from him!

D'ANDREA

Why did he do that?

ROSINELLA

I don't know why. He knows. Ask him. He's like a crazy man, I tell you! Make him do it, make him drop this case, please!

There's a knocking at the door.

D'ANDREA

Who is it? Come in.

MARRANCA *looks in, trembling.*

MARRANCA

He's – he's here, Your Honor! What – what shall I do?

ROSINELLA

My father?

Leaping to her feet.

Oh, my God! Don't let him find me here, Your Honor! Please!

D'ANDREA

Why not? What's wrong? Would he eat you up if he found you here?

ROSINELLA

No, sir. But he doesn't want us to leave the house. Where can I hide?

D'ANDREA

Over here. Don't worry.

He opens the secret door.

Go out this way, then down the corridor, and you'll find
an exit.

ROSINELLA

Yes, sir. Thank you, thank you. And don't forget, Excellency. Your servant.

She exits quickly. D'ANDREA *shuts the door behind her.*

D'ANDREA

Show him in.

MARRANCA *opens the main door as wide as possible and
hides behind it.*

MARRANCA

Come in, come in. . . . His Honor's waiting. . . .

As soon as CHIÀRCHIARO *enters,* MARRANCA *rushes out,
shutting the door behind him.* ROSARIO CHIÀRCHIARO
*has made himself up to look as much like a man with
the Evil Eye as possible; his face alone is a miracle to be-
hold. On his gaunt, yellow cheeks grows a rough tangled
beard; a pair of huge, bone-rimmed spectacles perches
on his nose, giving him the look of a marauding owl. He
is wearing a glossy, mouse-colored suit that bulges out
in every direction, and he carries a bamboo cane with a
handle made of horn. His pace is funereal and at every
heavy step he strikes the cane on the ground. He comes
to a halt in front of* D'ANDREA's *desk.*

D'ANDREA

Irritated, violently shoving the documents to one side.

Just what do you think you're doing? What is all this nonsense? You ought to be ashamed of yourself!

CHIÀRCHIARO

Not at all ruffled by D'ANDREA's *outburst, speaking in a
low, menacing voice through clenched teeth.*

So you don't believe in my power?

D'ANDREA

I say it's all a lot of nonsense! Come now, this is no time for

jokes, my dear Chiàrchiaro. Sit down. Sit down over here.
*He goes up to him and is about to put a hand on his
shoulder.*

CHIÀRCHIARO

Quickly drawing back and trembling.
Don't touch me! Be careful! Do you want to go blind?

D'ANDREA

After a pause, staring at him coldly.
Keep it up as long as you like. I'm in no hurry. . . . I sent
for you for your own good. There's a chair over there. Sit
down whenever you're ready.

CHIÀRCHIARO *takes the chair, sits down, looks at*
D'ANDREA, *then begins to roll the cane back and forth on
his lap, nodding heavily.*

CHIÀRCHIARO

Muttering.
For my own good . . . For my own good, you said. . . .
You dare to say it's for my own good, Your Honor, when
you tell me you don't believe in the Evil Eye?

D'ANDREA

Also sitting down.
You want me to say I do believe in it? Then I'll say I believe in it. All right?

CHIÀRCHIARO

Firmly, very seriously.
No, sir, it's not all right. I want you to believe in it absolutely. Ab-so-lute-ly. Not only that, but I want you to
prove it by the way you handle the case.

D'ANDREA

Now that, you see . . . Ah, that's going to be a little more
difficult.

CHIÀRCHIARO

Rising and starting for the door.
Very well, then I'll be going.

D'ANDREA

Oh, come on! Sit down! I told you this is no time for jokes!

CHIÀRCHIARO

Jokes? You think I'm joking? Don't trifle with me or you'll find out. . . . I warn you! I warn you!

D'ANDREA

Do you expect me to jump up and down and make an idiot of myself? You're wasting your time.

CHIÀRCHIARO

I said I'm warning you! I can be very terrible, you know!

D'ANDREA

Severely.

That's enough, Chiàrchiaro! I'm bored with this. Sit down and let's see if we can talk sensibly. I sent for you because I want you to realize that the course you've taken is not one calculated to bring you safely into port.

CHIÀRCHIARO

Your Honor, I'm standing in a blind alley with my back against the wall. What port, what course are you talking about?

D'ANDREA

The one I see you embarked on in that costume and the other one you've taken with your libel suit. I'm sorry, but you seem to be headed in two different directions at once. Opposite directions, in fact.

He brings the tips of his index fingers together to drive home his point.

CHIÀRCHIARO

No, sir. It just seems that way to you, Your Honor.

D'ANDREA

How can you say that? In your charges here you accuse two people of libel because they believe you have the Evil Eye. Then you come here, dressed in that ridiculous costume and made up to look the part, and you even announce that you expect *me* to believe in your Evil Eye.

CHIÀRCHIARO

Yes, sir. Exactly.

D'ANDREA

And you don't see any inconsistency in these two attitudes?

CHIÀRCHIARO

I see something else, Your Honor. That you've understood nothing.

D'ANDREA

Well, speak up, speak up, my dear Chiàrchiaro! What you've just said may be a gospel truth, but at least you'll be good enough to explain why I don't understand anything.

CHIÀRCHIARO

Gladly. I'll not only show you that you've missed the whole point, but I'll prove to you that you're my enemy.

D'ANDREA

I? Your enemy?

CHIÀRCHIARO

Yes, you. You. But first, tell me: do you or don't you know that the mayor's son has hired Lorecchio, the best lawyer in town, to defend him?

D'ANDREA

I'm quite aware of it.

CHIÀRCHIARO

And are you aware that I — I, Rosario Chiàrchiaro — that I myself went to see Lorecchio to make sure that he has all the evidence he needs to win? In other words, I not only told him that I've known for more than a year about everyone making signs against the Evil Eye, and other more or less insulting gestures, whenever I go by, but I also gave him proofs, Your Honor, documented proofs — irrefutable evidence, you know, ir-re-fu-ta-ble — concerning the terrible events on which my reputation as a bearer of the Evil Eye is unshakably founded. Un-sha-ka-bly, Your Honor!

D'ANDREA

What? You what? . . . You mean to say you went and gave this testimony to the opposing lawyer?

CHIÀRCHIARO

To Lorecchio himself. Yes, sir.

D'ANDREA

More nonplused than ever.

Well . . . I must admit I understand even less than I did before.

CHIÀRCHIARO

Less? You've never understood anything!

D'ANDREA

Forgive me, but . . . You went and testified against yourself to the lawyer for the other side. . . . Why? To make certain you'd lose the case? Then why did you sue these two men in the first place?

CHIÀRCHIARO

That very question, Your Honor, proves you've understood nothing. I brought the case into court because I want official recognition of my power. Now do you understand? I want this terrible power of mine to be officially recognized, to be legally established. It's the only capital I have left, Your Honor.

D'ANDREA

As if to embrace him, deeply moved.

Oh, Chiàrchiaro! My poor Chiàrchiaro! Now I understand! A fine capital! My poor man, what good is it?

CHIÀRCHIARO

What good is it? What do you mean, what good is it? You, my dear sir, when you set out to be a judge – even allowing for the fact that you're a poor one – now tell me, didn't you have to have a diploma, some sort of license?

D'ANDREA

Oh, yes, certainly. A diploma . . .

CHIÀRCHIARO

Well, that's it! I want *my* diploma! I want *my* license to practice! My license to be a full-fledged menace! Signed, sealed, and delivered by this court!

D'ANDREA

And so? What will you do with it?

CHIÀRCHIARO

What will I do with it? Can you really be so simple-minded? I'll stamp it on my visiting cards, I'll print it on my stationery! You think it's so unimportant? My whole life is at stake! I'm a ruined man, Your Honor! The poor father of an innocent family. For years I worked hard and honestly. They threw me out, kicked me into the gutter because they said I had the Evil Eye! In the gutter, with my wife a paralytic, bedridden for the past three years, and with two young daughters who, if you could just see them, Your Honor, it would break your heart, they're so pretty, both of them. But no one will have anything to do with them because they're mine, you understand? And do you know what we live on now, all four of us? On the bread my son takes out of his own mouth, and he a family man with three children of his own to feed! How much longer do you think the poor boy can go on sacrificing himself for me? Your Honor, there's nothing left for me to do but go into business with this Evil Eye of mine. I'm forced to practice the only profession I have.

D'ANDREA

What will you get out of it?

CHIÀRCHIARO

What will I get? I'll show you. Here, look at me: you see what sort of an impression I make. I frighten everyone. This beard . . . these glasses . . . As soon as you give me my license, I'm in business! You ask me how? That's be-cause − and I'll say it again − that's because you're my enemy!

D'ANDREA

Your enemy? Is that what you really think?

CHIÀRCHIARO

Yes, sir. You are. Because you refuse to believe in my power. Everyone else believes in it, you know. All of them, they all believe in it. And it's lucky for me they do! For instance, there are quite a few gambling casinos in town. All I have to do, Your Honor, is put in an appearance. I won't have to open my mouth. The proprietor, the players, everyone will pay me to go away. I'll buzz around this town like a huge fly. I'll stand in front of one shop window after another. . . .

Acting out his program.

Is that a jewelry store over there? Well, I plant myself in front of the window and I start eyeing everybody who goes by, like this! Who's going to enter that store, or even stop long enough to glance in that window? So the owner comes out and slips me a few lire to go away. A few more lire and I go and do guard duty in front of his competitor's place down the street. Now do you see? It's a new kind of tax I'm going to make people pay.

D'ANDREA

A tax on ignorance!

CHIÀRCHIARO

On ignorance? Oh, no, my dear sir! A tax on the public safety! Because I've accumulated so much spite and so much hatred against the whole of this disgusting humanity of ours that I really do believe, Your Honor, that here, in these eyes of mine, I have the power to reduce an entire city to rubble! Look out for me! Don't say I didn't warn you! You see? Look at you, standing there, frozen . . . like a pillar of salt!

D'ANDREA, *overcome by deep pity, has indeed remained motionless, struck dumb in the man's presence.*

Come now, let's get on with it! Let's get on with this case of mine! It's sure to be a famous one. Of course you'll acquit both these defendants, since they've obviously committed no crime. The decision of the court will be an official recognition of my professional standing.

D'ANDREA

Rising.

Your license?

CHIÀRCHIARO

Striking a grotesque pose and pounding his cane on the floor.

My license! Yes, sir!

The words are barely out of his mouth when a shutter opens, as if blown by the wind, and strikes against the stand, toppling both stand and bird cage to the floor with a great crash.

D'ANDREA

With a cry, running to the spot.

Oh, God! The goldfinch! My little goldfinch! Oh, my God! He's dead . . . dead. . . . The only thing my mother left me. . . . Dead . . . dead . . .

At his cries, MARRANCA *and the three* JUDGES *come running in. At the sight of* CHIÀRCHIARO, *they go pale and freeze in their tracks.*

ALL

What is it? What is it?

D'ANDREA

The wind . . . that shutter . . . my little goldfinch . . .

CHIÀRCHIARO

Triumphantly.

What wind? What shutter? I did it! He wouldn't believe in my power and I proved it to him! I did it! No one else! That's how the bird died!

The others back away from him in terror.

And that's how you'll all die, one by one!

ALL

Protesting, imploring in chorus.

No! God help us! I hope you choke to death! I have a family to support! For the love of God!

CHIÀRCHIARO

Imperiously, holding out his hand.

All right, then come over here! Pay your taxes! All of you!

ALL

Giving him money.

Yes, yes, of course! Right away! Here! Just get out! Leave us alone! Go away!

CHIÀRCHIARO

Turning triumphantly to D'ANDREA *and holding out his hand to show him the money.*

You see? And I don't even have my license yet! Get on with the trial! I'm rich! I'm rich!

Curtain

CHEE-CHEE

(Cecè, 1920)

THE CAST

CESARE VIVOLI, nicknamed Chee-Chee
COMMANDER CARLO SQUATRIGLIA
NADA

A room in a first-class hotel in Rome.

A combination sitting room and study in a first-class hotel, furnished in the latest style. At rear, the main entrance into a corridor; at left, another exit leading into a bedroom; at right, a window. A telephone hangs on the back wall, to the right of the door.

At curtain the room is empty. The telephone rings three times. On the third ring, CHEE-CHEE, *dressed in pajamas and holding a shaving brush, his cheeks covered with lather, runs in from the bedroom. He is thirty-five years old. Although his face shows signs of dissipation, there is a restless vitality in everything he does. His habitual expression, though not blank, is somewhat absent-minded, as if he had a hundred things on his mind. His features rapidly change expression, reflecting every twist and turn of his active imagination. He is smooth-shaven, extremely attractive, with sparkling eyes and a warm mouth. He is a born gentleman and dresses with scrupulous elegance.*

CHEE-CHEE

And three! Just a minute, Christ, can't you tell I'm shaving! Hello! . . . Who? Louder, I can't hear you. . . . I'm shaving. . . . Ah, Squatriglia? What? No . . . I was talking to myself, I'm in the middle of shaving. . . . Yes, send him up.

He turns back toward the bedroom, then pauses, doubtfully.

Who did he say? Squatriglia? Mmm! He has some kind of a title, Commander, I think. Commander? Of what?

Exits into the bedroom. A few moments later there's a knock at the front door.

CHEE-CHEE

From within.

Come in!

No one enters. A pause. Another knock at the door.

CHEE-CHEE

Coming to the doorway, angrily.

Come in, I said!

The door opens and COMMANDER CARLO SQUATRIGLIA *enters, closing the door behind him.* SQUATRIGLIA *is about fifty, a big, rough-looking man who seems uncomfortable in his new suit and would doubtless be more at home in working clothes. He has only one eye and there is no trace of the other one. He lost it in a mine explosion and has had the wound closed by a skin graft. He is very rich and most able in the world of business, but a complete simpleton outside of it.*

SQUATRIGLIA

My dear Chee-Chee!

CHEE-CHEE

Oh, so it's you! I'll be with you in a moment. Sit down, Commander. As you can see, I'm in the middle of shaving.

SQUATRIGLIA

I'm not disturbing —

CHEE-CHEE

Of course not! No sense standing on ceremony with you, is there? I'll just finish up.

Indicating the next room.

The door is open, so go ahead and talk. In fact, you can come in, if you want to.

SQUATRIGLIA

No, thanks. Take your time. I'll wait.

CHEE-CHEE

Five minutes. I'm almost done.

He exits. SQUATRIGLIA *sits down. He waits a moment, then from his briefcase he produces a piece of paper and begins to scan it.*

CHEE-CHEE

From within.

Aren't you going to talk?

SQUATRIGLIA

Go ahead, finish up. I have a bill to go over. . . .

Shaking his head as he stares at the paper.

My God, if I don't get out of here soon . . .

Looks at his watch, rises.

Chee-Chee, I have to go soon, you know. I just came to say good-by and thank you. I'm leaving at eleven.

CHEE-CHEE

Entering in the act of hurriedly getting dressed.

So soon? You got everything done?

SQUATRIGLIA

Yes, thanks to you.

CHEE-CHEE

To me? What did I do?

SQUATRIGLIA

If it hadn't been for you, I'd never have gotten in to see His Excellency as soon as I did!

CHEE-CHEE

And I was the one who fixed it?

SQUATRIGLIA

What? Don't you remember?

CHEE-CHEE

Which Excellency was it?

SQUATRIGLIA

Which Excellency do you think would waste time on a humble little contractor like me? Go on, you clown! You're pretending you don't remember! You know it all, don't you?

CHEE-CHEE

Pretending? Me? I know it all?

SQUATRIGLIA

What's the matter? Did I offend you?

CHEE-CHEE

You don't offend me, you make me angry! Because I swear to you that I don't know a soul! Not one single solitary soul, understand? Look, that's just what I was thinking about in there while I was shaving: I certainly do lead one hell of a life! Chee-Chee, Chee-Chee, Chee-Chee! Everyone calls me Chee-Chee! Like a flock of sparrows! A hundred thousand people chirping Chee-Chee! In Milan, Turin, Venice, Genoa, Bologna, Florence, Rome, Naples, Palermo! Everybody! Everywhere!

SQUATRIGLIA

No wonder! Everybody knows you.

CHEE-CHEE

So everybody knows me, but then tell me: who can *I* possibly know? You laugh, eh? And yet, my friend, if I think about it, I'll go crazy! Now tell me, isn't it hell to realize that you live chopped up into a hundred thousand pieces for a hundred thousand other people? People who know you and whom you don't know? Who know everything about you and whose names you can't even remember? Whom you have to smile at, slap on the back, and say "dear" or "darling" to, and all the time you're up in the air, trying to pretend you aren't, while you do your best to remember, to be interested? And meanwhile you're asking yourself, "And who's he? Where does he know me from? Who am I to him?" Because you'll have to admit we're never the same! Depending on how we feel, what time of day it is, what the circumstances are, we're first one thing, then another. Gay with one man, sad with the next. Serious with this man, a joker with that one. They all come up to you, they all call you Chee-Chee. Just you try and remember how you are with this man and how you are with that one, if you're known to him this way or that way. You see some of them gape at you and you can't shout, "Oh, I'm so sorry, my friend, I forgot, I forgot! I'm not supposed to be like this for you, I'm supposed to be someone else, aren't I?" Who? How do I know, if I'm chopped up into a hundred thousand different people, as I said? If I begin to think about it, word of honor, I'll go crazy! My God, sometimes I bump into somebody's wife and she calls me Chee-Chee, and then five minutes later I'm liable to be in conversation with her husband and I begin to talk about her to him as if – well, you know. . . . You're laughing, eh? You think it's funny, do you?

SQUATRIGLIA

I'm laughing because I just realized – now tell the truth – you don't know who I am, do you?

CHEE-CHEE

Oh, I don't mean you! What an idea! You I know – I know you very well – No? You say no? – But of course I know you! Only – well, maybe – now that I think about it – I'm not sure if –

SQUATRIGLIA

Rocking with laughter.
You see, I'm right! I'm right!

CHEE-CHEE

Loudly, annoyed.
The hell you are! I know you! You have a brother, damn it!

SQUATRIGLIA

Filippo, yes.

CHEE-CHEE

Filippo, that's it! You see, I remember! Which of you has the title? You're the Commander, right?

SQUATRIGLIA

Right, right.

CHEE-CHEE

And didn't I call you Commander? Commander of what?

SQUATRIGLIA

Purely honorary.

CHEE-CHEE

You see, I remember. Yes. Filippo. He has only one eye and you – that is, he has only one hand and you have only one eye, yes, that's it! A mine disaster, wasn't it? Yes, a mine explosion! But they really patched you up magnificently, didn't they? Nice and smooth, you'd hardly notice it. You ought to be glad of that anyway. I remember everything now. We met at – wait! You had something to do with some job in a port somewhere, or something like that. . . .

SQUATRIGLIA

That's right! In Palermo. I had a contract to repair the breakwater in the harbor.

CHEE-CHEE

That's it, yes, yes! Palermo! The breakwater! You see, I – so I did you a favor? Imagine that! Well, I'm glad. With His Excellency the Minister of Public Works, was it?

SQUATRIGLIA

First you got me in to see the Undersecretary, then the Minister.

CHEE-CHEE

Ah, first the Undersecretary, eh? Now tell me, I mean, a day of your time must be worth a couple, a few thousand lire, eh? Maybe more . . .

SQUATRIGLIA

Well, you know – not being always on the spot – in work like mine – always dealing with a bunch of thieves –

CHEE-CHEE

Distractedly.
Yes, I'll go put on my jacket.

SQUATRIGLIA

Confused.
What for?

CHEE-CHEE

You said I was always in shirtsleeves.

SQUATRIGLIA

No, I didn't! I said I was always dealing with a bunch of thieves!

CHEE-CHEE

Oh, I see! And so I must have saved you a tidy little sum, admit it!

SQUATRIGLIA

Well, of course you did! They'd been giving me the run-around for a week. It distresses me that I really don't know how to thank you.

CHEE-CHEE

It does? It distresses you? You're about to leave in distress because you don't know how to thank me?

SQUATRIGLIA

Well, of course – Chee-Chee, if I can – I mean, as a friend . . .

He starts to reach for his wallet.

CHEE-CHEE

Immediately stopping him.

Hey! Are you joking? Commander, what do you take me for?

SQUATRIGLIA

I'm sorry. We're such good friends. And you're such a wild man, always so tangled up in so many things. . . .

CHEE-CHEE

Thoughtfully.

Wait a minute! You're right! But not like this. I mean, the move you just made, Commander, was a little crude, if you'll excuse my saying so. . . .

SQUATRIGLIA

Among friends I – I thought that –

CHEE-CHEE

But I treat my friends well! Even if it costs them some little sacrifice, it's never anything quite like that. I don't want you to think I'm offended! I'm simply trying to find a way now to relieve you of this distress. Yes. I have it! I'm going to give you a great pleasure, a pleasure I've never been able to enjoy myself. But I'm sure it must be a very great one indeed: the pleasure of being able to speak as badly as you want of a friend behind his back. Now what do you think of that? Wouldn't you like to give that a try?

SQUATRIGLIA

Chee-Chee, I haven't time. I have to leave at eleven. And I still haven't packed.

CHEE-CHEE

You can't leave now!

SQUATRIGLIA

Chee-Chee, if I don't leave, they'll murder me! I'll show you —

CHEE-CHEE

Oh, come on now! You came here to thank me?

SQUATRIGLIA

Yes.

CHEE-CHEE

And you said you didn't know how? Now that I'm showing you how, you say you have to leave?

SQUATRIGLIA

As long as it's quick, the way —

CHEE-CHEE

The quickest! Where are you going? Leghorn? Fine. Instead of the eleven o'clock, you'll take the three o'clock train.

SQUATRIGLIA

Impossible!

CHEE-CHEE

Damn it, you ought to be ashamed of yourself! You admit I've saved you I don't know how many days and you don't want to give up even a few hours for my sake? Favor for favor now! The more I look at you, the more I realize you're exactly the man I need. Yes. Age – height – bearing – and then – yes – you're indulgence personified. . . .

SQUATRIGLIA

How can I help it? With one eye permanently closed!

CHEE-CHEE

Kissing him.

Sweetheart! You're a good sport, that's why I like you! Now listen: you're a friend of Daddy's.

SQUATRICLIA

Daddy's? Whose Daddy?

CHEE-CHEE
Mine.

SQUATRIGLIA

I thought your father was dead.

CHEE-CHEE

Don't be an idiot! You have to be a friend of my father's,
see? He's in business, right? And I'm in the firm with him.
But we're bankrupt. Worse than bankrupt. And it's all
my fault. Because I'm – which would you prefer? – a
crook, a rascal?

SQUATRIGLIA

Rascal.

CHEE-CHEE

So I'm a rascal, then. But a crook, too, see? It sounds
stronger. Use them both. And a gambler, too. And –

SQUATRIGLIA

And a Don Juan.

CHEE-CHEE

No, that's no insult! What's the matter with you? Wait –
something else – a swindler! How does that sound?

SQUATRIGLIA

Oh, come, come!

CHEE-CHEE

No, I mean it. If you like the sound of it, say it. Say all the
bad things you like behind my back, all the abuse, all the
insults you can think of. Then it's up to you to pay for this
pleasure just as little as you can get away with.

SQUATRIGLIA

Pay? But to whom? Why? Are you serious or is this another of your jokes?

CHEE-CHEE

Patience. It's true, I haven't told you yet – but I haven't any
time either! My God, it's nearly ten o'clock! She'll be here
any moment! All right, I'll tell you quickly, in two words,
what it's all about. A couple of weeks ago, I was alone, as
usual, in this mob of friends. Chee-Chee, Chee-Chee, Chee-

Chee! In a café on the Pincio, on the terrace. A cab drove by with a girl in it. My friend, the original Eve! One of those girls to want to make you kiss the tips of your fingers. "Hey, Chee-Chee," they say to me, "that girl, old man, she's not for you!" "Why not?" I answer. "You don't imagine there's a girl in the world I can't have, do you? You do? All right," I say, "let's bet on it!" And they all shout back, "Let's bet on it!" "If in three days," say I, "here, at this very same time, I haven't given you absolute proof that I've gotten to her, I'll buy you all dinner. Otherwise, you'll buy me dinner!" As you can easily imagine, three days later, at exactly the same time, I drove past sitting next to her and bowing to all my friends up there on the café terrace waiting for me. See?

SQUATRIGLIA

Well – yes – I suppose so. . . .

CHEE-CHEE

You don't see it at all. Now listen! To get to her, my friend, well, that was easy. I know all the routes. With my connections, the easiest thing in the world. But once there – oh, once there! Sometimes it's harder to come down than to go up! If you're loaded on the way up, you can usually float down. But if you aren't, my friend . . . Well, I had a little trouble, that's all. And to get out of it, I did a foolish thing, something I've always been careful to avoid. I got her to accept – in place of anything else, but greatly exaggerating their actual worth – three little I.O.U.s of two thousand lire each.

SQUATRIGLIA

That's all?

CHEE-CHEE

You don't seem very impressed. Oh, no, my friend, I don't want any of these little scraps of paper chasing me around. I've always been scared to death of them! I swear I haven't slept the past four nights thinking about them. I absolutely must get hold of those three I.O.U.s today. I wrote Nada yesterday to bring them to me and –

The telephone rings.
Here she is! So we're agreed now.

SQUATRIGLIA

Wait a minute! Agreed on what? What do I have to do?
You want me to pay her the six thousand lire?

CHEE-CHEE

No! What's the matter with you? Six thousand lire? Of
course not!

He is near the telephone.
Come here. Answer it.

SQUATRIGLIA

Me? But who is it?

CHEE-CHEE

Nada, of course! Who else?
Drags him to the telephone.

SQUATRIGLIA

Are you crazy? Me?

CHEE-CHEE

She won't bite you! Come on, if we're agreed! Pay six
thousand lire! Hah!

SQUATRIGLIA

Agreed on what?

CHEE-CHEE

That you'll spout everything bad about me that comes
into your head – crook, rascal, villain, thief – you'll tell
her my father is on the verge of bankruptcy – that those
I.O.U.s she has are worthless. You'll get them back from
her and in exchange you'll give her – let's see – oh, four
hundred, five hundred lire. Not more, understand? It
wouldn't be worth it!
The telephone rings again.
Come on, come on! Pick it up!
Handing it to him.
Say hello! Go on now!

SQUATRIGLIA

I will not! I can't do this kind of thing! With some
woman I never –

CHEE-CHEE

Woman or no woman, go on!
  Another ring.
Say hello! And good luck, eh! I'm off!
  Runs out the front door.

SQUATRIGLIA

  Into the phone.
Hello . . . All right, send her up.
  He hangs up, panting, shrugs helplessly, takes out his handkerchief, wipes his brow, and waits very nervously, muttering from time to time.
Good God! . . . Good God! . . . This is crazy! . . . Caught in a trap . . . Now what do I do? . . . What'll I say? . . . Oh, what a mess! . . . What a mess! . . .
  A knock at the door.

SQUATRIGLIA

Come in!
  NADA *enters. She is twenty-two, but she could be older. She is a girl who lives off the delicate arrangements she is able to make with gentlemen friends and she tries to pass for a great lady, but when aroused she drops her pose to become either ill-mannered or naïve.* SQUATRIGLIA, *very embarrassed, bows clumsily to her.*

NADA

  As embarrassed as he at sight of this stranger.
Mr. Vivoli?

SQUATRIGLIA

Mr. Vivoli, Miss – Mr. Vivoli is – is not here.

NADA

What? But who answered the telephone?

SQUATRIGLIA

I did. I answered because – excuse me, you're – yes – you are Miss Nada, aren't you?

NADA

Nada, that's right. And you? What are you doing here and why did you ask me to come up?

SQUATRIGLIA

Well, you see, I – that is – no, I – let me explain – there's – there's been a mistake.

NADA

I don't want to hear about it. This *is* Mr. Vivoli's room?

SQUATRIGLIA

Oh, yes indeed! If you'll let me explain – I heard a woman's voice on the telephone and – and I thought it – it was Mommy.

NADA

Laughing at his comical embarrassment.
Mommy? Whose mommy? Yours?

SQUATRIGLIA

No! Not mine!

NADA

Well, I didn't think so. Mistaking me for your mother!

SQUATRIGLIA

Please, let's leave my mother out of this. She hasn't anything to do with this, thank God! She's been in heaven for some time now! I'm sorry if I seemed a little angry. I meant *his* mommy – uh, his mother.

NADA

Chee-Chee's? Here?

SQUATRIGLIA

Yes, Chee-Chee's. Let me explain –

NADA

But Mr. Vivoli? I'm sorry, but –

SQUATRIGLIA

I can explain. I – I'm a friend –

NADA

Of Chee-Chee's?

SQUATRIGLIA

No. That is – well, yes – Chee-Chee's, too. But I'm really more a friend of his father's, the poor soul. No, I don't mean "poor soul." I mean, he isn't dead. He's alive. Unfortunately. That is – yes – he's alive. I say unfortunately because he's alive to suffer – oh, believe me, miss – trouble, nothing but trouble.

NADA

I'm sorry, but I –

SQUATRIGLIA

I'll explain –

NADA

But I don't want to know, I tell you! That's their business, not mine. If Mr. Vivoli isn't in the hotel, then –

SQUATRIGLIA

Forgive me, miss, but it *is* your business!

NADA

It is?

SQUATRIGLIA

Yes, it is. Oh, it's not your fault, we're very sure of that! So sure that – look – that Mommy and I were going to come and see you –

NADA

See me? You and Mommy?

SQUATRIGLIA

His mommy! Chee-Chee's mother!

NADA

You were going to come and see me?

SQUATRIGLIA

To place ourselves in your hands, miss!

NADA

What kind of a joke is this? I've only known Mr. Vivoli about three weeks. I came here because he himself –

SQUATRIGLIA

For God's sake, say no more! We know that, I tell you! And that's why we wanted to come and see you!

NADA

Are you serious?

SQUATRIGLIA

Of course!

NADA

You are? You and his mother? To see me?

SQUATRIGLIA

Because we know that you, miss, have been vilely, basely –
I wish there were a stronger word for it – help me – you've
been shamelessly – yes – even that won't do it – shamelessly betrayed by that rascal, that crook, that scoundrel –
no, please, let me finish – that villain, that philanderer,
that forger, that robber, that murderer –

NADA

And you say you're a friend of his?

SQUATRIGLIA

Yes, miss. The closest. A family friend. Of his father's, that
jewel of a man, the greatest gentleman God ever put on
this earth! Miss, we found out, by his own confession,
that –

NADA

Chee-Chee's?

SQUATRIGLIA

Yes, miss, that Chee-Chee –

NADA

What?

SQUATRIGLIA

That at a crucial moment like this, when the least little
thing – I mean, the slightest push, the merest whisper, yes,
the merest whisper could – could turn everything upside
down – could cause the most terrible disaster –

NADA

Under her breath.
Oh, for God's sake!

SQUATRIGLIA

Disconcerted.
What did you say?

NADA

I said, "Oh, for God's sake!" You have a way of putting
things – if you could see yourself . . .

SQUATRIGLIA

I do? I – I get too excited?

NADA

Yes. Yes, you do. And – and, oh, God –
  Hiding her face in her hands.
I can't look at you – all red in the face. Try to keep calm.

SQUATRIGLIA

I'll try. I'm sorry. I feel so personally involved. And it was
the moment, I was saying – the – the catastrophe not only
of an entire family, but the honor, miss, the honor of a
poor old man destroyed by the infamous conduct, the most
disgraceful iniquities of a son who –

NADA

Keep calm! Please try to keep calm! You look like – like –

SQUATRIGLIA

Like what?

NADA

You ought to see yourself!

SQUATRIGLIA

All right, I'll try to keep calm, miss. At such a moment, I
was saying – this son has the audacity to sign – to put into
circulation – yes, imagine – you know what I mean – three
of them, aren't there? Of two thousand lire each, aren't
they?

NADA

  Starting.
How dare you? Shame on you!

SQUATRIGLIA

Shame – yes, you're right – yes! Shame is just the word for
it, miss! Shame, shame! And I'm sick with it, believe me!
God only knows what I'm going through, standing here
and talking to you like this! On the edge of catastrophe,
miss –

NADA

  Looking at him sharply.
Stop it! You know, you're really a scream!

SQUATRIGLIA

Disconcerted.

I am? A scream? Me? Oh, I see what you mean. And – and take my word for it, miss, I'm – I'm sweating all over!

NADA

I don't wonder. Acting like this. Pull yourself together! Dry yourself off! I'm going.

SQUATRIGLIA

No, please, don't go! Listen to me, I beg you, miss! I can't let you go!

NADA

What do you want from me? I've never been in anything like this before!

SQUATRIGLIA

I believe you. And I want you to know that I understand and appreciate how you feel. But please don't go. Hear me out. Oh, how I wish she were here! She ought to have been here by now! I mean, his mother, miss.

NADA

There you go again!

SQUATRIGLIA

She could join me in prayer!

NADA

Now this is too much! Really! Aren't you ashamed of yourself?

SQUATRIGLIA

Yes, miss, I'm so very ashamed! But I must explain the situation to you. These three I.O.U.s –

NADA

What? Again?

SQUATRIGLIA

But we haven't talked about them yet!

NADA

Don't you realize that even if I had been ready to come here today and throw them in his face, now that he's insulted me, by sending someone else to talk to me about them, I'm going to keep them in here –

Patting her purse.

– and cause all the scandal I can?

SQUATRIGLIA

Good for you! Good for you! Yes – oh, believe me, miss, if you really did hold a weapon against him, a gun to shoot him down with, only him, and to destroy him, annihilate him, we'd all – his father, myself, even his mother – we'd all shout, "Go on! Shoot! Hurry up! Destroy him! Annihilate him, this wretch! This freak of nature! This scum of humanity!" But you don't have a weapon against him. All you have is three worthless pieces of paper, that's all!

NADA

They're signed by him!

SQUATRIGLIA

And what do you think his signature is worth? Zero! What kind of scandal do you think you can cause, when the man's whole life has been one long scandal? When he's famous for being shameless, indifferent to everyone and everything?

NADA

Chee-Chee?

SQUATRIGLIA

Chee-Chee, Chee-Chee!

NADA

But if he moves in the best society –

SQUATRIGLIA

Because he plays the clown for them, miss! Because he worms and sneaks his way in everywhere! Because he's willing to lend his foul talents to anyone for anything!

NADA

Chee-Chee?

SQUATRIGLIA

Chee-Chee. You don't know, you can't imagine, miss, what that man is capable of! Already he's plastered his father's

venerable bald head with mud! The name, the honor of
his family! Broken his mother's heart! You see? The weapon
you hold there in your purse would only be turned against
these two poor old people, already crushed and trampled
into the dust by everyone. Even so I'd say to you, "Go
ahead, use this weapon of yours, strike down these two
helpless victims!" – if I knew that you could gain some
material advantage from it. But no! You'd only be committing an unnecessary cruelty! All the little that remains
to the family has already been mortgaged for some time,
mostly without any security whatever. Through my own
efforts, and with great difficulty, we've recently been able
to make an agreement with the creditors, but an agreement regarded with such suspicion by all the parties involved that the merest whisper could knock it over like a
house of cards. The least hint of a new I.O.U. in circulation and the crash would be inevitable. Crushed in the
debris would be a poor old man, a poor old woman. . . .
But not him! Oh, not him! If only he could be the sole
victim! But what does he care for the crash? What does
he care for the dishonor, the death of a poor old man? He
signs his I.O.U.s, goes on gaily signing I.O.U.s for six
thousand lire! Look, miss: I'm like a brother to that poor
old man, and for these three pieces of paper you hold,
which are worthless, absolutely worthless to you, useless
to strike at him, but which could cause great harm to
someone who is not to blame, who has not sinned – for
these three pieces of paper, I say – from which you can
derive no advantage whatever, not even the satisfaction of
revenge – I am disposed, miss, to . . .

*He produces his wallet, hesitantly opens it, and with-
draws a sheaf of banknotes.*

NADA

As he does so, scornfully.
Oh, a little deal, is that it?

SQUATRIGLIA

No, not a deal! I place myself entirely in your hands, miss,
trusting in your generosity!

NADA

Generosity? For such a piece of impudence? You expect generosity from me?

SQUATRIGLIA

Not for his sake!

NADA

What do I care about the others?

SQUATRIGLIA

But that's why, you see — that's why I permitted myself to make this offer —

NADA

A little money to pay for my generosity? How much? A few thousand lire?

SQUATRIGLIA

No. I'm relying on —

NADA

My dear man, you're mistaken. You think you can buy a sentiment like generosity from a woman like me at a bargain price?

SQUATRIGLIA

Well — you see — I'd heard —

NADA

That we're generous and big-hearted? Oh, but not like this! Not for this kind of thing! For love, if ever! Not for someone who sends a stranger to beg us for his parents' sake, who involves in his own shame his mother, his father, and his whole family! This is an outrage! What the hell do you think I care for your whole story? All I feel right now is disgust, and I'm so angry that if, instead of you, I had him here, that bastard —

SQUATRIGLIA

Quickly, with a sincere, very comical expression.
You'd kill him? I'd kill him, too, believe me!

NADA

You make me laugh . . . really you do. . . .
Bursts out laughing.

SQUATRIGLIA

Go ahead. Go ahead. Laugh. Laugh at me all you like. I'm not offended, miss. Believe me, I'm – I'm mortified, ashamed. . . .

NADA

You had some nerve, I'd say!

SQUATRIGLIA

I had to. I – I'm in the middle – help me, help me get out of this, please. I'm – I'm not really suited to –

NADA

I can see that. You want the I.O.U.s?

SQUATRIGLIA

If – if you don't mind.

NADA

You say they aren't worth anything?

SQUATRIGLIA

Nothing. That I can swear to you. Nothing, miss.

NADA

Then why didn't you just tell me so?

SQUATRIGLIA

I did tell you!

NADA

No, I mean that and nothing else. And you should have added that by trying to cash them in I'd have all my girl friends laughing at me for being such a nitwit as to accept them in the first place. See? That's all you had to say. Don't appeal to my generosity. I can't afford to be generous. I want my revenge. And believe me, I'll find a way to get it and I'll revenge myself hard. Oh, will I get even with him! This embarrassment, this ridiculous scene I've had to put up with, by God, he'll pay for them, all right!
  Suddenly, resolutely, she opens her bag, produces the I.O.U.s, and hands them to him.
Here they are! Now get out! Get out of here!

SQUATRIGLIA

Thank –

NADA

Don't thank me!

SQUATRIGLIA

No – but – let me – allow me –

Timidly, with trembling fingers, he draws several bills from his bankroll and puts them on the table, under the inkwell.

NADA

No! I don't want your money! I don't want it!

SQUATRIGLIA

Let me. Please. As a favor. I don't know whether I'm doing right or wrong, but –

NADA

I said I don't want it! Pick up your money!

SQUATRIGLIA

Please – look – for me – it's the least I can do – I – please let me – as a favor – a special favor – to me.

NADA

How much is that?

SQUATRIGLIA

Fif – fifteen hundred lire, miss, but –

NADA

Fifteen hundred lire?

SQUATRIGLIA

If – if it isn't enough –

NADA

Annoyed, she takes an open envelope out of her bag and hands it to him.

Look at this bill.

SQUATRIGLIA

Taking the envelope, embarrassed, uncomprehending, he removes a dressmaker's bill and looks at it.

Low cloche hat, with white Bird of Paradise feathers, one thousand six hundred and fifty lire.

Looks up at her. NADA *points to the hat she is wearing. He understands and speaks hurriedly.*

Ah – yes – immediately – gladly . . .

Adds another hundred and fifty lire to the pile on the table.

There you are. I'm sorry if I – And thank you, miss. With all my heart. Also in the name of –

NADA

That's enough, please!

SQUATRIGLIA

You're right. I must run. I have to tell them of your generous – no, no – not another word –

Offers her his hand.

May I?

Shakes her hand, bows.

It was an honor.

Exits out the back. Left alone, NADA *begins to pace furiously about the room, disgusted and enraged.*

NADA

Oh, he'll pay for this! He'll pay for this! Coward! What a thing to do! Coward! Coward!

She stops by the table, picks up the money, angrily and disdainfully counts it, thrusts it into her bag, then she pauses a moment to think, biting on one finger, her eyes threateningly ablaze. Finally, she rouses herself, sits down at the table, takes out a sheet of paper and an envelope.

You wait. . . .

She begins to write. A pause. As NADA *writes, with her back to the entrance, the door silently opens and* CHEE-CHEE *appears, his hat on and cocked to one side. He enters, shutting the door behind him without making a sound, tiptoes up to* NADA, *and throws his arms around her from behind.*

CHEE-CHEE

Nada, my sweet!

NADA

Oh, it's you, is it? How dare you come here now?

CHEE-CHEE

What's wrong?

NADA

You've got some nerve –

CHEE-CHEE

I'm sorry, did I keep you waiting too long? I didn't think
I'd be so late. Anyway, here I am!
  He presents a smiling face to her.

NADA

Take that!
  She slaps him hard.

CHEE-CHEE

Oh, God! Too hard! You hurt me! What for?

NADA

What for? You dare to ask me what for?

CHEE-CHEE

I'm sorry! I said I was sorry! So what's wrong? I kept you
waiting a half hour or so. . . .

NADA

Oh, you think that's all?

CHEE-CHEE

What else could it be? What is it?

NADA

Did you go and see Mommy?

CHEE-CHEE

Mommy? Whose mommy?

NADA

Yours. Wasn't she supposed to come and beg me, implore
me to have pity –

CHEE-CHEE

My mother? What are you talking about? Are you crazy?

NADA

Oh, so I'm crazy, am I? You cheat!

CHEE-CHEE

What's all this business about Mommy? Whose mommy
and where? What's she got to do with anything?

NADA

Liar! I know damn well she hasn't got anything to do with anything! You didn't think I believed any of it?

CHEE-CHEE

Any of what? Have you gone crazy? What's happened to you?

NADA

Bankruptcy! Ruin! Dishonor! Everything upside down because of your infamous doings! A poor father whose saintly old head you've doused with mud! A poor mother whose – swindler! Crook! Aren't you even ashamed?

CHEE-CHEE

Seriously, coldly.

You are out of your mind, my dear! I beg you to explain. I don't know what you're talking about.

NADA

No? You don't? You really don't?

CHEE-CHEE

What am I supposed to know? I find you in a howling rage, and I thought it was because I was late. But now . . .

NADA

Going over to him with her hands out, palms up, imploringly.

Is it possible? Could anyone keep such a straight face? How? What about the man with one eye walled up?

CHEE-CHEE

The man with one eye? Walled up?

NADA

Who was here instead of you?

CHEE-CHEE

A man with one eye walled up?

NADA

Your daddy's friend!

CHEE-CHEE

What are you talking about? You really have gone crazy!

Or you dreamt it all! I don't have a daddy and I don't
have a mommy. Now, what are you talking about?

NADA

What? Do you want to drive me crazy? Now you watch
out! If this is a joke —

CHEE-CHEE

What do you mean, joke? I tell you I don't know what
you're talking about! Explain yourself! Who was here instead of me? A man with one eye walled up? What do you
mean, walled up?

NADA

Walled up, walled up. Like this.
  She covers an eye with one hand.

CHEE-CHEE

You found him here? How did he get in?

NADA

How should I know? He was here. I telephoned from
downstairs, he told me to come up. I thought I'd find you
and I found him.

CHEE-CHEE

And who let him in?

NADA

You're asking me?

CHEE-CHEE

  Suddenly feigning dismay, then consternation.
With a walled-up eye? Oh, God! Here? Tell me, what did
he say?

NADA

That he was waiting for your mother. They were going
to come and see me together to beg me —

CHEE-CHEE

My mother? And you believed him?

NADA

I told you no!

CHEE-CHEE

To beg you to do what?

NADA

To give back the three I.O.U.s.

CHEE-CHEE

With exaggerated anxiety.
And you?

NADA

What do you mean? What about me?

CHEE-CHEE

You gave them to him?

NADA

He began talking to me about the ruin of your whole family —

CHEE-CHEE

The crook! What else?

NADA

He said your father was on the verge of bankruptcy.

CHEE-CHEE

My father? Oh, the swindler!

NADA

That the least little push, the slightest whisper would be enough to break up some sort of agreement he'd been able to make with the creditors —

CHEE-CHEE

Him? The murderer! The robber!

NADA

He got so excited I thought — God, it was disgusting! — I thought his one good eye was going to pop out of his head.

CHEE-CHEE

But tell me, you didn't give him those I.O.U.s, did you?

NADA

He told me, he proved to me they weren't worth any-thing, that I wouldn't be able to take any advantage of them —

CHEE-CHEE

And you gave them to him? You idiot! You've ruined me!

NADA

I did? But how? How could I?

CHEE-CHEE

Absolutely ruined me! You know who that man is? The biggest extortionist in the whole world, that's who! A bloodsucker! A vampire!

NADA

He is?

CHEE-CHEE

Yes, he is! He is! How could you believe him?

NADA

I didn't believe him.

CHEE-CHEE

Then how —

NADA

I thought you'd sent him.

CHEE-CHEE

I sent him?

NADA

To get the I.O.U.s back.

CHEE-CHEE

Me? But why? When I wrote you myself to bring them to me here! I was going to exchange them — I wanted to get them back — give you the money. How could you give them to him? Oh, what a crook! You've ruined me!

NADA

How did I know? Who even knew the man?

CHEE-CHEE

Couldn't you tell?

NADA

He got so excited — begging me and — and sweating all over the place. . . .

CHEE-CHEE

Of course, he's a marvel at playing the fool! There isn't a part he doesn't know how to play! From usurer to pimp, tyrant to slave, donkey to pig, snake to hyena, tiger to rabbit! And you believed him! And you fell into the web he spun for you! But it's my bones he's going to suck the marrow out of! He'd never been able to get any kind of hold on me to get even! For years he's been lying in wait for me, on the hunt for me! Because, you see, I've saved more than one victim from his clutches, and I once shamed him in public. . . . How did he ever find out about those I.O.U.s? How did he know you were coming here to give them to me? Tell me the truth, you didn't tell anybody about this, did you?

NADA

He told me he'd found out from you yourself.

CHEE-CHEE

From me? Does that make any sense to you? You must have mentioned it to some friend of yours.

NADA

No – well – I did – I mean – I did mention it –

CHEE-CHEE

To whom?

NADA

I don't remember – some friend of yours –

CHEE-CHEE

The man has his spies everywhere! Maybe – yes, of course, that must be it! He must have been the one who sicked that bore on me this morning, so I'd be tied up for half an hour, giving him just enough time to come here and surprise you. Oh, what a disaster! Now what will I do? What will I do? Three I.O.U.s. A hundred percent – he'll make me pay a hundred percent interest on that six thousand lire – unless – unless – but wait a minute! You just gave them to him? For nothing? Three I.O.U.s with my signature on them? For nothing?

NADA

No. He – he gave me a few hundred lire.

CHEE-CHEE

Oh, a few hundred? How few?

NADA

A thousand – a thousand six hundred – six hundred and fifty.

CHEE-CHEE

The crook! One thousand six hundred and fifty lire for six thousand, on which he'll make a hundred percent interest!

NADA

And he tried to give me even less!

CHEE-CHEE

You see? He even tried to beat you down!

NADA

No – actually – the minute I showed him the bill for the hat –

CHEE-CHEE

What hat? This one? But this is the one I bought for you, isn't it?

NADA

So what? You hadn't paid for it yet. I still had the bill.

CHEE-CHEE

I see. One thousand six hundred and fifty lire? So that means I'll have to pay for the hat twice. He'll add what he gave you to the interest rate.

NADA

No, no. Listen, Chee-Chee, at least let me pay –

CHEE-CHEE

Scornfully.

Go on! What are you thinking now?

NADA

Chee-Chee, please!

CHEE-CHEE

Shut up! Are you crazy?

NADA

Please let me –

CHEE-CHEE

Are you serious? I'm sorry for you. But it serves you right, you know. Did you really believe all the bad things he must have said about me? What did he say? What did he say?

NADA

With an expressive gesture of her hands.
My dear . . .

CHEE-CHEE

Absorbed.
And the notes weren't dated, you know. He can collect any time he wants to. But he won't! He isn't crazy! He'll hold me – like this, under the threat – free to collect interest whenever he wants – and he'll bleed me dry, just like all the others!

NADA

Poor Chee-Chee . . . Come here. . . .

CHEE-CHEE

Let me alone! You've ruined me!

NADA

I'll make it up to you, Chee-Chee. . . .

CHEE-CHEE

Running to embrace her.
Oh, my darling, I know you will! You'll make it up to me at the same rate of interest he'll make me pay, won't you?

NADA

Even more!

CHEE-CHEE

But it's anger, you see, anger as much as anything! To have fallen into his hands like this!

NADA

And I'll make you forget it, don't you worry. Now sit here.
She makes him sit down, then sits on his lap.
There we are!

CHEE-CHEE

How about a little down-payment? Quick, kiss me here!
Indicates his forehead.

NADA

Kissing him.
There . . .

CHEE-CHEE

Tell me, did he say a lot of bad things about me, the scoundrel?

NADA

Oh, lots. Lots.

CHEE-CHEE

For each thing he said, a kiss! And where I tell you. Let's start. Now what did he call me?

NADA

A rascal!

CHEE-CHEE

Quick! One here!
Indicates his right check. NADA *laughs and kisses him.*
Go on, go on! What else did he call me?

NADA

Wait – a freak –

CHEE-CHEE

A freak?

NADA

A freak of nature.

CHEE-CHEE

A freak of nature?
Leaps to his feet. NADA *skips away from him, laughing.*
Come here! Come here!

NADA

Let me take my hat off.

CHEE-CHEE

Sixteen hundred and fifty lire! And my change? Nada, come here!

NADA

I'm coming!

CHEE-CHEE

Sits down again with NADA *on his lap.*

Now, then, a freak of nature, eh?

Puts a finger to his lips.

This time right here, right here, my pet. . . .

NADA *leans down to kiss him on the mouth. At this point it seems prudent to bring down the curtain.*

Curtain

AT THE EXIT

(All' uscita, 1922)

APPARITIONS

THE FAT MAN

THE PHILOSOPHER

THE MURDERED WOMAN

THE LITTLE BOY WITH A POMEGRANATE

ASPECTS OF LIFE

A PEASANT

A PEASANT WOMAN

AN OLD DONKEY LOADED DOWN WITH HAY

A LITTLE GIRL

The back entrance to a country cemetery.

The back entrance to a country cemetery encircled by a white wall of rough stone. Beyond the wall and the gate, in the pale, misty light, a glimpse of tall, dark cypresses. The dead, having left their useless bodies in their graves, emerge lightly through the exit, still in the vain guises they assumed in life.

The apparition of the FAT MAN *is seated on a worn bench at the foot of a large tree, his hands leaning on his cane, his chin resting on his hands. He has been there for quite a few days, but he can't seem to make up his mind to move from the spot. Showing no sign of pleasure, he has been witnessing the stupor, the terror, the disillusionment, the nausea that the other apparitions display as they exit from time to time through the cemetery gate, and the way in which they then wander off – uncertain, afflicted, disgusted, dismayed.*

The apparition of the PHILOSOPHER *has just emerged. He is a thin man and, despite a prominent bald spot, has a thick head of hair. He, too, seems annoyed; he looks around, bewildered; then he sees the* FAT MAN *sitting under the tree, composes himself, and approaches him.*

PHILOSOPHER

Why surprised, my friend? Why surprised? This is the way it is. What could be more natural?

FAT MAN

You're telling me? That's a good one! You're the one who's surprised. I'm past that stage.

PHILOSOPHER

Me surprised? At what? I just said it's only natural.

FAT MAN

I heard you. You want me to think that you'd anticipated

it, that you knew all along that you'd be just as you are, still here.

PHILOSOPHER

No, that's not what I mean. In fact, if I was surprised at all, and I suppose I was at first, I assure you it was because I didn't anticipate it.

FAT MAN

I see. Because it seems so natural to you.

PHILOSOPHER

I can prove it very easily, if you want me to.

FAT MAN

No, please, never mind. What consolation do you think I can possibly derive from this posthumous exercise of your reason?

PHILOSOPHER

Posthumous? What do you mean, posthumous? I go on reasoning, just as you go on being fat, my friend. And for the sole fact that you and I are still here, I continue to see in us two vain forms of reason. Doesn't that comfort you?

FAT MAN

No, it humiliates me.

PHILOSOPHER

Poor man, perhaps it's because, when you were alive, you thought the forms were real – you could see and touch them – while all the time they were only the illusions necessary to your being, as to mine. To consist of something, you see, they had and still have to create an appearance for themselves. You really don't understand, do you?

FAT MAN

How can you expect me to understand? Your talk is too subtle for a fat man.

PHILOSOPHER

Listen, I'll give you an example. Take this cemetery here. When you were alive, you must have seen it who knows how many times.

FAT MAN

Every now and then, when I felt depressed, I'd stroll out this way.

PHILOSOPHER

And didn't it ever occur to you that the tombs were not built for the dead, but for the living?

FAT MAN

You mean the vanity expressed in the epitaphs?

PHILOSOPHER

No, that's an old story. I mean the need life has to build a house for its sentiments. You see, it isn't enough for the living to *feel;* they want to see their feelings expressed concretely, be able to touch them, and so they build a house for them. They want their feelings out, out where – naturally – well, what's in those tombs? Nothing, no one.

FAT MAN

What do you mean, no one? What about the dead?

PHILOSOPHER

My good man, after a few years what's left of us poor dead in those graves? At most a little dust. Nothing. Then what is a tomb? A tomb is meant to house a memory, an affection, a respect, a devotion – all sentiments, you see – sentiments that might not have lasted very long otherwise and that have been provided this way with a permanent home. But who or what can actually live in a tomb? If the living still feel the sentiments in themselves, then those sentiments survive there, too. If not, the graves are empty. They express merely a vanity, as you said, though vanity is, I hasten to point out, a kind of sentiment. Well, let's go on. Listen to this: I used to have a nice little dog.

FAT MAN

You built him a tomb?

PHILOSOPHER

No, no, of course not! He's still alive. Such a nice little dog! He was black and white and full of life! A little devil! He had a silver bell on his collar and I used to walk him everywhere. His thin legs would tremble so and his paws would

seem to skim over the ground. But he used to drive me to
distraction because he'd want to rush into every church
we passed. And I'd have to run after him, calling his name:
"Bibi, Bibi, here, Bibi!" He could never understand why a
nice-looking little dog like him wasn't allowed inside a
church. When I scolded him, he'd sit up and lift one of
his front paws and whimper, one ear cocked, the other
one flopping down, and he'd look at me as if to say that obviously the place was empty and of course he could go in.
"What do you mean, it's empty?" I'd say, petting him.
"That place contains the highest of human sentiments, Bibi,
a sentiment so high that it could not content itself with
living only in the hearts of men and had to build itself a
house outside, and what a house! With domes, naves, col-
umns, gold, marble, great works of art." Now you, my
friend, will perhaps understand what I meant. As a house
of God, the world itself is a far greater and richer place
than any church. The spirit of man in adoration of the divine mystery is incomparably more noble and precious
than any altar. But this is the fate of all sentiments that
wish to build themselves a home: they inevitably diminish
themselves and in their vanity also manage to seem a little
childish. The same fate, you see, overtakes the infinite that
is in each of us, whenever it chooses to house itself in this
semblance of reality we call man, an ephemeral form clinging to a whirling speck of dust lost in the heavens. . . .

FAT MAN

But then you and I and everyone who comes through that
gate over there, what are we now, I'd like to know? Apparitions of apparitions?

PHILOSOPHER

No, why? We're exactly what we were, but with this difference: that the shapes others gave us are buried back
there, in the graves; and the shapes we assumed ourselves
still survive here, for a little while, in you and me. We are,
in short, the fleeting relics of our vanity. A last shadow of
illusion still lives on in us. We are still so fond of our own

vain likenesses that we can't free ourselves of them, but have to wait for them gradually to fade and disappear. In fact, perhaps because of what I've been telling you, you already look a little less solid. Ah, you see? All I had to do was mention it and you immediately condensed again! Poor shadow, what's holding you here? You're the saddest fat man I've ever seen.

FAT MAN

I regret something. I don't know. I still see the sunny little garden of my house. A carpet of green from my window. There's a pool in the shade of some trees, and the goldfish rise to nibble at the surface. The plants all around gaze astonished at the spreading circles in the quiet water. I'm still back there, in the fresh green of the new leaves, like an old dead leaf that can't seem to let itself go. I can actually picture it. This dead leaf really does exist. I'm just waiting for a breath of air to blow it down. And then maybe, as you say, I'll simply fade away.

PHILOSOPHER

That's all you regret? This little garden of yours?

FAT MAN

No, but flowers in general always used to fill me with wonder. I mean, that the earth could produce anything so lovely. Go ahead and call them illusions, if you like. Every evening in May a nightingale came and sang in my garden, which was then in full bloom, bursting with roses of all kinds – yellow, white, red – with carnations and geraniums. All your philosophy, you see, couldn't prevent that nightingale from singing or stop those roses from blooming, from filling my garden with the magic of their perfume. You could have chased the bird away and torn up all my roses, but he'd only have flown into the next garden and continued every night to pour his song out to the stars. And you certainly couldn't have cut down all the roses in all the gardens. Yes, these things pass. But now my only regret is that I didn't know how to enjoy them. I'd breathe the air and it wouldn't remind me then that I was alive. In

May I'd hear the chirping of all the birds in all the gardens around my house, and neither their singing nor the fragrance of all those flowers would cause me to remember that I was alive. I was absorbed and locked in my own petty thoughts. I paid no attention to all the life my senses were so open to. And I used to feel sorry for myself. Over what? Why, over the very pettiness of my own thoughts, over some frustration, some disappointment already past. And meanwhile all the good in life escaped me. Well, no, I can see now that that isn't quite true. It didn't escape me, exactly. It escaped my consciousness, but not this body of mine, which tasted the pleasures of living without being able to tell itself so. That's why I'm still here, like a beggar at a door that has just been slammed in his face, still longing for the life I accepted, with all the disappointments, all the conditions my mind stupidly esteemed wretched and unbearable. Some Sundays, when my wife pretended to go to Mass and went, instead, to meet her lover —

PHILOSOPHER

Ah, poor man, you knew about it?

FAT MAN

There, you see? A reality and not an illusion.

PHILOSOPHER

You're wrong. I could prove to you it was an illusion, like everything else.

FAT MAN

That my wife was betraying me? It was a fact!

PHILOSOPHER

Yes. That you accepted as a reality.

FAT MAN

How could I do otherwise, since she was in fact betraying me?

PHILOSOPHER

Look, what you call a fact — the pleasure your wife took for herself with another man — can it possibly have had the same reality for her as for you, if it gave her pleasure and you pain? And what gave birth to your pain if not the illusion you entertained that your wife belonged solely to you? All vain ideas, my friend, just as life itself is a vain idea. Your wife was an idea of yours, her betrayal was an idea of yours, your pain was an idea of yours. The trouble is that life is only possible if we agree to provide a reality for all our empty ideas. We ought to make up our minds not to live, my friend.

FAT MAN

Maybe you're right. Whatever taste I had for life was certainly due to the little thought I gave to my troubles and the few illusions I made for myself. I don't want you to think that my wife's unfaithfulness was, after all, any great sorrow to me. I'd sigh over it, yes. And I'd tell myself it was in grief. But deep down I knew the sigh was one of relief. Not complete relief, never, because she wasn't really happy even with her lover, just as she couldn't ever be really happy with anything or anyone. It's bound to end badly for her. And that's another reason, you see, why I can't seem to move from this place.

PHILOSOPHER

You're expecting her?

FAT MAN

Yes, soon. They'll kill her. I'm sure of it. Her lover's going to kill her. Today or tomorrow. It may be happening this very moment, while I sit here telling you about it.

A pause. He stares blankly into space, then resumes.

I'm sure of it if only because she was so happy as I lay dying that she didn't even try to hide it. Her joy wasn't due so much to my imminent death as to the spectacle of black despair her lover provided as he stood at my bedside, racking his brains to find some way of keeping me alive.

PHILOSOPHER

What? He didn't want you to die?

FAT MAN

You may be a very learned man, but I see you know very little about life. He couldn't help but like me. And I as-

sure you that from the very first I felt terribly sorry for
this man, because no sooner had she betrayed me than
my wife turned on him with all the ferocity and hate she
had until then reserved for me. With me she resumed
the lightly affectionate, slightly bantering tone of our early
courtship, when she'd do such things as stick a flower in
my mouth and tell me I looked funny. It wasn't long before I had the satisfaction of knowing for certain that the
man who thought he had done me wrong by deceiving me
was being put through the same torment I had suffered,
and that his agony was further compounded by a cruel and
sincere feeling of remorse. For this man, you see, my dying
was the greatest of misfortunes, since through my death
my wife hoped to free herself, not so much from me as
from him. In a sense, you see, he was only my shadow,
not because he was always around me, but because my
status of husband provided him with his status of lover.
The kind of lover a woman takes depends very much on
the kind of husband she has. When the body dies, the
shadow dies with it. As long as I was around, he could be
sure of remaining her lover. But now? With me gone, why
limit herself to one? And that one the boring shadow of a
body that no longer exists. She'll take another. Perhaps
more than one.

PHILOSOPHER

And you think he'll kill her?

FAT MAN

To stop her from laughing. At the first laugh, he'll kill her.
Right now she's holding it back, restrained by having to
pretend grief over my recent death. But already I can feel
that terrible laugh bubbling deep down inside her, the
laugh that will come bursting out past her gleaming teeth
and cruel red lips to explode in his face! She laughs like a
madwoman. You remember I told you that all your philosophy couldn't wither the roses in my garden? Well, that
woman's laughter could! Every time I heard her laugh, I
could feel the ground tremble and my little garden dry up
into a patch of thorns. It boils up from her guts like some

raging, destructive frenzy. It's terrible, terrible the effect that laugh can have on the victim of it. Of course he'll kill her.

A pause. He seems to be listening to something, his hand raised and his eyes staring into space.

Maybe he's already killed her. In a minute we'll see her come out over there. . . . Yes, there she is! There she is! Oh my God, you see? It's her! Dancing, spinning like a top! It's her! And she's laughing, laughing! All disheveled! And on her left breast, you see that? Blood! She's splattering it all over the place! . . . Here, over here! Come here! Stop jumping around like that! Sit down over here!

MURDERED WOMAN

Falling into a seat on the bench.

You here? You? Oh God, how did that happen? No, no . . . But how? I'm back with you again?

She laughs wildly.

FAT MAN

Don't laugh! Don't laugh like that!

MURDERED WOMAN

What a fool! He sent me back to you! And he's coming, too, you know! After stabbing me, he stabbed himself! Here, look!

To the PHILOSOPHER.

Oh, you can look, too. What difference does it make now? I could be naked and it wouldn't make any difference!

Laughs again.

Look, look at my husband, how he suffers!

To the FAT MAN.

No, darling! What's the matter with you? You think I still have to defend my virtue? All right, all right, I'll cover it with my hair, like this. If you only had a comb, I could – it's all snarled. You know what, darling? He left me there, one whole morning, sprawled on the bed. Like this. Look. My breast bare. Like this. And so many people came in to look at me. And I think they could see my legs, too. Yes, I think so.

She laughs.

What a fool! He thought he could hurt me. And, yes, I thought so, too. And I was frightened. He tried to grab me. I ran away from him. I danced around him, whirling, like a lunatic. Did you see me? Like this. Suddenly – ah! – a blow, here – cold – I fell – he flung me on the bed – he kissed me, he kissed me – then, with the same knife, he stabbed himself – lying on me – I felt him slipping to the floor – groaning, gasping at my feet. And the warmth of his kiss stayed on my lips till the end. But maybe it was only blood.

PHILOSOPHER

Yes, in fact there's still a trace of it on your chin.

MURDERED WOMAN

Quickly wiping it away with her hand.

Ah, there. So it was blood. I thought so. Because no kiss has ever been hot enough. Lying there on that bed, while the white ceiling of the room seemed to close in on me and everything was going dark, I hoped, I hoped – oh God! – that that last kiss would finally give me the warmth I'd always longed for so desperately and always in vain. And that the heat would revive me, cure me. And it was my own blood I felt.

A silence. The FAT MAN *shakes his head bitterly, then, more sadly and dejectedly than before, again leans forward on his cane. The* PHILOSOPHER *continues to stare intently, and with some dismay, at the* MURDERED WOMAN, *who suddenly turns her gaze toward the cemetery gate. She shudders, then shouts wildly, joyfully.*

Oh, look, look! You look, too! Wake up! Get your chin up off that cane! Look who's coming over there, skipping along on rosy little feet!

PHILOSOPHER

A little boy.

MURDERED WOMAN

The darling! And what's he holding, what's he holding in his hands? A pomegranate? Oh, look, a pomegranate! Come here, come here, darling! Come to me, come on!

LITTLE BOY
This – it's for me – all for me.

MURDERED WOMAN
Yes, darling, give it to me. Here. The skin is tough. Let me peel it for you and get the seeds out. Then you can eat it. Yes, all of it. Wait. Now give it to me. Oh, my! What a nice big red one!

LITTLE BOY
Yes, yes – it's mine – all of it – for me.

MURDERED WOMAN
All of it, yes, wait. Here, eat the seeds first. Oh my, how your lips tickle my hand! Here, yes, the rest of it – all for you. Shall we give a piece, just one little piece, to this poor man here leaning on his cane? No? All right, we won't – it's all yours! There, eat it up. Oh, what a dirty little face!

LITTLE BOY
More – more – me.

MURDERED WOMAN
Just these last few seeds left, darling, you see? This is the skin – ah!

The WOMAN *screams. Having licked the last of the fruit from her hand, the child has simply vanished into thin air. All that remains is the skin of the pomegranate, part of which lies on the ground. The rest of it now slips out of the* WOMAN'S *hand and falls to earth.*

PHILOSOPHER
The pomegranate was his last desire. He clung to it with both hands. He was all there, in those last few morsels he hadn't yet tasted.

MURDERED WOMAN
And me? What about my desires? Oh God!

She bows her head and weeps bitterly, hiding her face in her hands and allowing her flaming hair to tumble wildly forward. Then, through her sobbing, she hears the FAT MAN'S *cane fall heavily to the ground. She raises her head, pushes her hair back and turns to stare in terror at the now empty space beside her. Meanwhile, the* PHILOSOPHER *has risen and gone behind the bench to lean against the trunk of the tree. He motions to her to look elsewhere, not into the void recently filled by the* FAT MAN, *but at certain solid-looking aspects of life now approaching from the countryside: a* PEASANT, *a* PEASANT WOMAN, *an* OLD DONKEY *staggering along under a huge load of hay on which sits a* LITTLE GIRL. *Instinctively the child hides her face in her hands, as if aware that the terrible gaze of the* MURDERED WOMAN *is fixed on her from the shadows of the tree. The* OLD DONKEY *halts to nibble at the scattered bits of pomegranate skin and snorts.*

MAN

Oh look, a cane. Someone must have lost it. Whoa there!

WOMAN

To the child.
What are you doing that for?

LITTLE GIRL

I'm scared.

MAN

Come on, come on, it's getting late. Giddap you!

WOMAN

We'll say a nice prayer together for all the poor dead people.

The PEASANT *whacks the* DONKEY *with the cane he has picked up. They proceed on their way. The* MURDERED WOMAN *rises, brushes the hair off her face, stretches out her arms in despair, and runs wildly out after the* LITTLE GIRL. *The apparition of the* PHILOSOPHER *remains, tall and erect in the shadows, flat against the trunk of the old tree.*

PHILOSOPHER

I'm afraid I alone will always remain here, still reasoning. . . .

Curtain

THE IMBECILE

(L'imbecille, 1922)

THE CAST

LUCA FAZIO

LEOPOLDO PARONI

A TRAVELING SALESMAN

ROSA LAVECCHIA

FIVE REPORTERS

LEOPOLDO PARONI's study at *The Republican Sentinel*, a newspaper published in the small provincial town of Costanova.

The very modest study of LEOPOLDO PARONI, *editor of* The Republican Sentinel *of Costanova.* PARONI *himself is head of the local branch of the party and the offices of the newspaper are in his own house. Since he lives alone and professes to despise all comforts, as well as cleanliness, evidently, disorder and filth are the rule. Rubbish is strewn all over the worn, battered furniture and even the floor. The desk is piled high with papers; the chairs, scattered here and there, are loaded with books and files; newspapers are everywhere; the bookcase bulges with volumes stuffed into the shelves at random. The main entrance is stage left. At rear, a glass door leads into the editorial office of the newspaper; at left, another exit leading to* PARONI's *living quarters.*

It's evening, and at curtain the room is almost dark, barely illuminated by the light filtering in from the editorial office through the opaque glass panes of the closed door. LUCA FAZIO *is sitting motionless on a dirty, torn leather couch from which the stuffing is coming out. He has his feet up and he leans back against a soiled bed pillow. He wears a gray woolen shawl over his shoulders and a cap with a broad visor is pulled down over his nose. His bony hands are temporarily hidden by the shawl and he clutches a rolled-up handkerchief. He is twenty-six years old. When the lights eventually go on, his face will appear drawn, yellow, gaunt, with a sickly little beard and a drooping blond mustache. From time to time he jams the handkerchief to his mouth and struggles with a deep, racking cough. The confused voices of* PARONI *and the* Sentinel REPORTERS *can be heard through the office door.*

PARONI

I tell you we have to hit him with everything we've got!

VOICES

Yes, yes, you're right! Attack him! That's it! All the way!
No! You're wrong!

FIRST REPORTER

Shouting over the hubbub.
You'll just play into Cappadona's hands!

VOICES

He's right! He's right! It's what they want! Who says so?
No! No!

PARONI

Thundering.
No one will believe that! We follow our own line of action!
We have to attack him as a matter of principle! And that's
final! Now let me get to work!
   Silence. LUCA FAZIO *has not stirred. The door at left
   opens a crack and another voice is heard.*

VOICE

May I come in?
   LUCA *does not answer. After a moment, the question is
   repeated.*

VOICE

May I come in?
   The TRAVELING SALESMAN *enters, looking puzzled. He
   is a Piedmontese of about forty.*

SALESMAN

Anyone in?

LUCA

Without looking around, in a hollow voice.
They're in there.

SALESMAN

Starting at the sound.
Oh! Excuse me. Are you Mr. Paroni?

LUCA

Indicating the glass door.
In there, in there.

SALESMAN

Can I go in?

LUCA

Annoyed.

Why ask me? Go ahead, if you want to.

The SALESMAN *starts for the door, but before he can get
to it another altercation breaks out in the other room,
soon followed in turn by the still faraway sound of a
popular demonstration that is apparently taking place in
some nearby piazza and coming closer. Disconcerted,
the* SALESMAN *stops.*

VOICES

From the other room.

There, there, you hear that? A riot! A riot, damn them!
Cappadona's crowd!

FIRST REPORTER

They're shouting hurray for Cappadona! Didn't I tell
you?

PARONI

Slamming his fist on the table and shouting.

And I tell you we have to kill Guido Mazzarini! What do I
care about Cappadona?

*The uproar in the streets temporarily drowns out the
argument in the office. The demonstrators, evidently
numerous, run past, shouting "Hurray for Cappadona!
Down with Mazzarini!" As soon as the noise dies down,
the argument becomes once more audible.*

VOICES

Dogs! Dogs! Traitors! Cappadona will pay for this!

Suddenly, two REPORTERS *burst out of the room and
rush toward the front door, jamming hats on their heads
and shaking canes in the air. They evidently plan to run
after the crowd.*

SECOND REPORTER

Furiously, on the run.

The bastards! The bastards!

Exits.

THIRD REPORTER

Coming face to face with the SALESMAN *and shouting at him.*

How dare they shout for Cappadona!
Exits.

PARONI

Off stage.

Go ahead! Go on, all of you! I'll stay and write the piece!
Three more REPORTERS *rush across the room, shouting.*

REPORTERS

Cowards! Dogs! Whores!
Coming up against the SALESMAN.

Did you hear that? Hurray for Cappadona! Did you hear them?
They exit.

SALESMAN

I don't understand. . . .
To LUCA.

What's going on?
LUCA *is seized by a violent fit of coughing and covers his mouth. The* SALESMAN *peers at him more closely, somewhat embarrassed by the disgust he can't help feeling.*

LUCA

They all stink of tobacco, damn them! Get away from me. . . . Air! Give me some air!
Then, more calmly.

Excuse me. You're not from Costanova, I take it.

SALESMAN

No. Just passing through.

LUCA

We're all just passing through, my friend.

SALESMAN

I'm with the Sangone Paper Company. I wanted to speak to Mr. Paroni, about where he buys his paper.

LUCA

This isn't a very good time.

SALESMAN

So I heard. A riot or something.

LUCA

Bitterly ironic.
Eight months since the election and they're still angry at
Mazzarini.

SALESMAN

A socialist?

LUCA

I don't know. I guess so. He couldn't win a majority here in
Costanova, but he got himself elected deputy anyway. The
others killed each other off and then, well . . .
*Rubs his thumb and forefinger together to indicate that
the man had money in back of him.*
A great man. And everyone's still angry, as you can tell,
because he's dissolved the City Council and brought in his
own people and – move back, move back, give me a little
air, for God's sake! – Thanks. – Big doings, you see, big
doings!

SALESMAN

Oh, so that's why they were shouting down with him!

LUCA

Yes. They don't want him. Costanova's a great place, my
dear sir. Try to remember that the entire universe revolves
around it. Go to the window and look up at the sky. Know
why the stars are up there? So they can leer down on
Costanova. Some people say they're really laughing at
Costanova. Don't you believe it. Every one of them is simply aglow with the desire to have a city like Costanova.
And you know what the fate of the universe depends on?
The City Council of Costanova. The City Council has been
dissolved and so the universe has been turned upside down.
You can see it in Paroni's face. Take a look at him, take a
look at him in there.

SALESMAN

Starts for the door, then stops.
I can't see through the glass.

LUCA

True. I forgot.

SALESMAN

You aren't on the staff of the newspaper?

LUCA

No. I'm a sympathizer. Or rather, I was. I'm about to leave here for good, my dear sir. And there are quite a few of us like me, you know, just as sick as I am, in this town. Two of my brothers used to work here, until they left for good one fine day. Up until a couple of days ago I was a medical student. I came back this morning, to die in my own house. And you? You're a paper salesman, are you?

SALESMAN

Yes. All kinds of paper. No one undersells us. We'll match any bid.

LUCA

So they can print more and more newspapers?

SALESMAN

Believe me, with the market what it is today, the price of pulp –

LUCA

Cutting him off.

I'm sure of it. If you only knew what a comfort it is to me to think that who knows how many years from now you'll still be going from town to town, peddling your paper from one little provincial weekly to another! To realize that you'll drift in here again one evening, maybe ten years from now, just like tonight, and you'll find this same dreary couch, but without me on it, and the town of Costanova perhaps calmed down at last. . . .

Three of the REPORTERS *who went out earlier now rush back in, shouting.*

FIRST REPORTER

Paroni! Paroni!

SECOND REPORTER

All hell broke loose out there!

THIRD REPORTER

Come on, come on, Leopoldo!

LEOPOLDO PARONI, *the proud Republican, now runs into the room. He is about fifty, with a leonine head of hair, a large nose, a turned-up mustache, a Mephistophelian beard, and he sports a red necktie.*

PARONI

What is it? A riot?

SECOND REPORTER

They're going wild!

FIRST REPORTER

A socialist mob brought in from the countryside!

PARONI

Quickly.

Beating up Cappadona's crowd?

THIRD REPORTER

No, our people! Our crowd!

FIRST REPORTER

Come on! Quickly! We need you!

PARONI

Wait a minute, damn it all! What are the police doing?

FIRST REPORTER

The police? You don't think they're going to interfere? They're delighted to see us get it! Come on! Come on!

PARONI

All right, let's go, let's go!

To the THIRD REPORTER, *who at once obeys him.*

Go and get my hat and cane! Conti, Fabrizi, where are they?

SECOND REPORTER

Out there, doing the best they can!

FIRST REPORTER

They're holding their own!

PARONI

Seems to me Cappadona's people could have called in the police!

FIRST REPORTER

They all ran away!

PARONI

And I can't see why all three of you had to come here after me. One of you would have been enough.

THIRD REPORTER

Entering from the office.
I can't find your cane!

PARONI

In the corner, near the clothes rack!

THIRD REPORTER

I looked. It isn't there!

PARONI

What do you mean, it isn't there? I put it there myself.

SECOND REPORTER

Maybe Conti or Fabrizi took it.

PARONI

My cane?

FIRST REPORTER

Come on, come on, I'll loan you mine!

PARONI

And what will you do? Out there in that fighting without even a cane?

MISS ROSA LAVECCHIA *rushes in, breathless and frightened. She is about fifty, ruddy-looking, thin, wears glasses, is dressed rather mannishly.*

ROSA

Dead tired, out of breath.
Oh God . . . Oh my God . . .

OTHERS

Anxiously, very worried.
What is it? What is it? What's happened?

ROSA

You haven't heard?

PARONI

They killed somebody?

ROSA

Staring at them uncomprehendingly.
No. Where?

FIRST REPORTER

What? Don't you know about the riot?

ROSA

The riot? No, I don't know anything. I just came from poor
Pulino's house. . . .

SECOND REPORTER

Well?

ROSA

He's killed himself!

FIRST REPORTER

Killed himself?

PARONI

Pulino?

THIRD REPORTER

Lulù Pulino's killed himself?

ROSA

Two hours ago. They found him hanging from the light
fixture, in the kitchen.

FIRST REPORTER

Hanged himself?

ROSA

What a sight! I sent to see him. . . . He was black, with
his eyes and tongue sticking out and his fingers clenched.
. . . He was so long, so long, just hanging there in the
middle of the room. . . .

SECOND REPORTER

Imagine, poor Pulino. . . .

FIRST REPORTER

He was already done for, poor devil. On his last legs . . .

THIRD REPORTER

But to go that way!

SECOND REPORTER

He put an end to his suffering, I suppose.

FIRST REPORTER

He could hardly stand on his own two legs.

PARONI

But, excuse me, if a man doesn't want to go on living, he's an imbecile if –

FIRST REPORTER

If what?

SECOND REPORTER

If he kills himself?

THIRD REPORTER

Why an imbecile?

FIRST REPORTER

If he knew he was going to die anyway!

SECOND REPORTER

What did he have to live for?

PARONI

That's exactly what I mean! By God, I'd have paid his fare myself!

THIRD REPORTER

Paid his fare?

FIRST REPORTER

What are you talking about?

SECOND REPORTER

To the next world?

PARONI

No. To Rome. As far as Rome. I'd have gladly paid his fare! When a man doesn't know what to do with his life and decides to kill himself, before doing it he could at least – By God, I'd have known what to do! I tell you I'd have made my death count for something! Picture this: I'm sick, I'm going to die, and there's a man who brings dishonor on my home town, a man who brings shame to each and every one of us. Guido Mazzarini. All right, first

I kill him and *then* I kill myself! There, that's the way to do
it! And if you don't do it that way, you're an imbecile!

Fprint THIRD REPORTER

Maybe it didn't even occur to him, poor man!

PARONI

How could it help but occur to him? Until two hours ago
wasn't he in the same boat with the rest of us? Sharing
the shame and disgrace that blankets the whole town and
poisons the very air we breathe? I'd have given him the
gun to do it with. Kill him and then kill yourself, imbecile!
The other two REPORTERS *now return. They are jubilant.*

FOURTH REPORTER

It's all over! It's all over!

FIFTH REPORTER

Driven off like a flock of sheep!

FIRST REPORTER

The police?

FOURTH REPORTER

Yes, but only at the last minute.

FIFTH REPORTER

Not till our people – they were great! – you should have
seen them! – like so many lions – fell on them!

FOURTH REPORTER

Beat the hell out of them!
Noticing that no one seems to be enthusiastic.
What's wrong?

ROSA

It's Pulino.

FIFTH REPORTER

What about him?

FIRST REPORTER

Hanged himself. Two hours ago.

FOURTH REPORTER

Really? Lulù Pulino? Hanged himself?

FIFTH REPORTER

Poor old Lulù. Yes, he's been saying, he told me he wanted

to put an end to it. . . . Well, he did. And I say he did the right thing.

CENTER{PARONI}

He could have done better. That's what we were just talking about. Since he felt he had to kill himself for his own good, he could also have done the whole town a favor by going to Rome and killing Mazzarini! It wouldn't have cost him anything, not even the fare. I'd have paid it for him, word of honor! This way he died like an imbecile!

CENTER{FIRST REPORTER}

Hey, let's close up! It's late!

CENTER{SECOND REPORTER}

Yes. We can write the story in the morning.

CENTER{THIRD REPORTER}

Anyway, we have until Sunday.

CENTER{SECOND REPORTER}

With a sympathetic sigh.
And we'll do a story on poor old Pulino, too.

CENTER{ROSA}

To PARONI.
If you want me to, Paroni, I could do the one on Pulino, since I actually saw him.

CENTER{FOURTH REPORTER}

Oh, we could all stop off and see him, for that matter.

CENTER{ROSA}

He may still be hanging there. They were waiting for the chief of police before taking the body away and he hadn't come back from Borgo yet.

CENTER{PARONI}

What a shame! Just think, we could have given him the whole issue next Sunday, if he'd only done the thing right!

CENTER{FIRST REPORTER}

Finally noticing LUCA *on the couch.*
Well, look who's here! Luca Fazio!
They all turn to look.

PARONI

Why, Luca!

SECOND REPORTER

You've been there all this time and never opened your mouth?

THIRD REPORTER

When did you get here?

LUCA

Curtly, indifferently.
This morning.

FOURTH REPORTER

How are you?

LUCA

Hesitates, then waves airily.
Oh, about like Pulino.

PARONI

Noticing the SALESMAN.
And who are you?

SALESMAN

Mr. Paroni, I came to see you about where you buy your paper.

PARONI

Oh, you're the man from Sangone? Well, come back tomorrow. If you don't mind, it's late now.

SALESMAN

Yes, sir, tomorrow morning. I'm hoping to get away sometime tomorrow.

FIRST REPORTER

Come on, let's go. Good night, Leopoldo.
All say good night.

FOURTH REPORTER

To LUCA.
Aren't you coming?

LUCA

I have something to say to Paroni.

PARONI

Apprehensively.
To me?

LUCA

It won't take long.
An uncomfortable pause as they all stare at LUCA, *realizing suddenly that everything they have just been saying about Pulino could apply equally well to him.*

PARONI

Couldn't you say it now, in front of everyone?

LUCA

No. To you alone.

PARONI

To the others.
Well, go on home, then. Good night, my friends.
More good-bys.

SALESMAN

I'll be here at ten o'clock.

PARONI

Come earlier, come earlier, if you like. Good night.
All exit except PARONI *and* LUCA, *who now sits up, swings his legs to the floor but remains seated, hunched over, staring at his feet.*

PARONI

Going over to him solicitously and starting to put a hand on his shoulder.
My dear Luca, well – my friend –

LUCA

Quickly, warding him off.
No. Get away from me.

PARONI

Why?

LUCA

My cough.

PARONI

You're really sick, aren't you? Yes, I can see that.

LUCA

Nods.

I'm just right for you. Shut the door.

Indicating the front door.

PARONI

Doing so.

Yes, of course.

LUCA

Lock it.

PARONI

Doing so and laughing.

Unnecessary. No one will come this late. You can speak freely. In strict confidence.

LUCA

Shut the other door.

Indicates the glass door.

PARONI

What for? You know I live alone. There's no one in there. I'll go turn off the light.

Starts for the office.

LUCA

Then shut the door. It's full of smoke in there.

PARONI *enters the office, turns off the light, and comes back, closing the door behind him.* LUCA, *in the meantime, has risen to his feet.*

PARONI

There you are. Now, what's on your mind?

LUCA

Not too close, not too close . . .

PARONI

But why? For my sake?

LUCA

Also.

PARONI

I'm not afraid.

LUCA

Don't speak too soon.

PARONI

Well, what's this all about? Sit down, sit down.

LUCA

No, I'll stand.

PARONI

You just got back from Rome?

LUCA

Yes. From Rome. As you see me. I had a few thousand lire
left, but I spent them all. I only saved enough to buy –
  *Reaching into his pocket and pulling out a large re-
  volver.*
– this gun.

PARONI

  *Becoming very pale and instinctively raising his hands
  as he sees the weapon in the hands of a man with noth-
  ing to lose.*
Oh! Is it – is it loaded?
  As LUCA *examines the gun.*
Hey, Luca – it's loaded?

LUCA

  Coldly.
It's loaded.
  Staring at him.
You said you weren't afraid.

PARONI

No, but – for God's sake –
  He starts toward him as if to take the gun away.

LUCA

Stand back, and let me finish. Where were we? Yes, in
Rome. I had locked myself in. I was about to kill myself.

PARONI

You're crazy!

LUCA

Crazy? Yes. I was really going through with it. Like an imbecile. Yes. Isn't that how you would put it?

PARONI

Stares at him, then his eyes light up with joy.
Oh. You mean – you mean you'd really –

LUCA

Quickly.
Wait. You'll find out what I'd really do!

PARONI

You heard what I said about Pulino?

LUCA

Yes. That's why I'm here.

PARONI

You'd do it?

LUCA

Right this minute.

PARONI

Exulting.
That's wonderful!

LUCA

Listen! I had the gun up to my temple, then someone knocked on the door.

PARONI

The door? In Rome?

LUCA

In Rome. I open it. You know who's standing there? Guido Mazzarini.

PARONI

He was? At your place? And so?

LUCA

He sees me with the gun in my hand and he looks at me and he realizes at once what I'm going to do. He rushes up to me. He grabs me by the arms, he shakes me, he shouts at me: "What? You kill yourself like this? Oh, Luca, what an imbecile you are! Come on now! If you want to kill yourself, I'll pay your fare home. Go back to Costanova and take that damned Paroni with you!"

PARONI

Intent up to now on this dreadful and strange speech, very disturbed at the prospect of some sudden violence, now goes limp and smiles vapidly, hideously.

You're joking.

LUCA

Steps back a pace, his cheek twitching, his mouth twisted.

No, I'm not joking. Mazzarini paid my fare.

PARONI

Paid your fare? What are you saying?

LUCA

And so here I am. First I'm going to kill you, then I'm going to kill myself.

PARONI

Terrified, his hands to his face, trying to escape.

Are you crazy? No, Luca! You're joking! You're crazy!

LUCA

Menacingly.

Don't move! Don't move or I'll shoot!

PARONI

Freezing.

All right . . . all right . . .

LUCA

Crazy, am I? You think I'm crazy? You call me crazy and a few minutes ago you were calling poor Pulino an imbecile because, before hanging himself, he didn't go to Rome and kill Mazzarini for you?

PARONI

Trying to control the situation.

But that's different, damn it! Very different! I'm not Mazzarini!

LUCA

Different? What difference can there be between you and

Mazzarini to someone like me or Pulino, who no longer
give a damn for either of you and all your buffooneries?
Killing you or someone else or the first man to come along,
it's all the same to us!

PARONI

No, it can't be! It can't be! It would be the most meaning-
less and stupid of crimes!

LUCA

So you expect us to become the instruments of your hatred
or of someone else's, of all your clownish schemes, and at a
time when everything is over for us, or else you call us
imbeciles? All right, I don't want to be called an imbecile
like Pulino, so I'm going to kill you.

Raises the gun and points it at him.

PARONI

Imploringly, squirming to avoid the muzzle of the gun.
Please! No, Luca – what are you doing? No! – But why? –
I've always been your friend – Please!

LUCA

His eyes bright with the insane desire to pull the trigger.
Don't move! Don't move! – On your knees! On your knees!

PARONI

Falling to his knees.
Yes – there! Please! Don't do it!

LUCA

Snorts contemptuously.
"When a man doesn't want to go on living . . ." Isn't that
what you said? Clown! Don't worry, I'm not going to kill
you. Get up. But keep away from me.

PARONI

Rising.
That was a dirty trick, you know that? You can get away
with it, you're armed.

LUCA

That's right. And you're afraid because you know it
wouldn't cost me anything to go through with it. Like any

good member of your party, you're a good liberal, too, eh?
Atheist! You must be. Otherwise you couldn't have called
Pulino an imbecile.

PARONI

But I said that – well, because – because you know how I
feel about things here in town. . . .

LUCA

Oh yes, of course. Very noble of you. And very liberal, you
can't deny that. It's in everything you write. . . .

PARONI

Haltingly.
Liberal, yes . . . You don't expect to be punished or re-
warded in some other world, do you?

LUCA

Oh no! I couldn't stand that! To have to bear the weight
somewhere else, too, of all the things I've had to go
through these twenty-six years of my life.

PARONI

Well, so you see I –

LUCA

Quickly.
I could do it, you know. I could kill you as if it were nothing at all, because there's nothing to hold me back. But
I'm not going to kill you. And I don't consider myself an
imbecile for not killing you. I'm sorry for you, for all your
buffooneries. I can look at you now – if you only knew –
from such a distance! And you seem so small and nice –
yes – a funny little man with red cheeks and that bright-red
necktie there. . . . But you know? I'm going to copyright
this clownishness of yours.

PARONI

Uncomprehendingly.
What? What's that?

LUCA

Copyright, copyright. Don't you think I should? I have
every right to, a sacred right, now that I stand between

life and death. And you'll do exactly as I tell you. Sit
down. Sit down over there and write.
Waves the gun toward the desk.

PARONI

Write? Write what? Are you serious?

LUCA

Very serious. Go sit down over there and write.

PARONI

But what do you want me to write?

LUCA

Again aiming the gun at him.
Get up and go sit down over there, I said!

PARONI

Doing so.
What, again?

LUCA

Sit down. Pick up your pen. . . . The pen, I said!

PARONI

Doing so.
What do I have to write?

LUCA

What I tell you. You're down now, but I know you. Tomorrow, as soon as you hear I've killed myself like Pulino,
you'll raise your head again and run around town for hours
shouting that I was an imbecile, a bigger imbecile than
Pulino.

PARONI

I wouldn't do that! How can you think I would? I was joking before!

LUCA

I know you. I'm going to avenge Pulino. It's not for me I'm
doing this. Write!

PARONI

Looking at the table.
What do you expect me to write on?

LUCA

Here, here, this piece of paper will do. . . .

PARONI

But what?

LUCA

Just a couple of words. A little declaration.

PARONI

A declaration? To whom?

LUCA

To no one. Never mind, you just write! It's the only condition on which I'll spare your life. Either you write or I'll kill you!

PARONI

All right, I'll do it. Go ahead.

LUCA

Dictating.
"I, the undersigned, am sorry and I apologize —"

PARONI

Rebelling.
Come on now, apologize? For what?

LUCA

Smilingly placing the gun against PARONI's *temple.*
You mean you won't even apologize?

PARONI

Moving his head slightly and gazing at the gun from the corner of his eye.
Let's hear what I'm supposed to apologize for.

LUCA

Dictating again.
"I, the undersigned, am sorry and I apologize for having called Pulino an imbecile —"

PARONI

Oh, so that's it.

LUCA

That's it. Take this down: "— an imbecile in the presence of my friends and colleagues, because Pulino, before killing

himself, did not go to Rome and murder Mazzarini." That's
the simple truth, isn't it? I even left out that you would
have paid his fare. Did you get it all?

PARONI

Resigned.

Yes. Go on.

LUCA

Dictating.

"Luca Fazio, before killing himself –"

PARONI

Are you really going through with it?

LUCA

That's my business. Write: "– before killing himself, came
to see me. . . ." Do you want me to add that I was armed?

PARONI

At the end of his tether.

Oh, yes, if you don't mind!

LUCA

Go ahead, say I was armed. Anyway, they won't be able to
arrest me for carrying a gun without a permit. So did you
add that? All right, take this down: "He was armed and he
said to me that in consequence, so he wouldn't be called
an imbecile by Mazzarini or anyone else, he was going to
shoot me down like a dog."

He pauses long enough for PARONI *to write it all down.*

Did you write "like a dog?" Good. New paragraph. "He
could have killed me, but he did not do so. He did not kill
me because he was revolted –

PARONI *looks up at him.*

No, take that down. "Revolted." And add "took pity."
That's right: "He was revolted and took pity on my cow-
ardice."

PARONI

Now wait a minute –

LUCA

It's the truth. Because I was armed, of course. That's why
you were a coward.

PARONI

Anything you say. I'm here to please you.

LUCA

Good, yes, to please me. Got it all down?

PARONI

Yes, yes! And I think that's about enough!

LUCA

No, wait! We need an ending! Two more words, just to end it.

PARONI

What else is there to say? An ending?

LUCA

Yes, I have it. Take this down: "All Luca Fazio wanted me to do was admit that I alone am the real imbecile."

PARONI

Pushing the sheet of paper away from him.
Now listen, that's really too much! Honestly!

LUCA

Peremptorily, through clenched teeth.
"— that I alone am the real imbecile!" You'll preserve your dignity better, my friend, by keeping your eyes on what you're doing and not on this gun. I told you I was going to avenge Pulino. Now sign it.

PARONI

There. Anything else?

LUCA

Give it to me.

PARONI

Giving him the paper.
Here. Now what will you do with it? If you're really going to do away with yourself . . .

LUCA

Ignores him, reads what PARONI *has written, then speaks.*
Fine. What am I going to do with it? Nothing. They'll find it in my pocket tomorrow.
He folds it up and puts it in his pocket.

You can console yourself, Leopoldo, with the thought that I am now going to do something a little bit more difficult than anything you've had to do here this evening. Open the door.

PARONI *does so.*

Good night to you.

Curtain

THE MAN WITH THE FLOWER IN HIS MOUTH

(L'uomo dal fiore in bocca, 1923)

THE CAST

THE MAN WITH THE FLOWER IN HIS MOUTH

AN EASYGOING COMMUTER

A WOMAN IN BLACK *nonspeaking*

The sidewalk in front of an all-night café in some large city.

At rear, a row of trees lining an avenue, electric lights gleaming through the leaves. On either side, the last few houses of a street that leads into the avenue. In front of the houses at left, on the sidewalk, the tables and chairs of a cheap all-night café; in front of the houses at right, a street lamp casts a cold light. Another lamp shines at the corner of the last house on the left, where the street and the avenue meet. A few minutes past midnight. In the distance, the occasional haunting sound of a mandolin.

At curtain, THE MAN WITH THE FLOWER IN HIS MOUTH *is seated at one of the tables,* THE COMMUTER *at the one next to him. The latter is peacefully sipping a mint frappé through a straw, unaware that he is being closely observed by the other man. A long, silent pause.*

MAN

Well, I've been meaning to talk to you. I hope you won't mind. I suppose you're an easygoing type and – you missed your train?

COMMUTER

By not more than a minute. I rush into the station and it pulls out before my very eyes.

MAN

You could have run after it.

COMMUTER

Of course. It's silly, I know. If I hadn't been loaded down with all those damned packages, bundles, boxes, God knows what else! Like a jackass! But you know women – errands, errands – it never stops! It took me three minutes, believe me, just to get out of the taxi and get my fingers through all those strings, two packages to a finger.

MAN

You must have been quite a sight. You know what I'd have done? I'd have left them in the cab.

COMMUTER

And my wife? Oh yes! And my daughters? And all their friends?

MAN

Let them scream. I'd enjoy it enormously.

COMMUTER

That's because you probably have no idea what women are like when they get to the country in the summer!

MAN

But of course I know. Precisely because I do know.

A pause.

They all begin by saying they really won't need anything.

COMMUTER

That's all? They're even capable of maintaining that they're going there to save. Then, as soon as they get to some little village around here, the uglier it is, the poorer and dirtier it is, the more they insist on dressing it up with all the most expensive and useless little fripperies! Ah, women, my dear sir! Anyway, it's their profession.

Imitating a woman.

"If you just happen to be going into town, darling, I really could use this – and a little bit of that – and you might also, if it's no trouble" – sweet, that "no trouble," isn't it? – "and while you're there you could stop by so-and-so's. . . ." My dear, how do you expect me to do all these things in just three hours? "Why not, just take a cab. . . ." The trouble is that I planned on being here only three hours and I didn't bring my house keys.

MAN

Oh fine! And so?

COMMUTER

So I left my mountain of packages in the station checkroom and went out to eat in some restaurant. Then, to soothe my nerves, I went to the theatre. It was hot as hell. On the way out I asked myself, "What now? It's nearly midnight and the next train is at four o'clock." For just three hours of sleep it didn't seem worth spending the money for a room somewhere. So I came here. This place stays open, doesn't it?

MAN

It never closes.

A pause.

So you really left all your packages in the checkroom?

COMMUTER

Yes, why? Aren't they safe there? They were all nicely wrapped –

MAN

Oh, there's nothing to worry about.

A pause.

Very well wrapped, I'm sure of it. With that special skill the young clerks have for wrapping up what they've just sold. . . .

A pause.

What hands they have! You see them tear off a great big double sheet of that shiny red paper – a pleasure just to look at it – so smooth you want to put it to your cheek to feel how fresh it is. . . . They spread it out on the counter and then, nonchalantly, gracefully, they put the material you've just bought, all nicely folded, right in the middle. First, from underneath, with the back of one hand, they raise one side of the sheet. Then, from above, they fold over the other one, double-folding it quickly, too, along the edges, that little extra touch for the sheer love of the art. Then they fold up the end flaps into triangles and turn the points under. They reach for the string, pull out enough to tie up the bundle, and knot it so swiftly you hardly even have time to admire their skill before you're handed the package, all wrapped and waiting for you to stick your finger through the loop.

COMMUTER

Well, I can see you pay quite a lot of attention to how they do things in these stores.

MAN

Me? My dear sir, I pass whole days at it. I can spend an hour just staring into a shop window. I forget myself. I feel like – I really would like to be that bolt of silk – that strip of linen – that red or blue ribbon the clerks measure out by the yard. Have you ever noticed how they do it? Before wrapping the thing up, they make an eight with the ribbon between thumb and little finger of the left hand.

A pause.

I watch the customer leave the store with his package hanging from his finger or under his arm. I follow him with my eyes until I lose sight of him. I imagine – oh, I imagine so many things! You couldn't guess how many.

A pause. Then gloomily, mostly to himself.

It helps. At least it helps.

COMMUTER

It helps? In what way?

MAN

Clinging like this – I mean, in my imagination – to life. Like a vine around the bars of an iron gate.

A pause.

I try never to let my imagination rest, not even for a moment. I use it to cling, to cling continually to the lives of others. But not people I know. No, no, I couldn't do that! The mere thought of it disgusts me! Nauseates me! I cling to the lives of strangers on whom my imagination can work freely. But not capriciously, no. I keep careful track of the least little hints I can spot in one person or another. If you only knew how well it works! I see somebody's house and I live in it. I feel a part of it, so at home I can even sniff – you know that particular atmosphere that every house has? Yours, mine? Except that in our own houses we're no longer conscious of it, because it's the atmosphere of our

own lives we breathe. Do you understand what I mean?
Yes, I can see you do.

COMMUTER

Yes, because — I mean, it must be fun for you to imagine
all these different things. . . .

MAN

Irritated, after having thought it over a moment.
Fun? For me?

COMMUTER

Yes, I should think —

MAN

Tell me something. Have you ever gone to a good doctor?

COMMUTER

Me? No, why? I'm not sick!

MAN

Don't be alarmed. I just wanted to find out whether you've
ever sat in some good doctor's waiting room.

COMMUTER

Oh, yes. I once had to go with one of my daughters, something to do with her nerves.

MAN

Good. I'm not prying. All I meant was, those rooms. . . .
  A pause.
Have you ever noticed? The sofa's usually dark, old-fashioned looking — those upholstered chairs that hardly ever
match — the little armchairs. . . . Furniture picked up
here and there, secondhand, stuck in that room for the
patients. It doesn't belong to the house. The doctor would
never entertain his wife's friends in there. *His* living room
is luxurious, handsome. What a contrast between his home
and his waiting room, for which this decent, sober furniture
seems adequate enough. When you accompanied your
daughter, did you pay careful attention to the chair or sofa
you sat on?

COMMUTER

No, not really.

MAN

Of course not. Because you weren't sick. . . .

A pause.

But even the sick don't usually pay much attention, they're
so wrapped up in their troubles. . . .

A pause.

And yet how often some of them sit there, staring intently
at their fingers as they trace vague patterns on the shiny
arms of those chairs! Lost in their thoughts and unable to
see . . .

A pause.

But what an impression it makes when you're through with
the doctor, you're on your way out, and you come face to
face with that chair again, the one you were sitting in a
little while before, when you were still in ignorance of the
verdict! You find it occupied by some other patient, he,
too, with his secret illness, or you see it there, empty, im-
passive, waiting for someone else to sit down. . . .

A pause.

But what were we talking about? Ah yes, the pleasures of
the imagination. Now how do you suppose I happened to
think of a doctor's waiting room?

COMMUTER

Yes, I really don't —

MAN

You don't see the connection? Neither do I.

A pause.

It's just that certain seemingly unconnected mental images
are peculiar to every one of us. They arise out of experiences and considerations so individual, so private that we
simply wouldn't understand each other, if we didn't tacitly
agree in everyday conversation to dispense with them.
Nothing more illogical than analogies based on such private
visions . . .

A pause.

But perhaps, in this case, there is a connection. Look, do
you think a chair gets any pleasure out of trying to guess

who the next patient will be to sit in it? To guess what his trouble is, where he'll go, what he'll do after the visit? No, of course not. And I'm the same way. The patients come and go, and the chair, poor thing, is there to be sat in. Well, I fulfill a similar function. For a while I do this, for a while I do that. At the moment it's your turn. But I want you to understand that I get no pleasure from your story, from hearing about how you missed your train, about your family waiting for you in the country, about all the bother I suppose you've had to put up with.

COMMUTER

It's been a nuisance, all right!

MAN

Thank God it's nothing worse. . . .

A pause.

Some people aren't quite so well off, my friend. . . .

A pause.

I told you I had to use my imagination to cling to other people's lives, but not for pleasure, not because I'm interested. In fact – in fact, I do it because I want to share everyone else's troubles, be able to judge life as silly and vain. If you can make yourself feel that way, then it won't really matter if you have to come to the end of it.

With sullen rage.

But you have to go on proving it to yourself, you know. Continuously, mercilessly. Because, my dear sir, we all feel this terrible thirst for life, though we have no idea what it consists of. But it's there, there, like an ache in our throats that can never be satisfied, because life, at the very moment we experience it, is always so full of itself that we can never actually taste it. All we can really savor is the past, which remains alive within us. Our thirst for life comes from the memories that bind us. But bind us to what? Why, to this everyday foolishness, to these petty irritations, to so many stupid illusions, dull occupations . . . Yes, yes. What now seems foolish to us or boring – I might even say, what now seems a real nightmare to us – yes, sir, who

knows how it will all taste to us in four, five, ten years —
what flavor these tears will acquire . . . And life, by God,
the mere thought of losing it — especially when you know
it's a matter of days . . .

At this point, the head of a WOMAN *appears from around
the corner, at right. She is dressed in black and wears an
old hat with drooping feathers.*

There — see that? Over there, at the corner — see that woman's shadow? There, she's hidden herself!

COMMUTER

What? Who — who was it?

MAN

Didn't you see her? She's hiding.

COMMUTER

A woman?

MAN

Yes. My wife.

COMMUTER

Oh, your wife?
    A pause.

MAN

She keeps an eye on me, from a distance. And sometimes,
believe me, I could kick her. But it wouldn't do any good.
She's like one of these stray bitches: the more you kick
them, the closer they stick to your heels.
    A pause.
You can't imagine what that woman is suffering on my account. She doesn't eat, she doesn't sleep. She follows me
around day and night, like this, always at a distance. If
only she'd at least dust off those rags she wears . . . She
doesn't even look like a woman any more, just dusty rags.
Dust all over her, on her hair, at her temples. Permanently
dusty. And she's barely thirty-four. . . .
    A pause.
She annoys me so, you can't imagine. Sometimes I jump on
her, I shout in her face: "Idiot!" I give her a shaking. She
takes it all. She stands there and stares at me with eyes —

eyes that, I swear to you, make me want to strangle her. It does no good. She waits for me to move away before taking up the trail again.

Again the head of the WOMAN IN BLACK *appears around the corner.*

There, look – that's her peering around the corner.

COMMUTER

Poor woman.

MAN

What do you mean, poor woman? You see, she'd like me to stay at home. Calmly, quietly. So I could benefit from her most loving and tender care. So I could bask in the perfect order of all the rooms, the spotlessness of the furnishings, that mirrored silence that used to characterize my house, measured by the ticking of the big clock in the dining room. That's what she wants! Now I ask you, just so you'll appreciate the absurdity – no, not absurdity! – the macabre ferocity of this pretense, I ask you whether you think it possible that the houses of Messina or Avezzano, knowing they were about to be smashed by an earthquake, would have contentedly remained where they were, lined up along the streets and squares, ever obedient to the rules and regulations of the town real-estate board? No, by God, these houses of wood and stone would somehow have managed to run away! Try to imagine the citizens of Avezzano or Messina placidly undressing to go to bed, folding up their clothes, putting their shoes away, and snuggling down under the covers to enjoy the freshness of clean white sheets, knowing all the time that in a few hours they'd be dead. Does that seem possible to you?

COMMUTER

But perhaps your wife –

MAN

Let me finish! Wouldn't it be nice, my friend, if death were merely some sort of strange, disgusting insect someone might unexpectedly find on you. . . . You're walking down the street and some passer-by suddenly stops you. Carefully, he extends just two fingers of one hand and he says,

"Excuse me, may I? You, my dear sir, have death on you!"
And with those two fingers he plucks it off and flicks it
away. . . . That would be wonderful, wouldn't it? But
death isn't like some horrible insect. Many of the people you
see walking around happily and indifferently may be carrying it on them. No one notices it. And they're calmly and
quietly planning what they'll do tomorrow and the day
after. Now I —

He rises.

Look, my dear sir. Come over here. . . .

He makes the COMMUTER *get up and leads him over to
the street lamp.*

Under this light . . . Over here . . . I'll show you something. . . . Look here, here, under the mustache. . . .
There, you see that pretty violet nodule? Know what it's
called? Ah, such a soft word—softer than caramel—Epithelioma, it's called. Pronounce it, you'll feel how soft it is.
Epithelioma. . . Death, you understand? Death passed my
way. It planted this flower in my mouth and said to me,
"Keep it, my friend, I'll be back in eight or ten months!"

A pause.

Now you tell me if, with this flower in my mouth, I can
stay calmly and quietly at home, as that poor woman would
like me to do.

A pause.

I scream at her, "I suppose you'd like me to kiss you!" —
"Yes, kiss me!" — You know what she did? She took a pin
last week and she scratched herself here, on the lip, and
then she grabbed my head and tried to kiss me — kiss me
on the mouth. . . . Because she says she wants to die
with me . . .

A pause.

She's crazy. . . .

Then angrily.

I will not stay at home! I feel the need to stand at shop
windows, yes, to admire the skill of the clerks. Because,
you understand, if I found myself for one moment faced
by the void inside me — Well, you understand, I could

even, like nothing at all, snuff out the life in some total
stranger. . . . Pull out a gun and kill someone who, like
you, has unfortunately missed his train . . .

He laughs.

No, no, don't worry, my dear sir! I'm only joking!

A pause.

Well, I'm going now.

A pause.

I would kill myself if I ever –

A pause.

But these wonderful apricots are in season now. . . . How
do *you* eat them? With the skin on, don't you? You break
them in half, you squeeze them in your fingers, slowly.
. . . Like a pair of juicy lips . . . Ah, delicious!

He laughs. A pause.

Give my regards to your wife and daughters in the country.

A pause.

I imagine them dressed in white and blue, standing on a
lovely, shaded, green lawn. . . .

A pause.

And do me a favor. Tomorrow morning, when you get
there. I suppose the village is some little distance from the
station, isn't it? At dawn you might easily want to walk it.
The first little tuft of grass you see at the edge of the road,
count the blades for me. As many blades as you can count,
that's the number of days I still have to live. . . .

A pause.

Be sure you pick me a nice fat one.

He laughs.

Good night, my dear sir.

*And he strolls off, humming to the sound of the distant
mandolin. He starts for the road at right, but then he
remembers that his wife is probably hiding around the
corner, waiting for him. Quickly he turns and scurries
off in the opposite direction, followed by the appalled
gaze of the* EASYGOING COMMUTER.

Curtain

THE OTHER SON

(L'altro figlio, 1923)

THE CAST

MARAGRAZIA

NINFAROSA

ROCCO TRUPIA

A YOUNG DOCTOR

JACO SPINA

TINO LIGRECI

GIALLUZZA

AUNT MARASSUNTA

MRS. TUZZA LA DIA

MARINESE

In Sicily, in the early 1900s.

A row of huts on the outskirts of the Sicilian village of Farnia, at a turn in a dreary little street leading off into the countryside. The one-story clay houses are set apart from each other, with vegetable gardens behind, and are windowless. The light from the street is admitted through dingy open doorways, each set above a short flight of worn steps. At left, directly opposite and off by itself, stands NINFAROSA's *house, not quite so wretched and old as the others.*

At curtain, four women of the neighborhood are sitting in their doorways, mending clothes, cleaning vegetables, sewing, or otherwise occupied. They have been talking. GIALLUZZA *is thin, about thirty, with faded blonde hair worn low on her neck in a bun.* AUNT MARASSUNTA *is an old woman of about sixty, attired in mourning in a faded black cotton dress, with a black kerchief over her head and knotted under her chin.* MRS. TUZZA LA DIA *is about forty, her eyes always fixed on the ground and her voice a permanent lament.* MARINESE *is redhaired and flashily dressed.* JACO SPINA, *an old peasant in a black stocking-cap and shirtsleeves, is stretched out on the ground at the end of the road, his head resting on a donkey saddle. He is smoking his pipe and listening to the conversation. A few very dark, sun-baked children wander about here and there.*

GIALLUZZA

And at sunset tonight, more of them leaving!

TUZZA

Whining.
Good luck to them, poor things!

MARINESE

They say more than twenty are going this time!
Through the houses at right comes TINO LIGRECI, *a young*

peasant who has just completed his military service.
He's a cocky type, wears bell-shaped trousers and a cap
tilted jauntily to one side.

TINO

To MARASSUNTA.

Evening, Aunt Marassù. Do you know if the doctor's come
by here yet? I know he was on his way to Rocco Trupia's,
the house with the column.

MARASSUNTA

No, Sonny, he hasn't been here. At least I haven't seen him.

MARINESE

Why? Who's sick?

TINO

No one, thank God. I wanted to tell him to keep an eye on
my mother.

He hesitates a bit, looking at them, then, in a worried
voice.

And you, too, keep an eye on her for me. She'll be all
alone, poor thing.

Meanwhile, MARAGRAZIA *appears from behind* NINFA-
ROSA's *house. She is over seventy and her face is a net-*
work of wrinkles. Her eyes are red from prolonged weep-
ing and her thin, wispy hair hangs in two small knots
over her ears. She looks like a bundle of rags, stained and
filthy, worn constantly winter and summer, torn and
patched, colorless and reeking of all the dirt of the
streets. On her feet she wears shapeless, worn shoes and
heavy blue cotton socks.

MARINESE

To TINO.

So you're leaving?

TINO

Tonight, with the rest of them. But not for San Paolo, like
the others. I'm going to Rosario de Santa Fe.

MARAGRAZIA

From behind him.

You're leaving, too?

TINO

Sure I'm going. I'm going so I won't have to look at you or hear you cry any more, you old crone!

MARAGRAZIA

Staring into his eyes.

To Rosario, you said? Rosario de Santa Fe?

TINO

That's what I said, to Rosario. What are you looking at me like that for? Want me to go blind?

MARAGRAZIA

No, I envy you! Because you'll be seeing —

She breaks into a silent sobbing, her chin trembling.

My boys! They're both there! Tell them how you left me, that they'll never see me again if they don't come home soon!

TINO

Sure, you can count on it! As soon as I get there. Things get done over there: you call and they come running! Now I've got to go and find the doctor.

MARAGRAZIA

Holding him by one arm.

Wait. If I give you a letter for them, will you take it?

TINO

Give it to me.

MARAGRAZIA

I haven't got it yet. I'll have Ninfarosa write it for me right away and I'll bring it to your house, all right?

TINO

Fine, bring it to me. And meanwhile, good-by to all of you. And if we never see each other again —

Suddenly moved.

— Aunt Marassù, give me your blessing!

MARASSUNTA

Rising and making the sign of the Cross over him.

God bless you and keep you, my son! And may the good Lord go with you by land and by sea!

TINO

To the others, smiling to disguise his real feelings.
And so long to all of you, then!
    He shakes hands with all three.

TUZZA

Have a good trip, Tinù.

MARINESE

Good luck! And don't forget us!

GIALLUZZA

And come back soon, in good health, with a sackful of
money!

TINO

Thanks, thanks. Stay well and good luck to all of you!
    Exits at left.

MARASSUNTA

Just back from the army and he leaves his mother here all
alone!

TUZZA

Asks the rest of us to keep an eye on her!

MARAGRAZIA

After having watched him go, turning to the others.
Is Ninfarosa in?

GIALLUZZA

She's home. Knock.
    The old woman does so.

NINFAROSA

From inside the house.
Who is it?

MARAGRAZIA

Me, Maragrazia.

NINFAROSA

Off stage.
All right, I'm coming.
    MARAGRAZIA *quietly sits down on the steps of* NINFA-
    ROSA's *house. As she listens to the conversation of the
    other women, she nods her head and weeps.*

GIALLUZZA

They told me Saro Scoma was going, too, and him with a
wife and three kids!

TUZZA

In her usual whine.
And a fourth on the way!

MARINESE

Unable to stand it any longer.
Jesus, what a voice! It's hard on the nerves, neighbor!
Turns my stomach! Three and one is four, and if they had
them, then it means they wanted to have them and I'll bet
they had a good time doing it! So stop your whining, let
them worry about it!

JACO SPINA

Sitting up and crossing his large hands over his chest.
If I was king —
And he spits.
— if I was king of this country, not one letter — a letter, I
said? — not even a postcard would I let them send from over
there!

GIALLUZZA

A fine idea, Jaco Spina! And what would they do, these
poor mothers, these wives, without news and no one to
help them?

JACO SPINA

Yes, a fine lot of help they get!
Spits again.
The mothers have to go and work like dogs and the wives
just go to hell! Over some houses I can see the horns growing right up to the sky! Why don't they ever write about
the bad things over there? Everything's rosy, according to
them. And every letter that gets here is like a hen clucking
to her chicks, as far as these ignorant lunkheads are concerned. Cluck, cluck, cluck, and off they all go! There's no
one left in Farnia to do the hoeing or prune the trees. Old
people, women, children. I have to sit and watch my piece
of land go to waste.

Holding out his arms.

What good is one pair of arms? And still they go and they
go! Rain on their faces and wind up their backs, say I! I
hope they all break their fool necks, damn them!

    NINFAROSA *emerges from her house. She is dark but has
a ruddy complexion, with black, shining eyes, red lips,
and a trim, solid-looking figure. She is proud and gay,
wears a large cotton kerchief, red with yellow moons,
over her breast and two heavy gold bands in her ears.*

NINFAROSA

What's the sermon today? Oh, so it's you, Uncle Jaco?
Listen, it's better here with only the women! The fewer the
men, the better the women! We'll work the land by ourselves!

JACO SPINA

You women are good for just one thing!

NINFAROSA

What's that, Uncle Jaco? Out with it!

JACO SPINA

For crying. And one other thing.

NINFAROSA

So that's two things we're good for! Not bad! But I'm not
crying, am I?

JACO SPINA

I know you, girl! Not even when your first husband died!

NINFAROSA

Right. And if it had been me instead of him, wouldn't he
have married someone else? So there you are!

    Indicating MARAGRAZIA.

Anyway, look at her. She cries enough for all of us.

JACO SPINA

That's because the old woman has water to spare and likes
to squirt it from her eyes!

    So saying, he rises, picks up his saddle, and exits.

MARAGRAZIA

Two boys I lost, beautiful like the sun, and I'm not supposed to cry?

NINFAROSA

They were beautiful, all right! And worth crying for! Swim-
ming in luxury over there and they leave you to die here
like a beggar!

MARAGRAZIA

Shrugging.
They're only boys. How can you expect them to understand
what a mother feels?

NINFAROSA

And anyway, why so many tears, so much suffering, when
everyone says it was you who drove them away in the first
place?

MARAGRAZIA

Beating her breast and getting to her feet, astounded.
Me? Me? Who said that?

NINFAROSA

It doesn't matter who, somebody did.

MARAGRAZIA

It's a lie! Me? Drove them away, when I —

MARASSUNTA

Oh, let her alone!

MARINESE

Can't you see she's joking?

NINFAROSA

I'm joking, I'm joking, take it easy! Now what do you want?
You knocked, didn't you?

MARAGRAZIA

Oh, yes. The usual favor. If you can.

NINFAROSA

Another letter?

MARAGRAZIA

If you can. I'm giving it to Tino Ligreci. He's leaving tonight for Rosario de Santa Fe.

NINFAROSA

So Tino's going, too, eh? Then good luck to him! Quick now, hurry up! I'm sewing something and I ran out of thread. I have to go and buy some.

MARAGRAZIA

Yes, listen: I want you to write about the little house, just the way you did last time.

NINFAROSA

You mean those four walls of mud and straw you call a house?

MARAGRAZIA

Yes, I was thinking about it all last night. Listen: "My dear boys! You must remember, I'm sure, the four walls of our house. They are still standing. Well, your mother will give them to you for life if you'll only come home to her very soon."

NINFAROSA

Oh, that's sure to send them flying back, especially if it's true they're both rich! Maybe they'll come back so fast the house will blow over before they can get into it!

MARAGRAZIA

Oh, Daughter, a single stone of your old home is worth a whole kingdom anywhere else! Write, write!

And she produces from the bosom of her dress a single sheet of cheap letter paper and an envelope.

NINFAROSA

Give it to me. You wait there, please.

Indicates the steps.

You'd dirty the whole room.

Exits into the house.

MARAGRAZIA

Sitting down again.

Yes, you're right. I'll stay here. Your house is clean. I walk the fields and roads. You'll wonder where I am one day and you'll find me back there, in my little house, eaten by the rats.

NINFAROSA

Off stage.
I've already written about the house. Anything else you
want me to add?

MARAGRAZIA

Just this: "My darling sons, now that winter is coming on,
your poor mother's afraid of the cold. Please send her – it's
not much – a ten-lire note so she can buy herself –

NINFAROSA

Emerging from the house with her shawl over her shoul-
ders and stuffing the folded letter into the envelope.
All done, all done! Here you are! Take it!
Offering her the letter.

MARAGRAZIA

Amazed.
What? So fast? Already done? But how?

NINFAROSA

It's all in here. Even the stuff about the ten lire, don't
worry. I have to go now.
She exits at left.

MARAGRAZIA

But how did she write it all down so fast, without even
knowing what I wanted to buy with the ten lire?

MARINESE

Oh, we all know that! Your dress! You've made her write
that at least twenty times!
Unconvinced and puzzled, MARAGRAZIA *pauses, still*
holding the letter. Meanwhile, from the end of the
street, a young DOCTOR *enters.*

DOCTOR

To GIALLUZZA.
Excuse me, but can you tell me where the house with the
column is, the one belonging to Rocco Trupia?

GIALLUZZA

What, Doctor, you just came from up there and you didn't
see it?

MARINESE

It's right on the edge of town. You can't miss it. There's a piece of an old column, some kind of old ruin, stuck in a corner of the wall.

DOCTOR

I didn't see any column.

MARASSUNTA

That's because the wall is hidden from the road by a bunch of cactus. Unless you know the place, you're liable to miss it.

DOCTOR

Well, I'm not going back there now and eat myself another ton of dust. Do me a favor, one of you: send one of your kids to tell this Rocco Trupia the doctor wants to talk to him.

MARASSUNTA

Is it about his aunt? Ah, the poor woman! Is she worse?

DOCTOR

About the same. He'll have to persuade her, or force her if necessary, to go to the hospital. She'll never get well at home. I've already filled out the application for her.

GIALLUZZA

To one of the boys.

You go, Calicchio. Go on, up to the house with the column, you know the one. Tell Uncle Rocco Trupia he's wanted here, that the doctor wants to see him. Go on now.

The boy nods assent and exits on the run up the road.

DOCTOR

Thanks. Send him to my house. I'm going home.

Starts to go.

MARAGRAZIA

Excuse me, Doctor, would you do me a favor and read me this letter?

MARASSUNTA

Quickly, to MARAGRAZIA, *in an effort to prevent the* DOCTOR *from reading the letter.*

No, no! Don't bother the doctor now, he's in a hurry!

MARINESE

To the DOCTOR.

Pay no attention to her, Doctor!

DOCTOR

Why not? I've got time.

To MARAGRAZIA.

Give it to me.

*He takes the envelope, removes the letter, and opens it.
After glancing at it, he looks up at the old woman as if
suspecting her of trying to play a joke on him. The
neighbor women laugh.*

What is this?

MARAGRAZIA

You can't read it?

DOCTOR

What is there to read? There's nothing written here.

MARAGRAZIA

Amazed and indignant.

Nothing? What do you mean, nothing?

DOCTOR

Just a couple of scribbles, scratched any which way. Look!

MARAGRAZIA

Ah, I knew it! She didn't write anything? Why? Why would
she do that to me?

DOCTOR

Indignantly, to the laughing women.

Who did this? And what's so funny?

MARASSUNTA

Because she finally caught on.

TUZZA

It took her long enough.

MARINESE

Ninfarosa, the dressmaker, fools her every time like that.

GIALLUZZA

To get rid of her.

MARAGRAZIA

So that's why, Doctor, that's why my boys don't answer my letters! She never wrote any of them, not even the other ones! That's why! They have no idea how I am, what's happened to me, not even that I'm dying just to see them! And I put the blame on them, when all the time it was her, her tricking me!

She begins to cry again.

MARASSUNTA

But it wasn't just out of spite, believe me, Doctor.

DOCTOR

To MARAGRAZIA.

Come on now, don't cry like that. Come to my house later and I'll write the letter for you. Go on, go on now.

He gently urges her off.

MARAGRAZIA

Still crying as she disappears behind NINFAROSA's *house.*
Oh, God! How could she do that to a poor suffering mother? What a thing to do, what a thing to do!

She exits. At this point, NINFAROSA *returns. She witnesses the old woman's departure and notices the penitent, embarrassed expressions on her friends' faces.*

NINFAROSA

Don't tell me she found out!

DOCTOR

Oh, so it's you, is it!

NINFAROSA

Hello, Doctor.

DOCTOR

Never mind that. Aren't you ashamed of yourselves, treating that poor old woman like that?

NINFAROSA

Before you jump to any conclusions, you'd better hear me out first.

DOCTOR

So what have you got to say for yourself?

NINFAROSA

She's crazy, Doctor. Don't get all upset on her account.

DOCTOR

And what if she is? What fun is there in playing a joke on a
lunatic?

NINFAROSA

No fun, Doctor, no fun at all. It's what you do with children
to keep them happy. She went crazy, Doctor, when
those two sons of hers left for America. She won't face the
fact that they've forgotten all about her. For years she's
been sending them letter after letter. I pretend to write
them for her. This way, a couple of scribbles on a sheet of
paper. People going there pretend to take them and forward them for her. And she, poor woman, believes it. Ah,
Doctor, if we all acted like her, you know what we'd have
here? A sea of tears, that's what, and all of us drowning in
it. Take me, for instance: that jumping jack of a husband of
mine, you know what he did? Sent me a picture of him and
his girl over there, with their heads close together, cheek
to cheek, and holding hands – here, give me yours – like
this! And laughing, laughing right in my face! Me they
sent it to! But you see that hand of mine? See how white
and soft and gentle it is? That's me. I take the world as it is.

GIALLUZZA

Lucky you, Ninfarò!

NINFAROSA

Lucky? You could all be like me. If you were, nothing
would bother you.

MARASSUNTA

You're too fast for us.

NINFAROSA

And you're too slow. But say anything you like about me.
It goes in one ear and out the other, you know that.

DOCTOR

You all have your lives still to live, but that poor old
woman –

NINFAROSA

What are you talking about? Her? She could have anything she wanted, be waited on hand and foot. If she
wanted to. She doesn't want it. Ask anyone here.

ALL

Yes! She's right! It's true!

NINFAROSA

In her own son's house!

DOCTOR

What do you mean? She has another son?

MARINESE

Yes, sir. That same Rocco Trupia you want to see.

DOCTOR

Really? She's the sister of that other crazy woman who
doesn't want to go to the hospital?

GIALLUZZA

Her sister-in-law, Doctor.

NINFAROSA

But don't mention it to her! She won't hear a word of it!
Not about her son or any of the relatives on the father's side.

DOCTOR

Maybe he treated her badly.

NINFAROSA

I don't think so. But here's Rocco Trupia now. You can ask
him.

In fact, ROCCO TRUPIA *now enters down the road, accompanied by the boy sent to fetch him. He walks like
a typical peasant, heavily and slowly, on bow legs, one
hand behind his back. He is red-haired, pale, and freckled. His deep-set eyes glance fiercely, fleetingly about
from time to time. He goes up to the* DOCTOR, *pushing
his black stocking cap to the back of his head as a form
of greeting.*

ROCCO

I kiss your hands, Your Excellency. What can I do for you?

DOCTOR

I want to talk to you about your aunt.

ROCCO

You want to send her to the hospital? Forget it, Your Excellency. Let her die in peace in her own bed.

DOCTOR

As usual, like everyone else, you think it's shameful for her to be cured in a hospital. Is that it?

ROCCO

Cured? Doctor, the poor don't get cured in hospitals. She'd only die of despair, without the comfort of her own things around her. She won't go and I'm not going to force her, not even if you paid me in gold. She's been like a mother to me, so you can imagine –

DOCTOR

And while we're on the subject of your mother –

ROCCO

Interrupting him sullenly.
Doctor, is that all you wanted to see me about? I'm always at your service, but if Your Excellency wishes to talk to me about my mother, I'll say good-by. I have work to do.
He starts to go.

DOCTOR

Detaining him.
Wait a minute! I know you're well off!

ROCCO

Heatedly.
Want to come home with me and see? It's a poor man's house, but you're a doctor and I suppose you've been in a lot of them. Maybe you'd like to see the bed I keep always made up just for her, that – that kind old woman! Yes, she's my mother! I can't deny it! You can ask these women here if it isn't true that I've always insisted my wife and children respect that old woman as if she were the Madonna Herself –
Making the sign of the Cross, then adding more softly.

– and me not even worthy to mention Her name! What have I done to this mother of mine that she should shame me like this before the whole town? Right from my birth I was brought up by my father's relatives, because she wouldn't spare me a drop of milk, not even to relieve the pain in her breasts! And still I always treated her like my mother! And when I say mother, I mean –

He suddenly removes his cap and falls to his knees.

– that's what I mean, Doctor, because to me a mother is sacred!

He rises.

When those damn sons of hers left for America, I immediately went to bring her home, where she'd have been mistress of my house, me and everyone in it. No, sir! She has to go begging through the streets, making a spectacle of herself and bringing shame on me! Doctor, I swear to you that if one of those damn sons of hers ever comes back to Farnia, I'll kill him for the shame and all the poison I've had to swallow for fourteen years on their account! I'll kill him, just as sure as I'm talking to you now in front of these women and these innocents here!

His eyes flaming and his face contorted with rage, he wipes his mouth on his sleeve.

DOCTOR

Now I know why your mother doesn't want to come and stay with you! It's because you hate your brothers!

ROCCO

Hate them? Me? Yes, now I hate them! But when they were here, they were closer to me than my own sons and I respected them as my older brothers, while they, instead, were a couple of Cains to me. They wouldn't work and I worked for all of us. They'd come and tell me they had nothing to eat, that my mother would have to go hungry, and I'd give. They'd get drunk and play around with whores, and I'd pay. When they left for America, I bled myself white for them. The whole town can tell you that.

WOMEN

It's true, it's true! Poor man! He took the bread out of his own mouth for them!

DOCTOR

But then why?

ROCCO

With a snicker.

Why? Because my mother says I'm not her son!

DOCTOR

Stunned.

What? Not her son?

ROCCO

Doctor, get these women here to explain it to you. I have no time to waste. The men are waiting for me and the mules are loaded up with manure. There's work to do and – look at me – you've got me all worked up. I kiss your hands, Doctor.

And he leaves the way he came.

NINFAROSA

He's right, poor man. So ugly and sullen-looking, from his eyes you'd think he was bad, but he isn't.

TUZZA

And he's a worker, too!

MARINESE

On that score – work, wife, and children, that's all he knows! And he never has a bad word to say about anyone.

GIALLUZZA

He's got a nice piece of land up there, by the house with the column, and it pays well.

MARASSUNTA

That old lunatic could live like a queen! But here she comes again, still crying.

MARAGRAZIA reappears from behind NINFAROSA's house, holding another sheet of letter paper in her hand.

MARAGRAZIA

I bought another sheet of paper for the letter, if Your Excellency will be so kind.

DOCTOR

Yes, all right. But meanwhile I've been talking to your son. Now why didn't you tell me you had another son here?

MARAGRAZIA

Terrified.

No, no, for God's sake, don't talk about it, don't talk about it! It makes my blood run cold just to think about him! Don't even mention him to me!

DOCTOR

But why? What's he done to you? Out with it!

MARAGRAZIA

Nothing. He hasn't done anything, Doctor. I have to admit that. Nothing. Ever.

NINFAROSA

Who had gone to get the DOCTOR *a chair, now offering it to him.*

Here, sit down, Doctor. You must be tired of standing.

DOCTOR

Sitting down.

Yes, thank you. I really am tired.

To MARAGRAZIA.

Well? If he hasn't done anything —

MARAGRAZIA

I'm trembling all over, you see? I can't — I can't talk about it. Because he — he isn't my son, Doctor!

DOCTOR

What do you mean, he isn't your son? What are you saying? Are you stupid or really crazy? Did you give birth to him or didn't you?

MARAGRAZIA

Yes, sir. I did. And maybe I am stupid. But crazy, no. I wish to God I were! Then I wouldn't be suffering like this. But there are some things Your Excellency can't understand, because you're too young. My hair is white. I've suffered here a long time. And I've gone through a lot, too much! I've seen things, things you can't even imagine!

DOCTOR

What have you seen? Speak up!

MARAGRAZIA

You'll have read about it in books, maybe, about how, many years ago, cities and whole countrysides rose up against all the laws of man and God!

DOCTOR

You mean the time of the Revolution?

MARAGRAZIA

That's when, yes, sir. They threw open all the jails, Doctor, all the jails in all the towns and villages. And you can imagine what kind of hell broke loose all over! The worst crooks, the worst murderers – savage, bloodthirsty beasts – mad from having been cooped up for so many years! And one of them was a certain Cola Camizzi. The worst of all. A bandit chief. He killed God's poor creatures like this, for the fun of it, like flies. To try out his gunpowder, he'd say, or to make sure his gun aimed straight. This man took to the hills, not far from where we were. He came through Farnia. He already had a gang with him, but he wasn't satisfied. He wanted others. And he'd kill anyone who wouldn't join him. I'd been married only a few years and I'd already had those two boys of mine who are now in America, blood of my blood! We had some land around Pozzetto that my husband, that dear soul, worked as a sharecropper. Cola Camizzi came by there and forced my husband to go with him. Two days later he came back, looking like a corpse. I hardly recognized him. He couldn't talk. His eyes were full of what he'd seen and he kept his hands hidden out of sight, poor man, because of the horror of what he'd been forced to do. Ah, good sir, my heart turned over when I saw him like that! "Nino, darling, what did you do?" I shouted at him. He couldn't answer. "You ran away? And what if they catch you again? They'll kill you!" From the heart, from the heart I was speaking to him. But him – not a word – sitting there by the fire, keeping his hands out of sight, like this, under his coattails, and his eyes staring straight ahead and seeing nothing. All he said was, "Better dead!" That's all. He stayed in hiding three days and on the fourth he went out. We were poor, he had to work. So he went out to work. Night came. He didn't come back. I waited and waited. Oh, God! I knew already, I'd foreseen it all! But I couldn't help thinking, "Who knows, maybe they haven't killed him, maybe they've only taken him away again!" I found out six days later that Cola Camizzi and his gang were staying near Montelusa, in an old abandoned monastery. I went there, I was half-crazy. It was more than six miles from Pozzetto. The wind was blowing that day, blowing like I'd never seen it before or since. Can you see the wind? Well, that day you could *see* it! It was as if all the souls of the people they'd murdered were screaming to God and men for vengeance. I went with the wind, all disheveled I was, and it swept me along. I was screaming, screaming louder than the wind itself! I flew! It didn't take me more than an hour to reach the monastery, which was high up, high up in a grove of black trees. Next to the monastery there was a big courtyard with a wall all around it. You went in through a tiny little door, almost hidden – I still remember – hidden by a big stump growing right out of the wall. I picked up a rock to bang as loud as I could on the door. I banged and I banged, but they wouldn't open. I kept on banging until they finally let me in. Oh, what I saw! In their hands – their hands – those murderers . . .

Overcome by the memory, she is unable to continue. She raises a hand as if about to throw something.

DOCTOR

Turning pale.
Well?

MARAGRAZIA

They were playing – there, in the courtyard – they were bowling – but with heads – the heads of men – all black, covered with dirt – they held them by the hair – and – and one of them was Nino's – he had it – Camizzi – and – and he held it up so I could look at it!

She screams and hides her face.

They were all trembling, those murderers – trembling so hard that when Cola Camizzi put his hands around my throat to shut me up, one of them jumped him. Then four, five, ten of them threw themselves at him and tore him apart, like so many dogs. They'd had enough, fed up even then with the way he used to bully them and make them do things. And I had the satisfaction of seeing him torn apart right there, under my very eyes, by his own friends!

WOMEN

Crying out spontaneously.

Good! Good! Tore him apart! The murderer! The vulture! God's vengeance!

DOCTOR

After a pause.

And what about this son of yours?

MARAGRAZIA

The man who first went for Camizzi, the man who came to my defense was a man named Marco Trupia.

DOCTOR

Ah, so this Rocco –

MARAGRAZIA

His son. But, Doctor, you don't think I could have become that man's wife, after what I had just seen? He took me by force, kept me tied up for three months, and gagged, because I used to scream. Whenever he came for me, I'd bite him. After three months they caught him and put him in jail, where he died not long after. But I had to bear his son. I swear to you I'd have torn out my guts to avoid having his baby! I couldn't even bear to hold him in my arms. At the mere thought of having to give him my breast, I'd scream like a madwoman. I wanted to die. My mother, bless her, wouldn't even let me see him. They took him away and he was raised by his father's relatives. Now what do you think, Doctor? Aren't I right to say he isn't my son?

DOCTOR

Perhaps. But how is he to blame?

MARAGRAZIA

He isn't. And when, in fact, have my lips ever spoken a word against him? Never, Doctor! In fact – But what can I do if every time I see him, even from far away, I begin to tremble? He's exactly like his father, even his voice. It's not me, it's my blood that denies him!

Timidly indicating the sheet of paper in her hand.
If Your Excellency would please do me the favor you promised . . .

DOCTOR

Rising.
Oh, yes. Come, come with me, to my house.

MARASSUNTA

If only it would do some good, poor woman . . .

MARAGRAZIA

Quickly, heatedly.
It will, it will! Because it's her fault –
Indicating NINFAROSA.
– her fault if my boys haven't come home yet!

DOCTOR

Come on now, let's go!

MARAGRAZIA

Quickly.
Yes, sir! I'm ready! A nice long, long letter . . .
And as she follows the DOCTOR *out, her hands joined as if in prayer.*
"My darling boys, your loving mother . . . !"

Curtain

THE FESTIVAL OF OUR LORD OF THE SHIP

(Sagra del Signore della nave, 1925)

THE CAST

A CATERER

A WAITER

A BUTCHER

A SCHOOLTEACHER

A DOCTOR

AN OLD SAILOR

MR. LAVACCARA

HIS WIFE

HIS DAUGHTER

HIS SON

AND ALL THE PEOPLE, INCLUDING THE MEMBERS OF THE AUDIENCE, WHO ATTEND THE FESTIVAL

A section of open space in front of a country church.

The production of this play requires a passage connecting the stage with the center aisle of the theatre. Many of the people who come to the festival do so down this main aisle, through the audience. The stage itself represents a section of open space in front of a little country church. This building stands at the back, set above a worn, grassy flight of steps that leads to the main portal. Neither the entire façade nor the steeple can be seen, due to the elevation: only the portal itself. Under the trees that line the square, booths and counters have been set up, decorated with fluttering sheets that look like sails and festooned with strips of embroidered, brightly-colored cloth; these are open-air refreshment stands, equipped with tables and benches, selling wine and edibles of all sorts – cakes and fruit and candies.

It must be supposed that the entrance down the aisle is merely a narrow side street and that most of the people attending the festival enter the square by a larger avenue. Though we are allowed to see only a portion of the square, crowd noises off stage, right and left, testify to the presence of a great number of people.

As soon as the curtain rises, a distant beating of drums is heard from behind the audience and it grows gradually louder and louder.

CATERER

He is very fat, sports a paper hat, is in shirtsleeves, the cuffs rolled up to his elbows, and wears a rough apron with blue-and-white stripes. Calling off right.

Hey, Libè-e-e! I mean you! Damn you! Come here and spread the tablecloths! People are starting to come already!

The singsong cries of vendors begin to be heard from off stage and will continue throughout the play, but will not distract from the action. Some of these cries are indicated below; others can be added at the discretion of the director, as long as they vary sufficiently in tone and cadence.

PASTRY VENDOR

Almond cakes and cookies here! Get your crunchy cakes and cookies here!

ICE-CREAM VENDOR

Ice cream, ice cream! A penny a cone! Ice cream!

MELON VENDOR

Melon here! Slice your own, nice and red! Melon here!

FISHMONGER

Fresh mullet, fresh cod, right out of the sea! Fresh mullet, fresh cod!

And also the faraway sound of tinkling mandolins, whirligigs, other noisy toys, as well as the constant bustle of people arriving.

CATERER

Seeing a BOY *coming up the aisle, panting, with a barrel on his back.*

Hey, look out there! Don't shake it up like that! Want the wine to go sour?

A WAITER *enters hurriedly.*

WAITER

Here I am! Here I am!

Leaping behind a bench and emerging with an armful of tablecloths.

Here we go!

And he begins to spread them over the tables. His sleeves are rolled up and he wears a beret cocked at a saucy angle, with a red carnation tucked over his right ear. Then, whistling to himself, he sets the tables with cheap silverware, thick glasses, and rough earthenware plates painted with splotches of red and blue that are supposed to represent flowers. The golden light of a still-warm autumn day illuminates the scene. Gradually,

*during the action, the light will become red, a flaming
red that will finally blend into a misty purple.*

BUTCHER

Appearing behind his counter and addressing the CA-
TERER. *He has a coarse red face with a large mustache,
and his muscular arms are bare to the shoulder. He
wears a fuzzy cap and a leather apron around his waist.*
So where is the doctor? Why hasn't he shown up yet?

CATERER

He ought to be here by now! I invited him myself!

BUTCHER

Fine, but until he does show up I can't kill my pigs!

CATERER

And neither can anyone else, so take it easy!
Turning to the BOY *carrying the wine barrel and helping
him unload it.*
Is this the last one or are there others?

BOY

*Divesting himself of the sack he has been using to pro-
tect his neck and shoulders.*
The last one! The last one!
*From behind the audience the sound of drumming in-
creases. Two* DRUMMERS *now enter, old men with sun-
baked faces and short, ragged beards. They are wearing
old pointed hats with dangling tassels, worn and faded
velvet suits, one green and the other brown, knicker-
bockers, heavy blue cotton socks, and hobnailed boots.
They are followed by two* SAILORS – *one old, one young –
who were once miraculously saved by Our Lord of the
Ship. The* OLD SAILOR *is tall but stooped, with dark,
wooden features; coarse, slicked-down gray hair; hard,
angry eyes; and a beard that frames his face like a necklace. The* YOUNG SAILOR *is thickset and strong, with a
broad, good-humored face. They are both barefoot,
their white canvas trousers rolled to their knees and held
up by flashy red-silk sashes wound tightly at the waist.
They are in shirtsleeves, their blue shirts open at the*

chest. Hanging from their necks are votive tablets on which are painted storm scenes: an impossibly blue sea at the height of a tempest and the wreck of a small boat bobbing among the waves, its name written on the stern in letters so large that no one could fail to identify it, while through a rift in the clouds above Our Lord of the Ship appears and performs the miracle. In addition to these tablets, the two rescued men are bringing, as gifts to the church, a tray full of wax tapers. The tray is supported by a gaudy ribbon slung over one shoulder at each end and covered by an embroidered cloth. The SAILORS *are followed by three* WOMEN *wearing shawls over their heads and carrying sacks of flour, and by two* BOYS, *awkwardly dressed in their best clothes, carrying flowers.*

YOUNG SAILOR

Hail Our Lord of Grace, good Christians!

WOMEN AND OLD SAILOR

Hail! Hail!

WAITER

Taking off his beret and waving it.

Hail forever and forever!

The little procession moves up the aisle, crosses the stage, and climbs the steps of the church. Leaving the two DRUMMERS, *who now stop playing, outside the portal, it enters the church to deposit its offerings and votive tablets. The* DRUMMERS *exit at left, hoping to come upon other miraculously rescued persons to escort to the church. At right, a* PROSTITUTE *rushes in flanked by two* LABORERS. *One of the men is a decent, respectable type, with a sickly-looking beard and a guitar slung around his neck; the other is badly dressed and slovenly. The woman, disgustingly fat and violently made up, is already drunk. The two men are trying to restrain her.*

PROSTITUTE

Come on, come on, let's sit down over here!

SECOND LABORER

No, not right next to the church!

PROSTITUTE

Flinging herself into a seat, her legs wide apart and opening her arms.

Ah, I feel so warm, happy, happy!

SECOND LABORER

Pulling her to her feet.

Come on, let's get out of here! This is no place for us!

FIRST LABORER

Easy, easy! She'll make up her own mind!

PROSTITUTE

Throwing her arms around his neck.

Darling, play! Play something and I'll sing! You play, I'll sing!

SECOND LABORER

To his friend, tugging him off left by the arm.

No, please! She's got such a horrible voice, if she starts to sing she'll scare everybody away!

Laughing loudly, the PROSTITUTE *follows them out.*

CATERER

It's a good thing they realized this was no place for them!

Meanwhile, from the back of the theatre, the SCHOOLTEACHER *and the* DOCTOR *enter, deep in conversation. The* SCHOOLTEACHER *is a thin, pale, blond young man dressed in black. A poet at heart, he defends himself against the empty ironies and obscene brutalities of daily experience by maintaining an incorruptible faith in life's ideals and, above all, in human dignity. The* DOCTOR *is a sprightly old man, carelessly dressed, with an old straw hat that has seen better days on his head and a shepherd's crook for a cane.*

SCHOOLTEACHER

You come to this festival regularly every year?

DOCTOR

Not for the festival, my friend. I'm on duty here. You know what they call me in these little towns? The Master Doctor.

It's my official duty to supervise the first hog slaughter, which takes place every year at this time.

SCHOOLTEACHER

And can you tell me what the connection is between this butchery and the festival of Our Lord of the Ship?

DOCTOR

I have no idea.

They have reached the stage and the WAITER *goes to meet them.*

WAITER

Good morning, Doctor. Would you like to sit down over here?

BUTCHER

Well, he's here at last! Worked up a good sweat, I'll bet! A liter of your best wine for the good doctor, on me! To your health, Doctor!

DOCTOR

Thank you, my friend, thank you! I never drink on an empty stomach.

CATERER

Oh, don't forget, Doctor! This year you promised me the honor of eating giblets the way I cook them!

DOCTOR

And I'll keep my promise, as soon as I'm through with what I have to do.

CATERER

They've given me a spot near the church, as you can see. There won't be so much rough stuff here.

BUTCHER

But we'll do a good business, don't you worry. This is where the best people come. Let the rest of them mill around over there. People who raise hell don't eat much, anyway.

WAITER

Meanwhile, why don't you sit down?

SCHOOLTEACHER

I'm supposed to join some people who reserved a table. Perhaps you can tell me where it is.

WAITER

Reserved? In whose name?

SCHOOLTEACHER

Mr. Lavaccara.

WAITER

Ah, then it's that one.

He indicates a table at right, downstage.

Here we are. Sit down. Mr. Lavaccara will be here any minute.

BUTCHER

You know he sold me his pig.

The DOCTOR *and the* SCHOOLTEACHER *sit down at the table.*

WAITER

Will you order something in the meantime?

SCHOOLTEACHER

No, thanks. I'll wait.

Down the aisle comes a humble CLERK, *his* WIFE, *their two* DAUGHTERS, *and a* YOUNG MAN, *a friend of the family. The* CLERK *has squeezed himself into an old frock coat buttoned up to his neck. He also wears a greenish-looking top hat, slightly tilted. His handsome mustache has been waxed, combed, and turned up at the ends. The wings of his stiff collar come up under his chin and he wears a large bow tie around his neck. His* WIFE *and* DAUGHTERS *are all plump and still dressed in summer clothes. The* YOUNG MAN *wears a straw hat and spats that are so large they make him look like a banded pigeon. He worries about his broad starched cuffs, evidently afraid they'll pop out of his sleeves.*

CLERK

Arriving in the square, turning to the YOUNG MAN.

Oh, you should have seen how dusty it was when the women wore long skirts that dragged on the ground.

Confidentially.

And you can imagine how dusty it got *under* their skirts!
He snickers.

WIFE

Martino! The girls!

CLERK

Looking about the square.
Here, maybe we could sit here.

ONE DAUGHTER

Oh, no, Daddy! You can't see anything from here!

WAITER

But you can see the procession come out of the church!
Sit down, sit down!

CLERK

Overly polite.
No, thank you. You know, we really came more to get a
little air than to eat.
Bows, tips his hat, and they all exit at right.

SCHOOLTEACHER

Turning to the DOCTOR.
If he's called Our Lord of the Ship, surely there must be a
legend of some sort in which hogs play a part.
Meanwhile, the two SAILORS, *followed by the* WOMEN
and BOYS, *have emerged from the church. The* OLD
SAILOR *has overheard the* SCHOOLTEACHER'S *remark and
addresses him indignantly.*

OLD SAILOR

What have hogs got to do with it? That's blasphemy! Our
Lord of the Ship is ours! He belongs to us sailors and we're
not hogs!

SCHOOLTEACHER

Trying to apologize.
But I didn't mean —

WAITER

Aggressively to the SAILOR.
Watch the way you talk, you! No one here meant to offend
you!

OLD SAILOR

But you do offend us, all of you, carousing and guzzling here in front of the church, where we come every year from the sea to bring offerings and give thanks for having been saved from a terrible death by the grace and will of Our Lord!

The younger of the two WOMEN *steps forward and, humbly and sadly, tries to lead the* OLD SAILOR *away.*

WOMAN

Let's go, let's go, Father.

OLD SAILOR

Tearing himself away from her, angrier than ever.
No, let me alone! I've been wanting to shout this in someone's face for a long time!

Turning again to the SCHOOLTEACHER.
Have you ever seen Him, the Christ in there, in the church? Go, go and look at Him!

WAITER

He's right. What a face! He'd scare anyone.

CATERER

Whoever made Him couldn't have made Him more like Christ Himself if he'd wanted to.

DOCTOR

He looks like He must have looked when the Jews got through with Him –

Making the sign of the Cross.
– praise be His name! But in this case it was the sculptor who did it. Went to work so ferociously he didn't leave Him an ounce of flesh that isn't a wound or a bruise.

BUTCHER

Some fun he must have had!

WAITER

All the same, He works miracles all right! The whole church is full of tablets and gifts of all kinds.

The drums are rolling again, off left.
Here they come, more people who've been saved by Him!

Three more SAILORS, *dressed much like the others, enter, preceded by the* DRUMMERS *and followed by a crowd of* WOMEN *with shawls and kerchiefs over their heads.*

A SAILOR

Hail Our Lord of Grace, good Christians!

The other two SAILORS *kneel with the* WOMEN *and* BOYS, *crying "Hail!" The others present remove their hats. The new arrivals enter the church, while the* DRUMMERS *remain outside and eventually exit. The* OLD SAILOR *rises to his feet with the others and immediately resumes talking.*

OLD SAILOR

I was a boy when I saw it brought here to the church. By a crew of foreigners, it was. They were running like madmen, shouting and crying, holding it up in the air. We found out later it was an old Crucifix they had nailed up under the hatch of their ship, a Levantine. The sea had split the ship open like a pomegranate. They'd found the Crucifix floating around and all held on to it. And this Christ carried them all to safety, every last one of them, floating along on His Holy Cross, His arms flung out and staring up at the sky — like this!

DOCTOR

But, my good man, I don't think anyone here means to offend Him —

OLD SAILOR

Interrupting angrily.

— when you go butchering a lot of hogs around His church?

Immediately taking both WOMEN *by the arms.*

Let's go, let's go! We'll lose our faith if we stay here!

He starts to leave with his group, heading for the audience, when from the back of the theatre comes the long drawling wail of an accordion being played by a YOUNG MAN *who doesn't know how. He has bushy hair, and he wears a tight little jacket and bell-shaped trousers. There's another* YOUNG MAN *with him and two* PROSTITUTES. *The* OLD SAILOR *turns away at once, dragging the*

WOMEN *along. The* YOUNG SAILOR *and the* BOYS *follow him off at left.*

This way! This way!

SECOND YOUNG MAN

As the two PROSTITUTES, *laughing wildly, take the accordion away from his companion.*

Give it to me, I said! Anyone can push this thing in and out. You have to move your fingers – look! – like this, pressing on the keys, like this.

And, swaying to the accordion music, they cross the stage and exit at right.

DOCTOR

To the SCHOOLTEACHER.

People are having a little fun! And I suppose the only connection, if there is one, is the time of year. Pork is supposed to be bad for you in summer, so now that it's autumn and the weather should begin to cool off – it never does! – everyone waits for this first Sunday in September to start slaughtering. And that just happens to be the day dedicated to Our Lord of the Ship.

Rising.

Well, it's my job to supervise, you know.

BUTCHER

And you do a good job!

CATERER

At least he doesn't expect the pigs to be brought to him all washed, combed, and perfumed --

WAITER

-- with little blue ribbons tied to their tails!

A pretty young SERVANT GIRL *comes quickly up the aisle, followed by a lovestruck young* SOLDIER.

SERVANT GIRL

I do all the cooking and I also clean up, sweep, and do the ironing. With four children in the family, big baskets of laundry like this!

Chattering and skipping along, she reaches the stage

where, recognizing the DOCTOR, *she greets him with a smile, but without stopping.*

Good morning, Doctor.

DOCTOR

Be careful, my dear. You know about going out with soldiers.

SERVANT GIRL

Exiting at left.

Oh, he's going away on leave in three days!

DOCTOR

To the BUTCHER.

Well, let's get on with it.

BUTCHER

Wait till you see the beauty I have this year!

DOCTOR

If it's Lavaccara's pig, I'm sure it must be.

BUTCHER

He actually cried when he sold him to me.

CATERER

And they say he still hasn't gotten over it.

BUTCHER

We'll see how he acts when he comes to pick up the head and his half of the liver, as we agreed!

CATERER

To the SCHOOLTEACHER.

If he invited you —

SCHOOLTEACHER

Yes, he did.

CATERER

Well, you won't have a very good time, I'll bet.

DOCTOR

Perhaps he expects you to console him.

SCHOOLTEACHER

It's possible. Because I don't eat meat, pork or any other kind. Never. I'm a teacher of the old school, you know. I tutor Mr. Lavaccara's son in the humanities. To tell the truth, I'm very sorry the boy is coming here today. I'm not sure I approve of all this. It's not really very clear to me.

DOCTOR

And it won't be to anyone else either in a little while.

BUTCHER

Picking up a whetstone and beginning to sharpen his knife on it.

Come on, Doctor, it's getting late. Everything's ready.

SCHOOLTEACHER

Leaping to his feet.

My God, you're not going to kill them here, I hope, right in front of our eyes!

BUTCHER

Brandishing his knife with ferocious gaiety.

Yes, sir, right here! Stick them, skin them, and split them open! Hey, look at him! He's turning pale just listening to me!

SCHOOLTEACHER

But it's horrible! At least you could butcher them away from the crowd!

DOCTOR

And you're a teacher of the old school, you say? The humanities, was it?

BUTCHER

Wait till you see what a clean cut I make of the liver, all shiny and quivering!

DOCTOR

You ought to realize that without this act the festival would be deprived of one of its traditional characteristics, perhaps even of its primitive religious significance.

SCHOOLTEACHER

Ah, yes. The blood sacrifice.

DOCTOR

And you might remind your pupil of Maia, mother of

Mercury, from whom this animal takes its noblest Latin
name: *maialis*.

To the BUTCHER.

All right, come on.

He and the BUTCHER *disappear behind the curtain of the
latter's booth.*

SCHOOLTEACHER

*Still on his feet, hands on the table, looking up, as if
seeking inspiration.*

Yes . . . Maia . . . Maia . . .

*But as he hears the voices of the men behind the booth
preparing to kill the animal and the first grunts of the
victim, he begins to tremble, despite his best efforts to
control himself.*

It's – it's really true that – that as civilization progresses –

A louder squeal now brings the cold sweat to his brow.

– oh, my God! – man gets weaker and – and weaker, and
always more out of touch, despite his best efforts –

Giving way completely to his trembling.

– oh, God! – with his primitive religious impulse!

Up the aisle comes MR. LAVACCARA, *holding his* SON *by
the hand and followed by his* WIFE *and* DAUGHTER. MR.
LAVACCARA *is a mountain of pink, quivering flesh. Heavy
eyebrows under a bulging forehead somehow impart an
air of bitter sadness to his otherwise coarse, stupid, and
vulgar face. He seems about to burst out of his dark-blue
jacket and white canvas trousers. He wears a flaming red
tie and, over his vest, a heavy gold chain from which
dangles a great coral horn and other charms against the
Evil Eye, and his thick bamboo cane also has a horn for
a handle. His* SON *is about ten and looks like a suckling
pig in his sailor suit. The* WIFE, *dressed in flowery green,
is every bit as fat and no less bestial-looking than her
husband. The* DAUGHTER, *on the other hand, is tall, thin,
and yellow. She is dressed, like a nun, in a purple robe
and a cape trimmed in black. Her great sad eyes seem
permanently fixed on the ground at her feet.*

WAITER

Oh, just in time! Here's Mr. Lavaccara and his family!

LAVACCARA

Panting, out of breath, calling to the WAITER.
Have they killed him yet? Have they killed him?

WAITER

Hearing, through the noise of rolling drums and the distant sound of an accordion, the screams of the pig behind the booth, mingled with the confused shouts of those in the act of slaughtering him.
There! They're doing it now!

LAVACCARA

Moving as quickly as his bulk allows, shouting at the
WAITER.
No! Hurry, tell them not to do it! I'll give him back the money! I'll give him back the money!

WIFE

Simultaneously, stopping her ears.
Oh, God! Poor Nicola!

SON

Crying, running beside his father.
Nicò! Nicò!
The screams of the animal become louder.

LAVACCARA

Reaching the stage, hands clapped to his head.
No! No!

WAITER

As the screams suddenly stop, through the murmur of voices from behind the curtain.
All done!

LAVACCARA

Collapsing onto a bench and hiding his face in his hands.
Oh! Oh!

DAUGHTER

Bending over him, in a droning, masculine voice.
This, too, will help to expiate your sin, Father.

WIFE

On the other side of him, distressed.

Get up, get up from there! You're soaked with sweat!

SCHOOLTEACHER

To the SON, *who, curious and frightened, shows signs of wanting to peek behind the curtain.*

Come here, Totò! What are you trying to do? You can't go back there!

LAVACCARA

Weeping for the animal as for a dead relative.

He could do everything, everything but talk! We could carry on a regular conversation with him! The boy used to call him – "Nicò, Nicò!" – and he'd come and eat the bread right out of his hand, like a little dog! He was smarter, smarter than a human being, he was!

SCHOOLTEACHER

In a whisper.

So he was lean, was he?

LAVACCARA

Almost offended, turning quickly to stare at him.

Lean? He weighed three hundred if he weighed an ounce!

SCHOOLTEACHER

Smiling, clasping his hands.

Well, then, he couldn't have been so smart, could he?

LAVACCARA

Why not? You think fat is a sign of stupidity? What about me, then?

SCHOOLTEACHER

What have you got to do with it, Mr. Lavaccara?

LAVACCARA

I weigh over three hundred pounds myself!

SCHOOLTEACHER

That may be, but you belong to another species. You're a man. Which means, when you think about it, just this: when you eat hearty, and may God keep you always in

good appetite, you eat for yourself. You don't fatten yourself up for others.

WAITER
*Suddenly dazzled by the argument and espousing it
wholeheartedly.*
He's right! He's right! While a pig thinks he's eating for
himself and instead he's being fattened up for others!

SCHOOLTEACHER
Suppose that, for all your brilliance, you were –

WAITER
Enthusiastically seconding the SCHOOLTEACHER's *words
and interrupting from time to time to insert his own ob-
servations.*
Yes – of course – he's right – a pig –

SCHOOLTEACHER
– would you eat?

WAITER
Not me! When I saw them bringing me food, I'd grunt –

SCHOOLTEACHER
– in horror!

WAITER
"Nix! No, thanks, gentlemen! Eat me lean!"

SCHOOLTEACHER
Exactly. A pig who fattens himself up obviously hasn't
grasped the point. So calm yourself, Mr. Lavaccara, don't
let it weigh on you like this. Your pig –

WAITER
– he may have been the best pig in the world, we don't
deny it –

SCHOOLTEACHER
– but he was certainly not very smart.

LAVACCARA
Angrily getting to his feet.
What are you talking about? How is a poor animal to know
he's being fattened up for others?

WIFE

Right! You tell them!

LAVACCARA

He thinks he's eating for himself. And to say he shouldn't, just so he'd have to be eaten lean, is nonsense!

WIFE

To the attack.
Nonsense! Sheer nonsense!

LAVACCARA

Because no pig would ever think of such a thing!

SCHOOLTEACHER

Agreed, agreed! But don't you see? It wouldn't occur to him! To a man, yes! So a man —

WAITER

— can allow himself the luxury —

SCHOOLTEACHER

— of eating like a pig —

WAITER

— knowing that no matter how fat he gets, he's not going to be butchered. But a pig, a smart pig —

SCHOOLTEACHER

— to prevent himself from being butchered, or at least to avenge himself on the men who'll kill him —

WAITER

— ought to remain thin, like an old lady on a diet! My God, it's so obvious!

SCHOOLTEACHER

So go on and eat in peace, Mr. Lavaccara.

CATERER

I'll bring you a troughful of macaroni like this, with a sauce that looks like dragon's blood! You're dying for some right now, I can read it in your eyes!

He runs behind the curtain of his booth.

WAITER

That'll make you feel better.

LAVACCARA

The hell it will! I was hoping to get here in time, that's all!

WIFE

How white and still he must be by now.

LAVACCARA

Turning angrily on the SCHOOLTEACHER.

You don't take into consideration the fact that that poor animal went on eating without ever suspecting he'd be slaughtered!

WIFE

Trusting, poor Nicola, in those who fed him.

SCHOOLTEACHER

Trust? Stupidity, I'd call it.

LAVACCARA

Stupidity? Why stupidity?

SCHOOLTEACHER

Because ever since the world began man has consistently demonstrated his appetite for pork.

WAITER

And how! I've seen people sample an ear or the tail while the animals were still alive!

CATERER

Returning with a huge plateful of steaming macaroni.

Time to eat! Time to eat!

The WAITER *hastens to set the plate down on the table. The* SON *can no longer restrain himself.*

WAITER

There! Eat! Eat!

SON

Me first, Daddy! Me first!

LAVACCARA

Banging his fist down on the table.

Sit down, Totò! I can't stand this! Look how greedy he is! A glutton! I should have sold him to the butcher instead of Nicola!

WIFE

Come now, he's only a boy, Saverio!

LAVACCARA

*Serving everyone else meagerly and reserving the big-
gest portion and most of the sauce for himself.*
Nicola had better manners.

Then, angrily, to the SCHOOLTEACHER.
It's no good your staring at me like that, Professor! You
can't convince me! Today I'll eat everything, but not one
morsel of my Nicola!

SCHOOLTEACHER

Forgive me for saying so, but you're wrong. Let's be fair.
If he didn't eat his pig, what obligation would a man be
under to raise such a dirty animal in the first place, wait
hand and foot on him, lead him to pasture, and so on?
What for? What service does the animal render for the
food it eats?

WAITER

One thing is sure: while he lives, a pig has it pretty soft!

SCHOOLTEACHER

And considering the life he's led, he can't complain about
being butchered, because it's equally sure –

WAITER

– that, as a pig, he didn't deserve to live that well!

SCHOOLTEACHER

All you have to do is look at him! That's an *intelligent*
animal? With a snout like that?

WAITER

And those ears?

DAUGHTER

Who hasn't touched her food.
Those eyes?

WAITER

And that funny little curly thing behind?
Suddenly, the DAUGHTER *throws back her head and
bursts into shrieks of mad laughter.*

WIFE

Sternly.
Serafina! Serafina!

SCHOOLTEACHER

Let her laugh. She's right to laugh. Would they grunt like that?

In fact, a great grunting is now heard from off stage, as if a whole drove of hogs were arriving on the run.

There! There! Hear that? Do they sound intelligent? The noise itself is the essence of swinishness!

To LAVACCARA.

And now, instead, take a look at the people here, the people all around us.

Up the aisle people continue to arrive, alone, or two and three at a time, or in larger groups. They proceed in various ways and at different speeds to disperse right and left, conversing. First, two well-dressed YOUNG MEN, *perhaps students.*

THE FIRST

Yes, women! When they want to lie, all they have to do is cry and the lie becomes truth. Anyway, the tears are real, more real than anything else about them!

THE OTHER

They make me so mad! "Aren't you ashamed of acting that way with me?" I'd shout. And she'd pay no attention, but just go on crying.

They exit.

SCHOOLTEACHER

How different they are from this Nicola you can't stop thinking about! The divine gift of intelligence is truly visible in their every movement!

Two tough-looking THUGS *enter.*

THE FIRST

Just before dark. Still light enough, you know, but not so anyone could have been sure he wasn't seen.

THE OTHER

He was standing there?

THE FIRST

I'll say! This girl with the squint was standing at the window, combing her hair, and I caught him just as he was getting ready to throw her a flower!

Laughing, they exit, but will return later.

LAVACCARA

Look at those two! Bums, both of them! While a pig, no matter what he does, is at least innocent!

SCHOOLTEACHER

No, never innocent. I'm sorry. But just as you can't say a pig is guilty, so you can't say it's innocent. Never! A pig is merely stupid, Mr. Lavaccara.

BUTCHER

Emerging from behind the curtain and shouting over the counter.

Magnificent! Stupendous! Want me to bring you the head now, Mr. Lavaccara?

LAVACCARA

Howling, arms upraised.

No! I don't want to see it! I don't want to see it!

BUTCHER

Don't get excited! I'll send it over to your kitchen later.

SCHOOLTEACHER

Look, look over here at our friend the lawyer, and the notary, with their gracious wives!

The new arrivals enter from the left. The LAWYER *is fat, red-haired, and freckled; is nearsighted and wears large blue eyeglasses; has a thick, rather short beard and is sloppily dressed in an old gray suit and a white vest, already soiled. His stomach protrudes and his hands are thrust into his trouser pockets. The* NOTARY *is as thin and stiff as a rail, with a hard, gloomy, chocolate-colored face; has pointed, bony shoulders and long, dangling arms; is dressed all in black. The* LAWYER'S WIFE *is thin and blonde, with birdlike features and a green, bilious-looking complexion. The* NOTARY'S WIFE *is short, as dark as he, plump, with a double chin; is stupid and rich;*

laughs at everything and everyone. Both the women are
pretentiously, tastelessly dressed.

LAWYER

Ah, my dear Lavaccara! So you're taking refuge here,
too? Such a crowd over there, you can't move. Good day
to you, madam, miss, my dear professor. With your per-
mission.

And turning his back to them, he sits down at a nearby
table, while the women greet each other with little nods
of the head. Immediately, the WAITER *runs to take their*
order, ad-libbing appropriate remarks, as he will later,
returning with their food and drink.

BUTCHER

I've just finished butchering Mr. Lavaccara's pig! A beauty!
How about some chops?

LAWYER

And why not, if it's Mr. Lavaccara's pig?

LAVACCARA

Confidentially, to the SCHOOLTEACHER.

Let me tell you something: he may be a lawyer, but he's
more of a pig than that pig of mine he's about to eat ever
was!

SCHOOLTEACHER

Don't say that, Mr. Lavaccara. A pig is a pig and that's
all, while – I'm sorry to contradict you – you see, he may
be a pig, as you say, but he's both a pig *and* a lawyer.
And the other one is a pig *and* a notary. And that man
over there, he's a pig *and* a watchmaker. And that one,
he's a pig *and* a druggist. There's quite a difference, believe me!

Other people have been arriving from left and right.
They are, for the most part, typical representatives of
the town's middle classes: merchants, clerks, professional
men, blacksmiths, shopkeepers, all of varying appear-
ance, age, and bearing. They converse quietly and sit
down at the tables. The two THUGS *return and stroll*
through the crowd, glancing furtively about. Four CARD

PLAYERS *sit down at one table, throw aside the table-cloth, order wine, and immediately begin to play with a deck of cards one of them produces from his pocket. Meanwhile, alone and in silence, a very tall, ghastly-looking* OLD MAN, *with a spectral and smiling face, moves very slowly up the aisle toward the stage. He wears an old coat that is too short in the sleeves, carries his hat in one hand and a handkerchief and stick in the other. He eventually crosses the stage and exits at right. As soon as he's gone, two more old people, a* BROTHER *and* SISTER, *enter up the aisle in conversation. They are dressed in strict mourning. The* BROTHER *is thin, wears a top hat, and has a goatee; the* SISTER *is a plump, placid woman. With them is an* OLD FRIEND, *who has been listening to them sympathetically.*

SISTER

Only a year ago she was here at the festival with us!

BROTHER

Already just a shadow of herself, poor thing!

SISTER

Still, no matter what we said to her – remember? – she always had an answer ready!

BROTHER

To the FRIEND.

Think what it means to believe in God! Her death – well, here's what it's done to me – it's destroyed me. But because she believes – look at her! – nothing. Because she's certain that someday they'll meet again in heaven!

OLD FRIEND

As they reach the stage, gazing about the occupied tables.

All the tables are taken.

BROTHER

Pointing off left.

Let's go over there.

SISTER

No, first to the church! First to the church! They're beginning to sing, don't you hear? The procession will be
coming out soon.

*They mount the steps and disappear into the church,
from which, barely audible, can now be heard a slow,
nasal chanting accompanied by the organ.*

SCHOOLTEACHER

See those two? That's truly human! Mourning a relative
who only last year was happily with them at the festival!

LAVACCARA

A fine way to act! They ought to be ashamed of themselves, dressed in black like that when everyone else is having a good time!

SCHOOLTEACHER

But they were going to church first!

*At this point, the noise off stage grows louder until little
by little it becomes an uproar, the din of a mob indulg-
ing in a bestial orgy. The screams of animals being
slaughtered are all but drowned out by the cries of stroll-
ing vendors, the calls of caterers summoning revelers to
their tables and of butchers selling their fresh-killed
meat, by the sound of drunken brawling and high-
pitched laughter and the discordant harmonies of the
various instruments being played by sidewalk musicians.
Once again the* SCHOOLTEACHER *tries to defend human
values and speak up for the dignity of man to* MR. LAVAC-
CARA, *despite the massacre taking place under his very
eyes, but in the end his faith is badly shaken and he
collapses, utterly crushed by the obscene and terrifying
spectacle of bestiality triumphant.*

LAVACCARA

Rising, threateningly, already a little drunk.

And they were wrong! Stop trying to defend this humanity
of yours! To those bigots I prefer anyone who comes here
to prove he's more of a pig than any real pig could be!
Look, look over there! Can't you hear them **shouting**?

SCHOOLTEACHER

What does it sound like to you? Shouts of happiness, of joy?

LAVACCARA

They sound more like animals than the poor pigs they're butchering!

SCHOOLTEACHER

Exactly! Exactly! Shouts torn from them by the violence of a terrible pain! Without knowing it, they're in tune with the screams of the poor animals they're killing! That's a form of sensibility! And I can still recognize the human element, I can recognize man in that sound!

No sooner has he said this than a fight breaks out among the CARD PLAYERS. *Three of them leap to their feet, shouting, overturning their chairs, and attack the fourth, who gets up in his turn and fights back. A general uproar.*

CARD PLAYERS

Crook! – You cheated! – Grab him! – Bastard! – It's not true! Let me go! – Give me the cards! Crook! Robber!

The two THUGS *seize this opportunity to give the* LAWYER'S WIFE *a push and tear away her pearl necklace.*

LAWYER'S WIFE

Screaming like an eagle.

My pearls! My pearls! Those two crooks! My pearls!

To her husband.

Hurry! Hurry! Catch them!

The LAWYER *tries to break through the crowd to pursue the thieves, who have run off at right. His* WIFE *continues to scream, but no one pays any attention to her. The man accused of cheating at cards has now produced a knife to attack the other three players, and women scream in fright, children cry. Others are trying to break up the combatants. Meanwhile, a* CLERK, *wild-eyed with grief, runs up the aisle, shouting.*

CLERK

They've gone! They've gone! My wife! My daughter! Gone!
While I was sleeping!

*No one pays any attention to him either. After the fight
has been broken up, amid an increasing tumult, through
the overturned tables, a wild, drunken crowd of screaming, rioting men and women rushes back and forth across
the stage. Accompanied by a small band of wandering
musicians, some of the mob begin a frenetic, meaning-
less dance. The light over the scene has become flaming
red.* MR. LAVACCARA *shouts triumphantly at the* SCHOOL-
TEACHER, *who has collapsed in the face of events.*

LAVACCARA

There's your humanity! There, look at it! Now what do
you see? Still recognize it?

*Suddenly, from on high is heard the dark, solemn, enor-
mous tolling of a bell, and immediately, as if the sun
had unexpectedly set, the light changes from red to a
deep purple. All stop in their tracks, as if petrified, in
wretched postures of contrition, their shouts transformed
into a bestial wailing, a desperate, sorrowing, soulful
whining. The tremendous tolling of the bell continues
and now it is answered by the rumbling of the organ
and the singing of the worshippers inside the church.
In the open portal a very tall, ghostly-looking priest in
robes and stole appears holding on high Our Lord of the
Ship: the great, macabre, blood-soaked Crucifix. Two
other priests, equally ghostlike, stand at either side and
two more kneel before him, swinging censers. The crowd,
sobbing, trembling, wailing, falls to its knees, beating its
breast in anguish. Slowly the priest descends the steps,
followed by the praying worshippers and other priests
holding lighted tapers on long black staffs, and he begins the procession, crossing the stage and then descend-
ing from it to move up the aisle of the theatre. Many
rise and come staggering behind the Crucifix, still crying and beating their breasts; others, unable to get to*

*their feet, remain prostrate on the ground like wounded
beasts, muttering: "Mea culpa! Mea culpa! Christ, forgive us! Christ, have pity!" Then the* SCHOOLTEACHER,
who has remained beside MR. LAVACCARA, *both of them
stunned by the sight, now slowly rises and points to the
tragic procession.*

SCHOOLTEACHER

No, no, you see? They're crying! They're crying! Yes, they
were drunk, they became animals, but look at them now!
Look at them weeping behind their blood-stained Christ!
Could any tragedy be more tragic than this one?

*The procession disappears up the aisle, the bell ceases
tolling, and the curtain falls.*

Curtain

BELLAVITA

(Bellavita, 1927)

THE CAST

BELLAVITA, owner of a café and pastry shop
DENORA, a notary
CONTENTO, a lawyer
MRS. CONTENTO, his wife
A CLERK
MR. GIORGINO
SEVERAL OF CONTENTO'S CLIENTS

A sitting room in CONTENTO's house, in a small town of southern Italy.

The scene is a sitting room between CONTENTO's *private
living quarters and his professional studio. At rear there
is an entrance opening into a corridor; at right, an exit
leads into the lawyer's apartments; at left, two exits —
one into a clients' waiting room, the other into the lawyer's office.*

As the curtain rises, the CLERK *is admitting the notary*
DENORA. *The* CLERK *is young, shabbily dressed, but with
a pretense at elegance. He has a small, sleek head on a
long, scrawny neck.* DENORA *is fat, about forty, with
thinning reddish hair and a large, purplish, pimpled
face.*

CLERK

Make yourself comfortable in here, sir.

DENORA

Menacingly, barely able to control his agitation.
Will I have to wait long?

CLERK

Well, a few minutes, I'm afraid. But I'll tell Mrs. Contento you're here.

He starts for the door at right.

DENORA

Detaining him.
No, never mind. What's she got to do with it?

CLERK

To keep you company.

DENORA

Thanks a lot! I can wait by myself!

CLERK

The lawyer's orders, sir.

DENORA

Shouting.

And I say the hell with them!

Then, checking himself, contritely.

I mean, I don't want to inconvenience her.

CLERK

No, not at all. You see, I have reason to believe that she herself —

DENORA

— wants to keep me company?

CLERK

Yes, because she said —

DENORA

— she wants to have a good laugh on me like everyone else? I see!

CLERK

No. How can you think that, sir? She told me to notify her as soon as you arrived, that's all. But here she is.

MRS. CONTENTO *enters from the door at right. She is about thirty, pretty, with a straight little nose and bright eyes. The* CLERK *exits at left.*

MRS. CONTENTO

My dear Denora, so we've come to this, have we?

DENORA

For God's sake, Mrs. Contento, leave me alone or I'll go out of my mind!

MRS. CONTENTO

Taken aback.

Why? What did I say?

DENORA

Nothing, nothing. But I beg you not to ask me anything! I want you to bear in mind that if your husband's studio is full of clients and he's now doing so well, he owes much of his success to me! If I close up my office and go bury myself in the country, leaving you all without a notary

public, he'll suffer as much as anyone. That's what I want
you to keep in mind!

MRS. CONTENTO

I don't understand why you speak to me this way.

DENORA

Because I can tell from the way you came in here that you
too want to bask in the spectacle of my exasperation.

MRS. CONTENTO

Not at all. You're not being fair to me, Mr. Denora.

At this point, CONTENTO *enters from his office. He is
about forty, thin, all legs, with clear eyes that dart continually about as if he hears himself being called on all
sides. He has a wide, wet, smiling mouth; gray hair
worn rather long, bristly in front; and an abstracted,
rather absent-minded expression.*

CONTENTO

What is it? What is it, my dear fellow?

MRS. CONTENTO

I don't know! I came in to keep him company, just as you
told me to —

CONTENTO

I still have so many people in there!

MRS. CONTENTO

— and he took offense.

CONTENTO

What? What?

MRS. CONTENTO

A suspicion — I'm sorry, my dear Denora — it really isn't
worthy of you.

CONTENTO

A suspicion? What suspicion?

MRS. CONTENTO

He thinks we're all making fun of him, even us.

CONTENTO

Making fun?

DENORA

I didn't say that!

MRS. CONTENTO

You said we all want to enjoy the spectacle —

DENORA

Yes, that it amuses you. There. That's all!

CONTENTO

But where, for the love of God, did you ever get such an idea? How can you even think such a thing?

DENORA

Because it's only natural! Only natural! Do you think I don't know? This is the frightening thing, that I can see myself how ridiculous my position is. I'd be the first to have myself a good laugh on anyone else, even my own brother, if he were in the same position! The fact that I'm the victim, while I'd be among the first to laugh at anyone else — well, that's what is driving me crazy! Yes, crazy!

CONTENTO

But I'm here to help you, my dear Denora! To rescue you from this state of mind that distresses me so, as it distresses everyone who is fond of you and esteems you for the fine gentleman you are! Come, come. I've already sent for that bore in order to get rid of him for you. He'll be here soon. So you wouldn't have to wait alone, I asked my wife . . .

DENORA

Please forgive me, Mrs. Contento. Try to understand. I'm obsessed with this thing.

MRS. CONTENTO

Of course. I understand perfectly.

CONTENTO

Let me handle it. I'll have you free of him in a jiffy. Just as soon as he gets here. Yes, indeed! I've already arranged for him to be shown right in. You'll wait in there —
   Indicating the exit at right.
— with my wife and I'll talk to him, as we agreed.

DENORA

The best school in Naples, tell him that!

CONTENTO

Leave it to me! I understand everything. And keep calm. Until soon now.

He exits the way he came in.

MRS. CONTENTO

I don't think you ought to admit right away that the boy is your son. I'd at least express a few doubts. That's what I told my husband.

DENORA

No, no! It doesn't matter! Even if he weren't, it makes no difference! I admit everything! I accept everything!

MRS. CONTENTO

But why? If you could prove he wasn't yours —

DENORA

How can I prove it? It's not only the father, my dear lady, who can never know for sure. Not even the mother herself could say with any certainty whether her own son was fathered by her husband or her lover. It's all guesswork.

MRS. CONTENTO

Does the boy resemble you?

DENORA

So they say. Sometimes I think he does, sometimes I think he doesn't. You can't put much trust in resemblances. Anyway, as I said, I don't want to argue the point. I'm ready to do everything: adopt him, change my will in his favor, anything! I don't have anyone else. And I don't care any more about anything! I want to get rid of him — the father, I mean — at any cost! But the sound of money falls on deaf ears with that man, and it won't do any good to try that tack. He's never acted for profit. That's why I'm so desperate.

MRS. CONTENTO

It's really unheard of!

DENORA

Leaping to his feet.

Unheard of! Unheard of! And it had to be just my luck to have to deal with a husband like him!

MRS. CONTENTO

Why do they call him Bellavita? It must be some kind of nickname, isn't it?

DENORA

Yes, given him out of envy. People used to pass in front of his shop and see it always full of clients, his wife sitting behind the counter like a great lady, and they'd say, "Eh, *bella vita!* The good life!" They've been calling him that ever since.

MRS. CONTENTO

I was by the shop only yesterday. It was pitiful. Those beautiful white counters and the coffee machine that used to be so bright and shiny, why you wouldn't recognize the place! Everything's yellow and dirty. And the sad, faded curtains, one pink, the other blue, stretched across those dried-up cakes and moldy pies! No one goes there any more. Was it you who kept the shop going for him?

DENORA

Me? Certainly not! Not a word of truth in it, if that's what you heard! He wouldn't even let his wife accept the time of day from me. He'd let me pay for an occasional coffee, when I'd show up there with my friends, because it would have been unnatural for him not to. But I'm sure he hated it.

MRS. CONTENTO

It seems hard to explain.

DENORA

What is there to explain, Mrs. Contento? Some things just can't be explained.

MRS. CONTENTO

How can anyone be like that?

DENORA

When we don't want to know something – it's easy – we
pretend we don't know it. And if we're more concerned
with fooling ourselves than others, believe me, it's exactly,
exactly as if we don't really know. . . . He's even over-
flowing with gratitude for me.

MRS. CONTENTO

Gratitude?

DENORA

Oh, yes. For the way I stood up for him, from the beginning of the marriage.

MRS. CONTENTO

Yes, he was sickly-looking, always in poor health. . . . I
don't know why she married him. She came from a good
family.

DENORA

Fallen on hard times.

MRS. CONTENTO

I can't imagine what she saw in him.

DENORA

She used to accuse him of poor judgment, of being tactless
with their customers, even of stupidity.

MRS. CONTENTO

Well, he really is stupid. . . .

DENORA

You're telling me? – The scenes they'd have! – Well, you
understand, I was in the habit of dropping in with my
friends for a coffee. . . . I'm a peaceful type – it used to
upset me. . . . It began with my trying to make peace
between them and . . .

MRS. CONTENTO

. . . peace today, a friend the next, and eventually . . .

DENORA

Unfortunately, these things do happen.

MRS. CONTENTO

Unfortunately. She was so pretty! I can still see her, sitting

behind the counter, smiling and so full of life, with her pert
little nose all powdered white and that red-silk shawl with
the yellow moons on it around her neck, those big golden
hoops in her ears and the dimples she had when she smiled!
She was adorable!

At this description of her, DENORA *begins to sob with
his stomach, then, all choked up with emotion, to wheeze
through his nose. He raises a hand to his eyes.*

Poor Denora, you really did love her!

DENORA

Yes, yes, I did! And I hate this man because it wasn't
enough for him to poison my life; now he has to poison
my grief at losing her! And you know how? By reveling
in it! Yes. As if he were providing it for me to feed on,
to suck on, like a mother offering her breast to her baby!
That's why I hate him! Because he won't let me do what
I want, to mourn her by myself! You can understand, can't
you, the disgust I feel in having to share even her death
with him? He came to see me before the funeral, with the
boy, to tell me that he'd ordered two wreaths, one for him
and one for me, and that he'd arranged for them to be
placed next to each other on the hearse. He said they
talked.

MRS. CONTENTO

Bewildered.
Who talked?

DENORA

Those two wreaths. Next to each other like that. He said
they talked louder than words. He must have seen the
hate in my eyes. He threw himself on my neck, crying
and wailing at the top of his lungs, and he began shouting and begging me not to abandon him, for heaven's sake,
and to have consideration and pity for him, because only
I could understand him, because only I had had the same
loss to bear. I swear to you, Mrs. Contento, that his eyes,
as he spoke, were those of a madman, or I'd have been
tempted to push him away and boot him out of my sight.

MRS. CONTENTO

I can't believe it! I just can't believe it!

DENORA

I can still feel the horror of touching him. I had to take him by the arms – they were like sticks under the furry cloth of that black dyed suit of his – and free myself of that desperate grip he had around my neck! Funny, isn't it, how at certain times you notice little things that stay with you forever? There he was, crying on my neck like that. I turned toward the window, as if looking for a way out, I suppose, and somebody had traced a cross in the dust on the windowpanes. The whole sad business of this ruined bachelor life of mine, it was summed up for me in that cross, on the panes of that window, on that cloudy sky beyond. Ah, Mrs. Contento, that cross, those dirty windowpanes, I'll never get them out of my sight!

MRS. CONTENTO

Come now, my poor Denora, calm yourself! You'll see, my husband will –

She is interrupted by the CLERK, *who enters hurriedly.*

CLERK

He's here! He's here!

DENORA

Leaping to his feet.
He is?

MRS. CONTENTO

Let's go in there.
She points off right.
Come on.

CLERK

Yes, madam. Your husband asked me to usher him in here.

MRS. CONTENTO

Let's go then. Let's go.

DENORA

I could kill him! I could kill him!
He follows MRS. CONTENTO *out right. The* CLERK, *mean-*

while, has exited through the rear door and he returns a few moments later, followed by BELLAVITA. BELLA-VITA *is almost disgustingly thin, waxily pale, with keen, smitten, staring eyes. He is attired in strictest mourning, in an old furry-looking suit, recently dyed, and he wears an old black wool scarf about his neck, its ragged strands hanging down before and behind.*

CLERK

Make yourself comfortable, sir. The lawyer will be right with you.

The CLERK *exits again through the first door at left.* BELLAVITA *remains standing, motionless, spectral, in the middle of the room for a very long moment. Finally, with another sigh, he sits down on the edge of a chair beside a small table. After a minute,* CONTENTO *enters from the other door at left.*

CONTENTO

My dear Bellavita! Here I am at last!

BELLAVITA

Jumping to his feet at the sound of his voice.

You're much too kind, sir!

Immediately overcome by his sudden ascent into space, he covers his eyes with one hand and leans with the other for support against a table.

CONTENTO

Rushing to him.

My dear Bellavita, what is it, what is it?

BELLAVITA

Nothing, sir . . . sheer joy . . . when I heard your voice . . . I – I got up so quickly and . . . I'm so weak, sir, so weak. But it's nothing, it's all over now.

CONTENTO

Poor Bellavita! Yes, I can tell, you're very run down. Sit here, sit here, my dear man!

BELLAVITA

After you, after you. Please!

CONTENTO

Yes, of course. I'll sit here. Now then, I sent for you so we could resolve – or rather – so we could finish resolving, so to speak, a most painful and delicate situation.

BELLAVITA

What situation? Mine?

CONTENTO

Well, yes. Yours, the boy's, and the notary's. Both painful and delicate, my dear Bellavita. The – the – how shall I say it? – the misfortune you've both endured – yes, that's what I mean – this misfortune did, to some extent, suddenly resolve – brutally – at one blow – most painfully – but from a certain point of view – well, you could say, almost surgically! – you never wanted to – well, anyway, let's come to the point!

BELLAVITA

Yes, sir. Because I, you know –
Tapping his forehead with one finger.
– my – my mind isn't what it was. Of this whole speech you've just been so kind as to make to me, I've understood absolutely nothing.

CONTENTO

I see, I see. Well then, I'll put it another way. It's going to be a great relief to you, my dear Bellavita. A great relief, which I know you'll welcome. You need it, I can see that. You need it as much as food.

BELLAVITA

Yes, sir. I haven't eaten for days, I can't sleep. I sit all day on one of those iron stools in my café.

CONTENTO

Yes, well – that's what I –

BELLAVITA

As if it weren't really me sitting there, you know?

CONTENTO

Of course!

BELLAVITA

As if somebody else had just propped me up and left me there, like a puppet.

CONTENTO

Now let's discuss –

BELLAVITA

Cutting him off with a gesture.
Wait a minute. They won't come.

CONTENTO

Confused.
What won't come?

BELLAVITA

The words, sir. And you want to discuss something with me. . . . I'm – I'm half deaf, half paralyzed. Let me try to get hold of myself a little. It's been so long since I talked to anyone! Now that I have the chance . . . Oh, you've no idea, sir, no idea what my days are like, sitting there in the café, at that table! I run my fingers over it like this, fingers full of dust. There's nothing but dust in my café any more!

CONTENTO

Well, it's a windy spot, our town! The dust blows all over the place.

BELLAVITA

And the flies. The flies eat me alive. I can hear them buzzing even in my head. I find myself shooing them away even when they aren't there. And I sit with my back to the counter, so I won't have to look at my scales. There's a single brass weight on one of the plates, the last sale my poor wife ever made – a kilo of sweets to the lawyer Giumìa.
His thin face wrinkles up into a horrible grimace and he begins to cry. He takes a black handkerchief out of his pocket and raises it to his eyes.

CONTENTO

My dear Bellavita, if you keep on like this, before the month is out you'll be going to join the poor soul!

BELLAVITA

If only I could! If it weren't for Michelino!

CONTENTO

Ah! – At last! – That's it! – Michelino! – You see, I sent
for you –

BELLAVITA

Quickly, apprehensively.
– to discuss Michelino?

CONTENTO

I imagine the boy must be a great worry to you.

BELLAVITA

If you could see him . . .

CONTENTO

Naturally! Left motherless . . .

BELLAVITA

If you could see what's become of him, the poor little
thing, in just a few days . . . All I can do is weep, weep,
weep. . . .

CONTENTO

Well now, isn't that grand! I mean, I have a proposition
to make to you, my dear Bellavita.

BELLAVITA

A proposition? Concerning Michelino?

CONTENTO

Exactly. On behalf of the notary.

BELLAVITA

What proposition?

CONTENTO

I'm getting to it.

BELLAVITA

But excuse me, the notary felt he had to come to –

CONTENTO

I'm his lawyer.

BELLAVITA

So much the worse!

CONTENTO

But I'm only acting for him as a friend in this matter.

BELLAVITA

That's what I mean! He goes to you and asks you to make a proposal concerning Michelino? Couldn't he come to me directly?

Becoming excited.

Good Lord, Mr. Contento —

CONTENTO

Don't get so excited until you hear what I have to say!

BELLAVITA

Why shouldn't I get excited? If the notary had to go to you —

CONTENTO

But I'm also your friend and —

BELLAVITA

That's very nice of you. My friend? No, that's too kind. My benefactor! But you see, I — oh — I'm — I'm fainting — I'm fainting. . . .

CONTENTO

No, no! Come now! What the devil! Listen to me!

BELLAVITA

Oh, God, I think you must be trying to take away even the air I breathe. . . .

CONTENTO

By proposing something for the boy's own good?

BELLAVITA

On behalf of the notary?

CONTENTO

Who's always been very fond of him — you can't deny that — and is still very fond of him!

BELLAVITA

His eyes suddenly full of tears.

Really? But then why, why —

CONTENTO

Raising his hands to cut him off.

Let me finish, for God's sake! Mr. Denora proposes to send
the boy to boarding school, in Naples.

BELLAVITA

Send the boy to Naples?

CONTENTO

The best boarding school in Naples.

BELLAVITA

Staring at him.

What for?

CONTENTO

What do you mean, what for? To give him a better education, of course.

BELLAVITA

In Naples?

CONTENTO

He'd pay all the expenses, that's understood. All you have
to do is give your consent.

BELLAVITA

Give my consent? What are you saying?

CONTENTO

Well, why not?

BELLAVITA

Consent to send the boy away? My dear sir, what are you
saying?

CONTENTO

That's what the notary proposes.

BELLAVITA

But why?

CONTENTO

I told you why.

BELLAVITA

But the boy is going to school here. He's doing very well.
And the notary knows that. Send him to Naples? And what

about me? Ah, so the notary doesn't take me into account at all any more!

CONTENTO

Who said so?

BELLAVITA

I'd die without the boy, sir! I'm dying now, dying of a broken heart, abandoned by everyone and I don't know why! What have I done to the notary that I should be treated like this, not only by him, but by all his friends?

CONTENTO

No one's mistreating you. You're just imagining it.

BELLAVITA

Then why doesn't he come to the café any more?

CONTENTO

Because he hasn't the time.

BELLAVITA

He always used to have the time.

CONTENTO

And now he doesn't.

BELLAVITA

Now that I've been overwhelmed by misfortune he doesn't have the time? And to top it all off, he wants to take the boy away from me?

CONTENTO

You won't let me finish!

BELLAVITA

What is there to finish? You shouldn't even have begun! You listen to me, sir! It's not true, you know, that he cares about Michelino's education. No. It's something else! And I know what it is! What? He talks about expenses? Him? He dares to talk about expenses to me? To me? When did I ever ask him for a cent to help bring the boy up? I did it, alone! And the boy has had nothing but the best! As long as I live, he'll never have anything but the best, you tell him that! I can't send him to Naples. Even if I could, I wouldn't. Why does the notary force you to ask me such a thing? Was he afraid I'd show up with the boy to beg him for something?

CONTENTO

Of course not! Such a suspicion is not only unworthy of the notary, but of yourself!

BELLAVITA

I'm sorry, but why does he do this then? Doesn't he even want to see the boy any more? He's been avoiding me for some time now. You think the suspicion is unworthy of me?

CONTENTO

Unworthy and absurd!

BELLAVITA

Oh, no, not absurd! I understood, you know. I understood quite well that my visits to the notary were no longer welcome. I kept control of myself, bit my tongue not to scream, and I stayed out of sight. I'd send Michelino in to see him and I'd sit down, quiet as a mouse, in the anteroom – you know, where that green armchair is? Right next to it. You know how it is when you cry and you feel like giving your nose a good hard blow? Well, do you know how I'd blow mine? Very, very softly, so I wouldn't disturb him, so he wouldn't hear me. But you know how it is: the more you hold yourself in, the more you get to feeling sorry for yourself at the shabby treatment you get for all your trouble! I wouldn't want to cry and I'd find myself crying all the harder! I'm melting, melting in a pool of tears, my dear sir!

CONTENTO

That's enough now! Let's get to the point! I'm going to tell you once and for all, my dear Bellavita, what I have to say and that will be the end of it!

BELLAVITA

Yes, sir. Fine. Speak out. I'm all ears.

CONTENTO

I'd like to ask you first, since I can see it isn't going to be easy, to please do your very best to understand without forcing me to be too specific. That's all. For your sake more than mine.

BELLAVITA

For my sake? What is it? Tell me what's happened!

CONTENTO

Nothing's happened! Except what had to happen. You know what I mean, I'm sure.

BELLAVITA

You're referring to my wife's death?

CONTENTO

Exactly. And now you ought to set your heart at rest!

BELLAVITA

How, sir?

CONTENTO

Make the sign of the Cross and put all this behind you!

BELLAVITA

Make the sign of the Cross? Behind me?

CONTENTO

I don't mean that you should stop mourning your wife. Mourn her all you want! I mean that your – what should I call it? – your forgive – yes, that's it – your spirit of forgiveness, my dear Bellavita, is a bit exaggerated in regard to the notary.

BELLAVITA

Forgiveness?

CONTENTO

Yes. It weighs, it weighs very heavily. Try to bear that in mind.

BELLAVITA

What do you mean, spirit of forgiveness? I'm sorry, I don't understand.

CONTENTO

For God's sake, try!

BELLAVITA

Is it because I've always respected him?

CONTENTO

Yes, partly! Too much!

BELLAVITA

Too much respect?

CONTENTO

And because you insist on keeping it up!

BELLAVITA

He doesn't want me to?

CONTENTO

No, he doesn't want you to!

BELLAVITA

It weighs on him?

CONTENTO

Yes, of course. Because the relationship, you see, had some
substance and was tolerable, my dear Bellavita, while your
beloved wife was alive. But now that, alas, she has been
taken from us – well, be reasonable! – you can't expect the
notary to go on being bound to you by your common
grief, by the loss you've both sustained!

BELLAVITA

Why not?

CONTENTO

Because it's ridiculous!

BELLAVITA

Ridiculous?

CONTENTO

Ridiculous! Ridiculous! I can't understand why you don't
see it!

BELLAVITA

And it weighs on him, you said?

CONTENTO

The death of your wife has altered the situation, my dear
Bellavita! Try to understand! If the notary grieves for her,
and he grieves for her, all right –

BELLAVITA

Oh, he does?

CONTENTO

But of course he does! And if he wants to mourn her —
and he mourns her, all right, in his heart — there's no reason, let's be fair, why he should mourn her with you!

BELLAVITA

Because he's afraid of looking ridiculous? I see. I respect
him and he's afraid of looking ridiculous! The man who
for over ten years made me the laughingstock of the whole
town, now *he's* afraid of looking ridiculous!

CONTENTO

The situation — try to understand!

BELLAVITA

I understand, I understand. And you can't imagine how
sorry it makes me! So that's the reason he wants to wash
his hands of me and Michelino!

CONTENTO

Not wash his hands of you!

BELLAVITA

Get rid of us! Get the boy off to Naples and me — I'm supposed to pass him in the street and pretend I don't see him,
pretend I don't know him, isn't that right? So people won't
laugh if I tip my hat to him. . . . I understand, I understand. . . . Fine, Mr. Contento. Tell him, then, that as for
going to see him at home, I won't go any more, either
alone or with the boy. All right? . . . But as for showing
my respect, well, as for that — I'm sorry — I can't do without that. Tell him so.

CONTENTO

What do you mean?

BELLAVITA

Ah, my respect for him — can he stop me from expressing
it? I always respected him, I was always correct, at a time
when it brought me nothing but shame and mortification.
And now, this very moment, all of a sudden he expects me

to stop paying my respects to him? Impossible, my good sir! I'll always respect him, I'll always honor him. I have no choice. Tell him so.

CONTENTO

Why? Simply out of spite?

BELLAVITA

No, what spite? Excuse me, but he himself shows me how to avenge myself and he expects me not to profit by it?

At this point DENORA *enters in a rage from the door at right, followed by* MRS. CONTENTO.

DENORA

Oh, so you intend to get even with me, is that it?

BELLAVITA

Not I, Mr. Denora! I never wanted any such thing!

DENORA

You just admitted it to him!

BELLAVITA

Only because now you want me to, Mr. Denora! All *I* want to do is respect you, as I've always done, that's all!

DENORA

But it's to get even with me!

BELLAVITA

No, sir! It's genuine respect! But you're turning it into a vendetta by trying to stop me!

DENORA

But I don't want your respect!

BELLAVITA

You may not want it, but I want you to have it! I'm sorry!

DENORA

Oh, you do, do you!

BELLAVITA

How do you expect me to stop? I've always respected you.

DENORA

Trembling.

I warn you, Bellavita! I'll give you a good kick in the pants!

BELLAVITA

Go ahead, go ahead, Mr. Denora! You kick me! I'll let you!

DENORA

Watch out, Bellavita, or I'll really do it!

BELLAVITA

Go ahead, go ahead! I told you I'd let you, and I'll even thank you for it!

DENORA

Oh, you will, will you? You villain!

He hurls himself furiously at BELLAVITA.

Then take this! And this! And this! You dirty rotten swine!

CONTENTO

Holding him off.

No, for God's sake! What are you doing, Denora?

BELLAVITA

Go on, go on! Let him kick me! I'll let him! I couldn't ask for anything better! And not only here, but out in the street! That's where he's got to do it! Come on! More! More! And I'll thank him in public!

DENORA

Raising his cane.

Get him out of here! Get him out of here or by the Madonna I'll break every bone in his head!

Attracted by the shouting, seven or eight of the lawyer's CLIENTS *rush in from the first door at left. Among them is* MR. GIORGINO.

CLIENTS

What is it? What is it? What's going on? The notary? With Bellavita?

MR. GIORGINO

To BELLAVITA, *kindly.*

He's been kicking you?

BELLAVITA

Yes, you see? Because I want to respect him, he kicks me around!

DENORA

That's not true! He wants revenge! Revenge!

BELLAVITA

For what? For all the affection and kindness I've always
shown him? You can all testify to that!

DENORA

Yes, yes, but that's how you revenge yourself, you dog!

BELLAVITA

By repaying him with affection for all the harm he's done
me?

DENORA

Yes, yes! I'm drowning in your stinking kindness!

BELLAVITA

Because it makes him look ridiculous? Oh, what a relief!
What a relief, my friends! I can laugh, I can laugh again!
All I've done is cry and now I can laugh! Laugh and make
everyone else laugh, too, for all the tears I've shed over this
ingrate! Ah, what a relief!

CLIENTS

Why? What does he mean? What's he talking about? Has
he gone crazy?

BELLAVITA

Revenge, the new revenge of all betrayed husbands! Don't
you see? Mr. Giorgino, you, too!

The other CLIENTS *burst out laughing.*

MR. GIORGINO

Me? What are you insinuating?

BELLAVITA

Yes, step out, step out! You, too! Come forward, Mr. Giorgino!

MR. GIORGINO

Me? What are you talking about, you scoundrel?

BELLAVITA

Come on, Mr. Giorgino, everyone knows!

MR. GIORGINO

Furious, hurling himself at BELLAVITA.
Know what, you wretch?

BELLAVITA

Come on! Don't pretend you don't know anything! Don't you hear? They're all laughing! And you know it, too! Go on with you! Horns, the same horns I wear! We're a couple of goats, you and I! But don't let it bother you, it's nothing! You want revenge? Worship, worship, start worshipping, start bowing in public in front of your wife's lover! Watch, here's what I do with Mr. Denora! Watch, watch! Like this! You bow, you smile, you take off your hat – like this!

DENORA

Furiously.
Stop it! Stop it, Bellavita, or I'll kill you!
He starts for him but is held back.

BELLAVITA

Yes, yes, kill me, kill me! I'll bow, I'll scrape, I'll kneel!

DENORA

Freeing himself.
Let me go! Let me go or I'll really kill him!
Having freed himself, DENORA *runs out, amid gales of laughter.*

BELLAVITA

There, you see? He runs away! Laugh, laugh away! Let him run, and you all keep laughing! And now I'll go after him! Down every street, nods, bows, curtsies, until he hasn't a moment's peace! I'll go to my tailor! I'll order myself a mourning suit, something spectacular, and follow him around in it, impaled on my grief, two steps behind him all the way! He stops, I stop. He goes on, I follow. He the body and I the shadow! The shadow of his remorse! My new profession! Let me out! Let me out!
He pushes his way to the door amid general joking and laughter.

Curtain

I'M DREAMING, BUT AM I?

(Sogno [ma forse no], 1931)

THE CAST

THE YOUNG LADY
THE MAN IN EVENING CLOTHES
A WAITER

The YOUNG LADY's room, somewhere in a large city.

A room, perhaps a living room, but is it? There is cer-
tainly a YOUNG LADY *lying on a bed, but is it a bed? It*
seems more like a couch, the back of which, for some
reason, has been lowered. In any case, nothing can be
clearly discerned because the room is dimly lighted by
an odd-looking lamp that stands on a bright-green scat-
ter rug at the head of the couch. This lamp gives the
impression that it could disappear at any moment, at
the slightest stirring in her sleep of the dormant YOUNG
LADY. *In fact, the lamp belongs in the* YOUNG LADY'S
dream, just as in her dream the living room has been
transformed into a bedroom, the couch into a bed.

In the wall at rear is a closed door, and next to it a
small cabinet with glass doors. At right, a large mirror
hangs over an artistically carved bracket in the shape of
a small gilded chest. At the moment, this bracket is in-
visible; the mirror, too, at present looks more like a win-
dow. The reason for this deception is simple: the mirror
reflects the window opposite, in the wall at left, but
naturally, in the YOUNG LADY'S *dream, the window is*
where the mirror reflects it. And this dream window will,
in fact, be opened later by the MAN, *who has yet to*
appear.

Under the mirror a curtain is drawn across the shelf
of the bracket. This curtain is of the same stuff and pat-
tern as the wallpaper and cannot, therefore, be distin-
guished. Thus drawn, it serves to hide completely the
void into which, during the dream, the bracket has van-
ished. It will only become visible again when the dream
is over and the mirror has once more become a mirror.
From the ceiling hangs a chandelier, now unlighted, with
three rose-colored globes of polished glass.

At a certain point, in the **shadows of the** *room so*

dimly illuminated by that dream lamp, a hand, an enormous hand, emerges from under the couch now converted into a bed and raises up the lowered part of it. And as the back of the couch gradually rises into place, a man's head, also enormous, emerges behind it. The expression on the huge head is one of terrible distress: the hair is tousled, the forehead wrinkled into a deep frown, the eyes terrifyingly gloomy and fixed in a hard, menacing stare. It's a face out of a horrible nightmare.

It continues to rise until it is high enough over the couch to reveal the figure of a MAN *dressed in evening clothes, with a black cape and a white silk scarf. The face hovers over the* YOUNG LADY, *who has opened her eyes and is shielding herself in fear behind her raised hands, sitting up and shrinking as far away from it as she can.*

The floor lamp dims and the head suddenly disappears behind the couch. Then the three globes of the chandelier are lighted, casting a very soft, tenuous rosy light about the room, and there, standing stiffly by the couch, is the MAN IN EVENING CLOTHES, *no longer a figure out of a nightmare but of normal proportions. This does not mean that he should seem real; he is still someone who is being dreamed about, with the same menacing expression on his face. However, his appearance is now more normal.*

The scene that follows, changeable and almost completely suspended in the inconsistency of a dream, will be continually interspersed with pauses of varying length and also with certain sudden halts in the action, during which the MAN IN EVENING CLOTHES *will not only abruptly stop moving but will also become immediately expressionless, in his eyes as well as in his whole face and body, remaining in position like a posed puppet. He will recover from these cessations of activity, just as suddenly assuming each time expressions and attitudes that are often in violent contrast with the previous ones, according to whatever new aspect and new idea the* YOUNG LADY *forms of him as she remembers him at random in the fickle inconstancy of her dream.*

YOUNG LADY

You here? How did you get in?

At first the MAN *remains motionless, then he turns slightly to look at her. From a small vest pocket he removes a shiny key and shows it to her, then returns it to his pocket.*

Oh, so you found it again. Just as I suspected. Remember when I asked you for it, after that last indiscretion?

The MAN *smiles.*

Why are you smiling?

He suddenly stops smiling and gazes at her darkly, to make her understand that it's useless to lie to him and expect him to believe that the key was taken from him because of "that last indiscretion" he supposedly committed.

YOUNG LADY

Again afraid, dominating the uneasiness caused in her by his gaze.

That's the only reason I asked you for it. I cared so little about having it back that I slipped it into my pocket without paying any attention. It must have slipped out and fallen on the rug, when I stepped out of the room for a moment.

As soon as she turns her head to look the other way, as if indicating the act of leaving the room, the MAN, *with the speed of a sneak thief, commits the act imagined by her: he bends down as if to snatch up a key and slip it into his pocket. As he carries out this action, his whole face is twisted into a mad smile. When he stands up again, he at once resumes his former attitude.*

YOUNG LADY

After waiting for him to say something to her.
What's the matter with you? Why are you looking at me like that?

MAN

The matter? Nothing's the matter. How am I looking at you?
And with these words he goes up to her, bends over her, leaning one knee on the edge of the couch, putting one hand on the back of it and the other, delicately, on her forearm.
I can't keep away from you. I can't live unless I can feel you like this, like this, close to me – unless I can inhale the perfume of your hair – the rapture of it – the smoothness of your skin – the scent of your whole being. You're everything to me, everything – my whole life!
The YOUNG LADY *jumps to her feet and moves away from him, brushing past him as she does so. In this way she shows him she can't bear hearing him repeat his usual words of love to her. But it was she who made him repeat them by remembering that he, in love with her, had appeared to her so often in the past with that same troubled expression that now, in her dream, is making her so afraid. Immediately sorry for her behavior, she expects him, having had this proof that she no longer loves him, to pretend that he has spoken those words in mockery. She, therefore, turns fearfully back to him.*
The MAN IN EVENING CLOTHES, *having remained suspended like a robot in his posture of courtship, kneeling there and leaning toward her vacant place, now, as soon as she turns to look at him, flings himself back on the couch, his legs and arms spread wide, throws back his head, and bursts into a long scornful laugh. As he laughs, the back of the couch gradually gives way behind him until it is again even with the seat. Simultaneously the rosy light from the chandelier dims slowly*

until, still laughing, the MAN *is supine. In the moment*
of darkness between the chandelier's going out and the
relighting of the floor lamp, the MAN *stops laughing and*
turns onto his side in what has once more become a bed.
It's as if he has been there a long time, talking calmly,
a sad smile on his lips, to the YOUNG LADY, *who is now*
sitting at his feet.

MAN

. . . of course a woman can't force a man, or a man a
woman, to return a love he no longer feels. But then one
should have the honesty to say, "I don't love you any
more."

YOUNG LADY

Very often you don't say it out of pity, not because you
aren't honest enough. It's sometimes very convenient to be
honest.

MAN

It can also be very convenient for a woman to think she's
keeping quiet out of pity. When a woman says that her
silence is motivated by pity, she's already deceiving the
man.

YOUNG LADY

That's not true!

MAN

Yes, it is. And herself as well. Under this so-called pity of
hers you'll always find some much more practical reason.

YOUNG LADY

Rising.

I see you have a high opinion of women.

MAN

But even if there weren't some practical purpose behind
it, don't you understand that this pity of hers can't help
but be false?

YOUNG LADY

No. I've always known that one can also deceive out of pity.

MAN

How? By making someone think you still love him when you don't? A useless deception. Anyone really in love notices right away the absence of love in his partner. And so much the worse for him if he pretends not to notice: it would be like opening the door to betrayal. Real pity, one that conceals no secondary motives, can be, in the person who feels it, only pity, no longer love. To pretend otherwise is to corrupt this pity. And pity will necessarily lead to contempt, and contempt to betrayal. It doesn't matter because, in any case, the original betrayal was committed by not wanting to admit the deception.

YOUNG LADY

Sitting down again at the foot of the bed.
So you think one should admit it?

MAN

Unruffled.
Yes. Loyally.

YOUNG LADY

Because a deception, even when motivated by pity, is really a betrayal?

MAN

Yes. When a person accepts it, as a beggar accepts charity.
A pause.
How would you treat a beggar who, to express his gratitude at your charity, would expect to kiss you on the mouth?

YOUNG LADY

Smiling ambiguously.
If the charity he received was love, a kiss is the very least the beggar could ask.

MAN

Standing up and angrily raising the back of the couch into place.
I forgot I was talking to a woman.
Walking excitedly about the room.
Loyalty, loyalty is a debt, the most sacred debt we owe to

ourselves, even more than to others. To betray is horrible, horrible.

YOUNG LADY

I don't know why you speak to me like this tonight or why you should be so excited by what you say.

MAN

Not by what *I* say, but by what *you've* said. I'm speaking in the abstract.

YOUNG LADY

But so am I, darling. You can't have any doubts about me.

MAN

You know very well I always have doubts about you and that I have every reason to doubt.

He goes resolutely to open the dream window; in doing so he admits an exaggeratedly bright ray of moonlight. The slight, caressing murmur of the sea is also heard.

Don't you remember?

And he remains by the open window, gazing out.

YOUNG LADY

Looking straight ahead, lost in her memories.

Oh, yes, I remember – last summer – by the sea. . . .

MAN

Still in front of the window, as if gazing out over the water.

. . . all shining in the moonlight . . .

YOUNG LADY

Yes, yes, it was really a madness. . . .

MAN

And I said to you: we're challenging the sea by allowing ourselves to feel so secure in this canoe; any wave could sink us from one moment to the next.

YOUNG LADY

. . . and you tried to frighten me by rocking the boat from side to side. . . .

MAN

Do you remember what else I said to you then?

YOUNG LADY

Yes. Something bad.

MAN

That I wanted you to feel the same fear I felt in entrusting myself to your love. You took it badly. And so I then tried to make you understand that, as we two, that night, were challenging the sea, by feeling ourselves so secure in that canoe, so it seemed to me that I was challenging you, by saying I felt safe in the small amount of assurance your love could give me.

YOUNG LADY

It seemed small to you even then?

MAN

Of course! From the very first, my dear. Necessarily. Not because that was the way you wanted it. In fact, you thought you'd given me every assurance. It still wasn't much, because you yourself, my dear, you yourself can't be certain that tomorrow or five minutes from now you'll still love me. There was a time when you first realized you loved me. There will also be a time when you'll realize you've stopped loving me. . . . Perhaps that time has already come. . . . Look at me! Why are you afraid to look at me?

YOUNG LADY

I'm not afraid. I know you're a reasonable person. You said yourself just a minute ago that no one can force anyone else to return a love he no longer feels.

MAN

Yes, I was being reasonable. But God help you, God help you if your love should die while it still has me in its grip, so vital and so strong!

YOUNG LADY

You've got to be reasonable!

MAN

Yes, yes, I'm trying. I'm trying. I'll reason as much as you like, if it makes you happy. So you won't be afraid of me, do you want me to prove I still have perfect control of my reasoning powers? Here, I'll prove it to you. I'll go on understanding everything perfectly, don't worry, just as long as the flame burns only up here.

He touches his forehead.

I understand perfectly, as you can tell, that your love can die as suddenly as it was born, for any reason at all, unforeseen, unforeseeable. What more can I tell you? I could even say: at a turn in the road, because of a chance meeting, a sudden blinding conglomeration of circumstances, an unexpected, irresistible intoxication of the senses . . .

YOUNG LADY

Oh, as for that . . .

MAN

Why couldn't it happen that way?

YOUNG LADY

Because, after all, we *are* able to reason, and reason immediately calls us back.

MAN

To what? To duty?

YOUNG LADY

To not allowing ourselves to be swept away.

MAN

Life, life is what sweeps us away! It always has! Why do you make me say this to you, me of all people, just as if you didn't know it already? God help you, God help you if the flame burns in here —

Touching his chest.

— and consumes your heart! You've no idea what ghastly smoke can rise from a burning heart, from blood, from burning blood, and what a horrible night this smoke causes in your brain, a storm cloud that blots out your reason! Do you think you can prevent that storm from breaking, keep it from setting fire to your house and killing you?

As he speaks, he has become terrible. No sooner has he mentioned the word "storm" than the distant but growing sound of one is heard through the open window and the moonlight becomes a livid flashing of sinister lights.

Terrified, the YOUNG LADY *hides her face in her hands. The instant she does so, the* MAN IN EVENING CLOTHES *is cut off in mid-gesture, his face becomes expressionless, robot-like. The storm sounds and flashing lights cease abruptly. The moonlight again falls softly through the window and everything remains in a mysterious state of suspension that lasts as long as the* YOUNG LADY *keeps her hands to her face.*

Still shielding her face in her hands, the YOUNG LADY *rises and moves a few steps toward the window as if to close it. The* MAN, *though still suspended in his posture of astonishment, turns only his head and arms in her direction, as if magnetically attracted to her. The* YOUNG LADY *finally takes her hands from her face and, gazing out the window, she too now pauses in amazement at the serenity of that moonlight. Overcome, she smiles: she is remembering the moment in which she began to fall in love with this man. It took place, of course, by a living-room window through which moonlight was streaming. She turns to him, still smiling.*

The MAN *immediately assumes the expression of the "moment." That is, he becomes a man who during a social gathering has seen from the corner of his eye the woman he's in love with go over to a window, and, pretending that he too was headed that way for a breath of air, he affects surprise at finding her there quite by chance.*

MAN

Oh, excuse me. You here? It's really unbearably hot, isn't it? Too hot to dance. We all ought to go out into the garden, under that lovely moon, and leave the orchestra behind. Down there we'd hear the music from a distance and we could dance out in the open, in the space around the fountain.

From far away, veiled, as if from above, the sound of a piano.

YOUNG LADY

I shouldn't think you'd want to go out there in a group.
Why don't you ask that beautiful lady in the pink dress,
the one you've been dancing with all evening.

MAN

How can you say that to me? You're the one who —

YOUNG LADY

Interrupting.
Hush! They can hear you.

MAN

Lowering his voice.
— who told me not to dance too much with you, that it
would seem too obvious, and now you have the nerve to
say —

YOUNG LADY

*First signaling him to be quiet, then murmuring very
softly.*
Go down to the garden, but don't let anyone see you. As
soon as I can, I'll join you.

MAN

*Happily, after gazing about to make sure no one is look-
ing, taking her hand and kissing it furtively.*
I'm going. I'll wait for you. Hurry!
*He leaves the window, moving cautiously across the
room toward the closed door. He reaches it, turns back
to gaze circumspectly about like someone waiting for
the opportune moment, opens it, and exits.*

The YOUNG LADY *remains as if hidden, framed by the
window and bathed in moonlight. Little by little the
rays fade along with the light from the floor lamp, and
the piano music becomes fainter and more distant, because her vision of that "moment" is dying slowly in
her. When it has died completely, and the sound of the
piano with it, in the instant of darkness that precedes
the relighting of the chandelier, the window is closed
and the* YOUNG LADY *sits down on the couch again. The*
MAN IN EVENING CLOTHES *is standing motionless by the*

couch, with exactly the same threatening expression on his face as before.

YOUNG LADY

After waiting for him to make up his mind to speak, tapping her foot impatiently.

Well, aren't you going to say something? Surely you aren't going to stand there all night with that silly frown on your face!

She is almost in tears now from the effort of having to curb the rage she feels.

MAN

It's not my fault. You put the frown there. You know very well I'm still in love with you. You know very well that if I turned now to look in the mirror, I wouldn't even recognize myself. The mirror would tell me the truth, reflecting an image of myself I've never seen, the one you've made of me. And that's why you've made the mirror disappear and turned it into an open window.

YOUNG LADY

Almost shouting.

No, no, it *is* the window! It *is* the window! I swear to you it's the window! You don't have to turn and look at it!

MAN

I won't, don't worry. It's the window, all right. Of course it's the window! Didn't I just open it? And isn't there a garden out there, where our lips met in a long, an endless kiss? And the sea we dared together one moonlit night last summer? – Nothing terrifies an uneasy conscience more than a mirror. – And you know there are other reasons, also your fault – when I think of what I've done because of you and what I'm doing – why, I don't dare look in a mirror. Right this moment, as I stand here in front of you, you know exactly where I am – you came there once with me – in the back room of my club – where the gambling is – and I'm cheating, cheating for you – luckily no one notices – but I'm cheating all right, swindling my friends –

just so I'll be able to make you a present of that pearl
necklace. . . .

YOUNG LADY

No, no, I don't want it any more! I don't want it! I told
you once it would have made me so happy, but only to –

MAN

To degrade me.

YOUNG LADY

No. To make you understand that I expected too much
from you.

MAN

You're lying again! You hadn't the slightest intention of
making me secretly contemptuous of your excessive demands. No, you wanted me to realize you were made for
someone richer, someone who could easily satisfy your expensive tastes.

YOUNG LADY

Oh, my God, you should have thought of that yourself,
right from the beginning! You knew who I was, what
kind of life I've been used to leading!

MAN

And you knew who *I* was when we became lovers. I've
never had money. I've done everything I could think of to
find the means to keep up with you, so you wouldn't be
forced to give up too much or make too many sacrifices.
And everything I've done, which, if you only wanted to admit it, you must certainly have guessed –

YOUNG LADY

Yes, I did.

MAN

Expedients of every kind . . .

YOUNG LADY

I know – I know – and I admired you for the way you
were able to hide every difficulty from me.

MAN

Because it didn't matter to me at all. I thought it was the least I could do for allowing me to love you.

YOUNG LADY

But you did expect me to –

MAN

To what?

YOUNG LADY

You know what! You appealed to my sincerity, you always expected me to remember what it was costing you –

MAN

I told you: nothing. Just as I expected it would cost you nothing to give up your most expensive desires.

YOUNG LADY

So I wouldn't force you to spend sums I knew you couldn't afford, yes. And I did give up a lot, you can't imagine how much!

MAN

I can, I do imagine it very well!

YOUNG LADY

You thought that was natural?

MAN

Yes, if you really loved me . . .

YOUNG LADY

It made me furious!

MAN

Because it seemed natural to me?

YOUNG LADY

Yes. That because I loved you I shouldn't expect anything any more! And that's why, when we passed in front of the jeweler's window that night – yes, I did it on purpose, I wanted to be cruel.

MAN

And don't you think I knew it?

YOUNG LADY

Did I seem cruel?

MAN

No. Female.

YOUNG LADY

Striking her fist against her knee and rising.

Again! Can't you understand it's your fault, you men, if we behave like that, because of this stupid idea you have of us? Your fault if we're cruel, your fault if we deceive you, your fault if we betray you?

MAN

Easy . . . easy . . . What are you so excited about? Do you think I don't realize you're simply trying now to justify yourself in some way?

YOUNG LADY

Turning to him, stunned.

Me?

MAN

Grimly.

Yes, you. Why look so surprised?

YOUNG LADY

Ill-at-ease.

Justify myself? For what?

MAN

You know very well *for what.* I said "female" in order to soften your word "cruel." It seemed quite just to me, not cruel, that, passing in front of the jeweler's window that night, you should half-jokingly moan like a greedy little child.

Imitating a child in the act of begging for some favorite delicacy.

"Oh, how I'd like that nice pearl necklace, Daddy! Please, Daddy, please!"

She laughs and suddenly, as she laughs, it becomes dark, absolutely dark. In the darkness, the doors of the cabinet against the rear wall open and a sudden shaft of brilliant light isolates it from everything else in the room. The interior of the cabinet has become the luxurious showcase window of a jewelry store displaying many

*pieces of jewelry, all of them quite fantastic-looking.
In the middle of the window, most prominently mounted
on a satin-covered prop, is the pearl necklace. It, too, is
much larger than life. At the very instant the window is
thus illuminated, like a hypnotizing vision, the* YOUNG
LADY *stops laughing. The vision lasts for a long moment
and in absolute silence. Nothing else in the room, including the two people, can be distinguished. In any case,
the two characters have turned their backs to the sight.
The vision of the jeweler's window is only for the audience, but for the two people in the drama it is as if the
window were in front of them. At a certain point, two
male but very white and delicate-looking hands part the
curtains within the cabinet window and carefully remove
the pearl necklace. Then, without causing the vision of
the window to disappear, the lights of the chandelier
come up slowly, revealing the* YOUNG LADY *and the* MAN
IN EVENING CLOTHES *standing exactly where they were,
hypnotized by the vision behind them. They speak
rigidly, softly, staring straight ahead.*

MAN

Want me to steal them?

YOUNG LADY

No, no. It was just an insanity on my part. I don't want
them, I don't want you to give them to me. I already told
you I was only being cruel. I know very well the only way
you can get them for me is by stealing them.

MAN

Or by stealing from others so I can buy them for you!
Which is what I'm doing! While – did you see that? – other
hands, other hands took the pearls from the window – for
you – and you know it – you know it!

He turns on her menacingly.

And you dare to say you don't want them from me any
more? Of course you don't want them from me! Somebody
else is going to give them to you! You've already betrayed
me, you bitch!

He grabs her by the arm as she gets up in order to get away from him.

And I know who it is! I know who it is! Bitch! Bitch!

He shakes her.

You've gone back to him, haven't you? Back to your first lover, now that he's home from abroad and become so rich! I've seen him! I know he's back! He stays away from us, but I've seen him!

                    YOUNG LADY

She has been struggling with him and finally succeeds in breaking away.

It's not true! You're wrong! Let me alone!

                    MAN

He seizes her again, flings her back on the couch, and leaps on her, his hands around her throat.

Not true? I'm wrong? When I tell you I've seen him, the scum! You're waiting for him to give you those pearls, while I dirty my hands by stealing from my friends at the club! You bitch! You bitch! Just to make you happy, to satisfy your cruelty!

He is on her and about to strangle her; she's already giving away beneath his furious onslaught. All the lights flicker, then suddenly go out, as she dreams that he is actually strangling her. Absolute darkness, but it lasts only a moment or two. During it there is a loud, unreal, heavy pounding on the door, as if the sound of it were echoing inside her head. Meanwhile, the doors of the cabinet close, the floor lamp disappears, the shelf of the bracket becomes visible, and the mirror becomes once more a real mirror. It no longer reflects the window, because the real window is now open and admits the warm light of the setting sun. The room is filled, in fact, with a limpid, soft daylight. The MAN IN EVENING CLOTHES has also vanished. Immediately, as this light comes up, the pounding on the door becomes a realistically discreet, rather gentle knocking. The YOUNG LADY wakes up from her dream and raises her hands to her throat, as if to rub

out the feeling of being choked. She takes several deep,
careful breaths, showing traces of the fear she experi-
enced in her dream. She is still dismayed by it and looks
around, as if unable to pull herself together and recognize
the reality of her surroundings. She tries to get up from
the couch, but falls back, her legs too weak to support
her. She hides her face in her hands and remains like
this for a short while. The knocking on the door is repeated.

YOUNG LADY

Standing up and pausing attentively before answering.
Come in.

She walks toward the window, straightening her hair a
bit. The WAITER enters, carrying a plate on which rests
a small box, expensively wrapped and tied with a silver
ribbon. He starts toward her, but she stops him with a
gesture.
You can leave it over there.

She indicates the bracket. The WAITER leaves the package on the shelf, bows, and exits, closing the door behind
him. The YOUNG LADY remains where she is for the moment, as if surprised. Inside that little box is the precious
gift she has been expecting. But her joy at receiving it
is tempered by the recent scare of her dream and the
threat it contains for her. What if the lover she has been
dreaming about should suspect her betrayal of him,
proof of which now reposes on that shelf? She hurries
over to the shelf, picks up the box, and glances furtively toward the door. Then, unable to resist the tempta-
tion, she tears away the wrapping and the ribbon. First
she removes a card from inside the box and reads what
is written on it, then, finally, she takes out the pearl
necklace. She looks at it, admires it, smiles, clutches it
with both hands to her breast, and closes her eyes. She
tries it on in front of the mirror, without, however, fasten-
ing the clasp behind her neck. Another knock at the

door. Immediately the YOUNG LADY *removes the necklace, picks up the card, stuffs everything back into the box, and hides it in a drawer below the shelf of the bracket. Then she turns back toward the door.*

Who is it? Come in.

The WAITER *enters and gives her a calling card.*

Show him in.

The WAITER *now admits the* MAN, *who in her dream was dressed in evening clothes. Now, however, he wears an ordinary business suit and his expression is serene enough.*

Oh, darling, come in, come in.

The WAITER *exits, closing the door.*

MAN

After kissing her hand fervently.

Have you been waiting long?

YOUNG LADY

Simulating absolute indifference.

No, no . . .

Sitting on the couch.

Can't you tell I've been napping?

MAN

Looking at her.

No. Really?

Softly.

Napping?

He sits down, too.

YOUNG LADY

Yes, I dozed off in here, just for a few minutes. . . . I was suddenly very sleepy. . . . Strange . . .

MAN

Any pleasant dreams?

YOUNG LADY

No, no. It was only a few minutes. But I must have – I don't know – I must have been lying in an odd position.

Again caressing her neck with both hands.

I – I suddenly felt I couldn't breathe.
She smiles.
Ring the bell, please. We'll have some tea.
*He rises and rings a bell next to the mirror, then sits down
again.*

MAN

I was afraid I was late. I really had quite a disappointment.
I'll tell you about it.
The WAITER *knocks and enters.*

YOUNG LADY

We'll have tea now.
The WAITER *bows and goes.*
A disappointment?

MAN

Yes. I was planning to surprise you.

YOUNG LADY

You? Surprise me?
She laughs.

MAN

Offended.
What are you laughing about?

YOUNG LADY

Still laughing.
A surprise? From you?

MAN

You don't think I can any more?

YOUNG LADY

Yes, darling. Anything is possible. But you know how it is:
when you've known someone too long, surprises are – and
anyway, you said it in such a gloomy voice. . . .
Imitating him.
. . . "I was planning to surprise you. . . ."
She laughs again.

MAN

I really did have a disappointment.

YOUNG LADY

I'll bet I can guess.

MAN

All right. What?

YOUNG LADY

Were you disappointed for me or for yourself?

MAN

For both of us. Because I couldn't give you the surprise I wanted to.

YOUNG LADY

Well then, yes, I've guessed it. Just to prove to you, darling, that you can't surprise me any more . . .

She goes behind him, puts her arms around his neck, and leans her face against his cheek.

So you really did want to give me that necklace?

MAN

I went into the shop to buy it.

Surprised suddenly.

Then you knew it was sold?

YOUNG LADY

Yes, darling. That's how I guessed.

MAN

But how did you know it was sold?

YOUNG LADY

Aren't you funny! How do you think? Last night, walking past the window, I saw it was gone.

MAN

It was there at four o'clock today. I saw it myself.

YOUNG LADY

You couldn't have. I went by about seven last night and it was gone.

MAN

Strange. They told me it was sold only this morning.

YOUNG LADY

Oh – you asked?

MAN

I went in, I told you, to buy it. And they said it was sold this morning.

YOUNG LADY

Simulating complete indifference.
To whom? They didn't tell you?

MAN

Totally unsuspecting and, therefore, attaching no importance to her question.
Yes. To some man, they said.
Pulling her around in front of him.
But as for you, if you were able – I mean, seeing how disappointed I was – if you were able to guess so easily that it had to do with that necklace, it proves you must have been thinking about it.

YOUNG LADY

No, no . . .

MAN

What do you mean, no? And it proves you expected me to give it to you.

YOUNG LADY

Oh, dear. Well, I knew you'd been gambling for some time at the club and winning incredibly. . . .

MAN

Yes, and you know why? I'm sure of it. Because of a kind of fever I've been in ever since you told me you wanted that necklace – a real clairvoyance, almost – so that everything I try comes out, one coup after another.

YOUNG LADY

Have you won a lot?

MAN

Yes, quite a lot.
With sincere elation.
And now you'll help me pick out some other beautiful thing – something for you, something you really want. . . .

YOUNG LADY

No!

MAN

Yes! Then I won't be so unhappy that I couldn't give you
what you wanted this time.

YOUNG LADY

No, darling. I never really thought seriously about those
pearls. I never really expected you to give them to me. It
was just – well – the caprice of the moment, that night,
passing by the window. . . . No, I'm going to be good.

MAN

I know – I know you're good – so good – to me. But everything I've won these past few nights is yours, all yours, I
can assure you. I owe it all to you, absolutely.

YOUNG LADY

Then so much the better! I'm even happier now – happy I
brought you luck and that you weren't able to buy the
pearls. Let's not discuss it any more, please.

A knock at the door and the WAITER *enters with the tea
tray.*

Here's our tea.

The WAITER *puts the tray down on a table near the
couch and sets it in front of her. As he starts to lay out
the service, the* YOUNG LADY *stops him.*

That's all right, I'll do it.

The WAITER *bows and exits.*

MAN

Falsely casual now, anxious to drop his piece of news.

Oh, by the way, guess what? I heard – I heard he was
back, home from abroad somewhere. . . .

YOUNG LADY

Pouring tea.

Yes, yes, I know. . . .

MAN

Oh, somebody told you?

YOUNG LADY

Yes, the other night. I don't remember who. . . .

MAN

I hear he's made himself an awful lot of money. . . .

YOUNG LADY

So casually.
Milk or lemon?

MAN

Milk – thank you.

Curtain

About the Authors

LUIGI PIRANDELLO wrote forty-three plays, eight volumes of verse, five scenarios, and three hundred short stories. He was awarded the Nobel Prize for Literature in 1934.

WILLIAM MURRAY is the translator of another volume of Pirandello's plays (*To Clothe the Naked and Two Other Plays*) and the author of several novels, including *The Fugitive Romans*, *Best Seller*, and *The Americano*.